THE
PLANT-BASED
SLOW COOKER

Other books by Robin Robertson

Vegan Mac & Cheese

Veganize It!

Vegan Without Borders

Cook the Pantry

One-Dish Vegan

1,000 Vegan Recipes

Vegan Planet

Vegan on the Cheap

Party Vegan

More Quick-Fix Vegan

Quick-Fix Vegan

The Vegetarian Meat and Potatoes Cookbook

The Nut Butter Cookbook

Plant Protein Revolution

THE
PLANT-BASED
SLOW COOKER

225 SUPER-TASTY VEGAN RECIPES

ROBIN ROBERTSON

HARVARD
COMMON
PRESS

Brimming with creative inspiration, how-to projects, and useful information to enrich your everyday life, Quarto Knows is a favorite destination for those pursuing their interests and passions. Visit our site and dig deeper with our books into your area of interest: Quarto Creates, Quarto Cooks, Quarto Homes, Quarto Lives, Quarto Drives, Quarto Explores, Quarto Gifts, or Quarto Kids.

First Published in 2020 by The Harvard Common Press, an imprint of The Quarto Group, 100 Cummings Center, Suite 265-D, Beverly, MA 01915, USA.
T (978) 282-9590 F (978) 283-2742 QuartoKnows.com

The Harvard Common Press titles are also available at discount for retail, wholesale, promotional, and bulk purchase. For details, contact the Special Sales Manager by email at specialsales@quarto.com or by mail at The Quarto Group, Attn: Special Sales Manager, 100 Cummings Center, Suite 265-D, Beverly, MA 01915, USA.

24 23 22 21 20   1 2 3 4 5

ISBN: 978-1-59233-990-7
Digital edition published in 2020

Content in the book was previously published in Fresh from the Vegan Slow Cooker by Robin Robertson (The Harvard Common Press 2012).

Library of Congress Cataloging-in-Publication Data available

Cover Design: Rita Sowins
Cover Image: Shutterstock
Page Layout: Megan Jones Design
Illustration: Neverne Covington

Printed in China

For the animals

Acknowledgments

Many thanks to Eve-Marie Williams, recipe tester superstar, for testing all the new recipes in this edition—your slow cooker was working overtime!

I also remain grateful to those who slow-cooked their way through the recipes in the previous edition of this book: Amanda Sacco, Andrea Zeichner, Barbara Bryan, Dave Melmer, Debbie Cowherd, Heather Galaxy, Jill Paschal, Joan Farkas, Jocelyn Kimmel, Jonathan and Nancy Shanes, Julie Smallwood, Lea Jacobson, Lori Maffei, Lyndsay Orwig, Melissa Chapman, Melissa West, Sabrina Butkera, Terri Merritts, and Zsu Dever. Your careful and enthusiastic testing and spot-on feedback made my job much easier.

Much gratitude goes to everyone at Quarto and The Harvard Common Press for their part in making this book a reality, with special thanks to Erik Gilg, Associate Publisher; Dan Rosenberg, Editorial Director; Nyle Vialet, Project Manager; and Marissa Giambrone, Art Director.

Thanks also to my longtime agent, Stacey Glick of Dystel, Goderich & Bourret and to my husband, Jon Robertson, for always being there.

Contents

Introduction

The irresistible appeal of a slow cooker is its convenience and simplicity. Turn it on, and it cooks dinner while you do other things. You have no pot to watch. It doesn't burn or spill over. Just set it and let it do its work. Next thing you know, your kitchen smells heavenly, and you feel like your personal chef did all the work.

Slow cookers first appeared in the 1970s, and you could get one in harvest gold, avocado green, or maybe decorated with orange flowers. Back then, the Crock-Pot (as the Rival Company, which is now a brand of Sunbeam Products, trademarked it) was mostly favored for cooking tough cuts of meat. The Crock-Pot left the limelight for a while, but in 2002, when I wrote my first slow cooker cookbook (*Fresh from the Vegetarian Slow Cooker*, The Harvard Common Press, 2004), slow cookers were enjoying a comeback. The goal of my first slow cooker book was to show how versatile slow cookers are for vegetarian cooking—they can be used to prepare everything from breakfast to dessert.

Fast-forward to 2012, ten years from writing that first book, and the popularity of slow cookers showed no sign of waning. Since those first two slow cooker cookbooks were published, I've written many other titles, but I never stopped developing new recipes, discovering new techniques, and exploring new ideas for using the slow cooker. As I've continued to develop new plant-based recipes for the slow cooker, and tweak my existing ones, I've come to realize that it was time to share them in a new volume.

In the eight years since *Fresh from the Vegan Slow Cooker* (The Harvard Common Press, 2012) was published, I have developed new recipes and explored the world's cuisines to discover more creative ways to prepare food using the slow cooker method. At the same time, more people are enjoying a plant-based diet than ever before, and they may be looking for a new take on a reliable cooking method.

I'm pleased and proud, therefore, to present this new book to you. It contains more than 225 recipes using only plant-based ingredients. While I've included much of the general information and the basic recipes from the first two books, this new volume contains many new recipes and lots of updated tips for making the most of your slow cooker experience. I've worked hard to make the recipes accessible using most sizes of slow cookers. In addition to being plant based, the recipes have helpful icons to indicate if they are also gluten-free, soy-free, or fat-free, or have options to make them so. I've also added a new chapter called "Not from the Crock" that contains recipes for ingredients used to enhance some of the slow cooker recipes that are not themselves made in a slow cooker, such as cashew sour cream and tempeh bacon.

We all know that a slow cooker is ideal for cooking beans, soups, and stews, but as you explore the pages of *The Plant-Based Slow Cooker*, you'll discover a whole new slow-cooking world. The slow cooker can be used to make braised vegetable dishes, comforting casseroles, luxurious risottos, and fun dips and snacks. It can even be used to "bake" potatoes, breads, pâtés, and desserts.

With chapters on everything from appetizers to main dishes, desserts, and beverages, there's something for everyone's breakfast, lunch, and dinner. *The Plant-Based Slow Cooker* picks up where my previous books left off and delivers healthy and delicious plant-based recipes. I love to cook in my slow cooker, and I hope that after you try some of these recipes, you will, too.

CHAPTER 1

Slow Cooker Basics

There is something almost primal about slow cooking that warms the soul. Perhaps this feeling is rooted in our ancestral iron-pot traditions around the hearth. Cooking food in closed ceramic vessels dates back at least to Roman times and is still done throughout the world, from the Moroccan tagine and the Italian *fagioliera* to the Pan-Asian clay pots (in Chinese, *shāguo* or *bàozai;* in Japanese, *donabe*). There is growing interest in another, even lower-tech method called "retained heat" or "haybox" cooking, in which food is brought to a boil and then allowed to continue cooking inside an insulated container.

The first modern electric slow cooker was originally developed for bean cooking. The "Beanery," made by Naxon Utilities Corporation, was redubbed the Crock-Pot by the Rival Manufacturing Company after it bought Naxon in 1971. This revolutionary kitchen appliance was marketed to working women as a way to make a home-cooked meal while they were at work, and they quickly put it to use in preparing pot roasts and other meat-centric dishes. A phenomenal hit at the time, the Crock-Pot fad faded, only to enjoy a resurgence some thirty years later. Since those early days, more than 80 million slow cookers have been sold, with more than 350 models and counting, from basic manual cookers limited to the two Low or High settings to fully programmable units with a variety of settings.

Why Use a Slow Cooker?

If you have been using a slow cooker in your kitchen with any regularity, then you know that there are many answers to that question.

For many years, I used my 1970s-era slow cooker for cooking beans or bean soups. However, when I got my first high-tech slow cooker, I was inspired to look beyond bean basics and began experimenting with all of the ingredients I love. To my delight, I discovered that the slow cooker cooked a seitan pot roast just as well as it had cooked traditional roasts, and it easily cooked many of my other favorite vegan dishes.

Most slow cooker enthusiasts would agree that convenience, economy, and great taste are what keep them coming back to their slow cookers time and again. When you cook in a slow cooker, the longer cooking times allow the flavors of the ingredients to meld into a deep complexity that is often unparalleled in other cooking methods. Slow cooking can be more nutritious, too, since the long cooking time allows the nutrients to concentrate in the food as it draws more flavor out of the ingredients. When you factor in the convenience quotient, you've got a kitchen helper worthy of the name.

Think about it: You simply assemble your ingredients in the slow cooker, turn it on, and that's it—several hours later, dinner is served. But the benefits don't stop there. For added convenience, your meal can be served directly from the ceramic pot in which it was cooked. In addition, the removable ceramic insert can be refrigerated, so you can prepare your ingredients the night before and refrigerate them overnight right in the insert so it's all ready to cook the next day. Slow cooking can be a terrific solution for busy people who are trying to eat healthier and for anyone who wants an easy way to eat more deliciously.

At the heart of slow cooking lies a paradox: Your food takes longer to cook, but it gives you more free time. I find it more liberating to get dinner cooking in a slow cooker than I do preparing even the quickest meal at the last minute, especially when I'm tired and hungry. Slow cooking can help you eat more well-balanced and economical meals on the nights when you're running late or too exhausted to cook. The reason is that those are the nights when you're tempted to order takeout, or eat junk food or a packaged convenience food. Simply by planning ahead, slow cooking can reward you with the ultimate convenience food.

Because of how well slow cookers cook many bean, grain, and vegetable dishes, the appliances are especially useful for preparing vegan meals. While some people may prefer using a pressure cooker for beans and other long-cooking recipes, I find the slow cooker more convenient since you can leave it unattended—something you wouldn't do with a pressure cooker or any stovetop cooking method. So even though meals prepared in a slow cooker take longer to cook, they can end up saving you time.

The flavor factor is also a good reason to use the slow cooker. Dishes that have been simmered for hours in a slow cooker taste better than the same recipe prepared quickly on top of the stove. The extended, gentle cooking time in a covered

10 GREAT THINGS TO KNOW ABOUT YOUR SLOW COOKER

1. It's a convenient way to prepare healthy home-cooked meals.

2. It allows you to cook and serve in the same vessel, so it saves on cleanup time.

3. It can have dinner ready and waiting for you at the end of the day.

4. The slow, gentle cooking adds depth of flavor to foods.

5. It keeps the kitchen cool on hot days.

6. It's an ideal way to cook beans and seitan from scratch.

7. It doubles as a chafing dish or hot punch bowl at parties.

8. It's economical because it uses less energy than oven cooking and makes great leftovers.

9. It can be used as a mini-oven to slow-bake cakes, casseroles, potatoes, and more.

10. It frees up stovetop burners when cooking for parties or for a crowd on holidays.

ceramic pot allows the flavors of the ingredients to fully bloom, mingle, and intensify. Using a slow cooker allows you to enjoy the intense flavors of hearty soups, stews, and other recipes without having to be tethered to a hot stove.

In addition, a slow cooker doesn't heat up the kitchen the way other cooking methods do, which is a great relief when you're cooking on hot days. Finally, the slow cooker uses less energy than other cooking methods, so you save money on utilities. And speaking of saving money, the slow cooker also makes it easy to cook larger quantities of food that can then be portioned and frozen. This is much preferable to relying on frozen convenience foods, which are more expensive.

While your main dish is simmering in the slow cooker, you also have more time to be creative with your side dishes, salads, or other accompaniments. Food doesn't burn when left unattended because the heating coils in slow cookers cook food gently and evenly from the bottom and sides. The lid keeps the heat and moisture inside. While the benefits of slow cooking make it ideal for when you're not home, it's also a great relief to busy stay-at-home moms and those who work at home and don't have the time to linger in the kitchen.

Versatility is another great reason to slow cook. Thanks to the wide variety of sizes now available, slow cookers can be used to make anything from appetizers to desserts. A slow cooker can also be a great help when company's coming, allowing you to keep the soup or main dish warm while you entertain your guests.

Using a slow cooker also lets you free up other cooking surfaces, which can be especially handy for holiday meals. If you're serving a buffet meal, you can place the slow cooker right on the table. It will keep the food at the proper serving temperature for hours while you enjoy the party. Slow-cooked dishes are also great for potlucks and other gatherings. Just prepare your dish in the slow cooker, bring along the entire unit (some come with their own carrying cases), and plug it in when you arrive at your destination to keep your dish warm for serving.

All Shapes and Sizes

The original Crock-Pot came in only one size (3½ to 4 quarts, or 3.3 to 3.8 L), one shape (round), and a few colors that now seem awful, such as harvest gold and avocado green. The stoneware crock was not removable, and the temperature settings were manual and limited to either High or Low. How things have changed!

Today there are many slow-cooker brands available, including the original Crock-Pot made by Rival (now a brand of Sunbeam Products) and similar units made by companies such as Proctor Silex, West Bend, All-Clad, and others. The removable ceramic inserts of most slow cookers are dishwasher-, oven-, and microwave-safe, but they typically cannot be used directly on the stovetop. One exception is the Hamilton Beach Stovetop-Safe Slow Cooker, which is designed to go from stovetop to slow cooker, allowing you to brown and cook in the same vessel.

You can find slow cookers in sizes ranging from 1 to 7 quarts (960 ml to 6.7 L). They are available in round or oval shapes with removable crockery inserts. The most popular sizes are the 4-quart (3.8 L; medium) and the 6-quart (5.7 L; large). The bigger models of slow cooker are great for large quantities of food and to hold racks and pans for "baking" inside a slow cooker.

Smaller 1- to 1½-quart (960 ml to 1.4 L) slow cookers are ideal for dips, hot drinks, and other party food, but they are impractical for most everyday cooking. Only two or three recipes for dips in this book call for the small cooker.

If you can buy only one slow cooker (and your household consists of more than one person), I recommend that you buy a larger model—at least 5 to 6 quarts (4.8 to 5.7 L). This will allow you more flexibility, because most recipes calling for a 4-quart (3.8 L) model can easily be made in the larger one, often with no adjustment to the recipe. The bigger slow cooker also enables you to make larger volume recipes, which you can then portion and freeze for further convenience. In addition, certain recipes (such as breads and desserts) call for a small (7-inch, or 18 cm) springform or other pan to be inserted in the cooker, and you will need a larger model to accomplish this. Even though I'm usually cooking for only two people, I most often use my 6-quart (5.7 L) slow cooker so that I can freeze plenty of leftovers.

While some slow cookers have basic manual High and Low settings, other cookers are completely programmable with integrated timers to start and stop the cooking, as well as a "Keep

Warm" setting to keep the food at a constant serving temperature once the allotted cooking time is over. You can also plug your cooker into a kitchen timer that you can set to switch on or off at a designated time, allowing for more peace of mind if you're late getting home.

Recent innovations in slow cookers include a three-in-one unit that features three different size crocks that fit into the same base, offering lots of flexibility. There are also models, such as the one described earlier, that have inserts that can be used on the stovetop as well as in the oven or freezer. This type of cooker is especially handy for browning onions and other ingredients on the stovetop before cooking in the slow cooker. In addition, there is the Instant Pot and other "multi-cookers," so named because they can be used for pressure cooking, sautéing, and other types of cooking. However, bear in mind the timing and temperature settings in a multi-cooker may vary greatly from a traditional slow cooker.

Slow Cookers Used for Testing These Recipes

More than twenty people tested the recipes for this book, using various brands and sizes of slow cookers, including several Rival Crock-Pots, a number of Hamilton Beach/Proctor Silex slow cookers, a few West Bend Crockery Cookers, a Betty Crocker slow cooker, a Cuisinart programmable slow cooker, and more. Some testers noticed, as I have, that their cookers have various quirks—some cook faster or slower than others, and some have a "hot spot" on one side. For that reason, most of the recipes in this book include a range of cooking times that you may need to adjust according to your own slow cooker's "temperament."

If you think that having one slow cooker is great, then you may find that having two is even better. I regularly use both 4-quart and 6-quart (3.8 and 5.7 L) models, and I sometimes use both sizes at once. As many slow-cooker fans have discovered, there is frequently a need for both. Sometimes you may need a large one for the main dish and a smaller one for a side dish, soup, or dessert. I have a total of three slow cookers in different sizes: one small (1½-quart, or 1.4 L) round, one medium-size (4-quart, or 3.8 L) round, and one large (6-quart, or 5.7 L) oval. They all get a lot of use, especially during one of my marathon cooking days when I prepare food for the following week and cook up some staples such as beans to portion and freeze for future use. Even if it's just to take advantage of the various recipes that are best prepared in one size or another, you may want to consider buying a second cooker.

What about the Instant Pot?

One of the most prominent changes to the world of small appliance cooking in recent years has been the widespread popularity of the Instant Pot, or multi-cooker. The Instant Pot boasts seven different cooking methods, including pressure cooking and slow cooking.

In my experience, I've found the Instant Pot to be great as an electric pressure cooker. When I'm in a hurry for a batch of beans or whole grains, I almost always reach for the Instant Pot to get the job done.

But I still love the flavors of foods cooked long and slow, so I was keen to see if the Instant Pot was as good at slow cooking as it was at pressure cooking. Let's just say, I wasn't impressed for several reasons.

The Instant Pot has different settings than a traditional slow cooker. While the Instant Pot and most slow cookers have three settings (most slow cookers settings are Low, High, and Warm and the Instant Pot's slow cooker settings are Less, Normal, and More), the actual cooking temperatures on those settings do not align with each other.

Another difference is that a slow cooker heats from the bottom with that heat spreading up the sides of the ceramic insert, which absorbs the heat and radiates from the sides. An Instant Pot also heats from the bottom, but its thin metal insert doesn't radiate the same way as a slow cooker. The heat in an Instant Pot comes from pressurized steam, which works well as a pressure cooker but less so as a slow cooker.

Bottom line, if you do decide to use your Instant Pot as a slow cooker, you will need to experiment with a few recipes to determine the time and setting you need to use. For me, the Instant Pot has proven to be a fabulous electric pressure cooker but less impressive as a slow cooker. I love both appliances for doing what they do best, and happily make room for each of them on my countertop.

It's Easy to Become a Slow-Cooking Expert

Because food cooked in a slow cooker virtually "cooks itself," this type of cooking is simple and stress free. By keeping a few basic tips in mind, you can become a slow-cooking expert in no time.

INGREDIENT VOLUME VERSUS SLOW COOKER SIZE

Each recipe in this book specifies a recommended slow cooker size. However, since the amount of the ingredients determines the volume, it is important to pay attention to how full your cooker is after adding all of your ingredients.

For example, since the range of what constitutes a "small" onion or a "large" potato may vary, you may find that the volume of ingredients in your cooker is too close to the top. Especially if you are preparing a soup or stew, there is a risk that the contents may bubble up and over onto your kitchen counter. You will need to assess this as you are preparing the recipe, keeping in mind that slow cookers perform best when at least half full but no more than three-quarters full.

RECIPE COOKING TIMES

When slow cookers first came on the market, the appeal to the working woman was the fact that most recipes listed an eight- to ten-hour cooking time—long enough for the dish to cook all day while she was at work. While this cooking time may be correct for certain recipes, particularly meat-centric ones, the fact is that many of them don't take as long to cook as once thought. This is especially true for a variety of vegan ingredients, including seitan, tofu, and plant-based sausage.

In developing the recipes for this book, my testers and I found that many recipes are actually ready to eat much sooner than the traditional eight hours, although some recipes do hold up well when left to cook for an additional hour or so. The forgiving nature of slow-cooker cooking times is one of the great features of the appliance.

I've done my best to provide realistic times for when dishes may actually be done while stressing that you may often tack on an additional hour or so for the food to cook without compromising flavor or texture. Most recipes will also be fine for a while beyond the cooking time when held at the Keep Warm setting.

If this still doesn't allow you enough time to get home and turn off the slow cooker (and if your slow cooker doesn't have a built-in timer), the solution is to purchase an inexpensive appliance timer to use with your cooker. Simply set the timer to start cooking up to two hours later. That way you can enjoy the convenience of shorter-cooking recipes if you're away from home all day.

If you're short on time in the morning, one of the easiest solutions is to prepare your ingredients and load your slow cooker insert the night before, then refrigerate the crock overnight. The next morning, you can then put the insert in the slow cooker and set the cooking time in just seconds.

HIGH ALTITUDES

If you are cooking at a high elevation (over 3,000 feet, or 1 km), you may find that food cooked in a slow cooker takes somewhat longer to get done than the cooking times recommended in this cookbook. To compensate, you can cook all recipes on High, although you will probably also need to cook your food a little longer as well. Once you calibrate the cooking time for your location, make a note of the changes for future use.

SLOW COOKER POINTS AND POINTERS

1. To save time in the morning, prepare your ingredients and load your slow cooker insert the night before and refrigerate it overnight. You can then quickly put the insert in the slow cooker and set the cooking time in the morning.

2. While slow cookers are designed for even heating, some have "hot spots." So, for all but very "soupy" recipes, it's a good idea to oil the insert of your slow cooker or spray it with nonstick cooking spray. If you have a slow cooker with a nonstick insert, oiling or spraying may not be needed.

3. Many recipes achieve a better flavor if some of the ingredients (specifically onions, garlic, and spices) are cooked for a few minutes before adding them to the slow cooker. Since some people won't want to dirty a skillet to do this, such recipes include the option of using the microwave for this step.

4. It's a fact that all slow cookers cook at different temperatures: sometimes slightly different, sometimes dramatically different. For this reason, you will notice a fairly wide time range for doneness—usually plus or minus two hours. For the most part, recipes will be cooked on Low, since many people want to be able to set it in the morning and forget it until dinnertime. A High cooking time choice is sometimes also provided. If the cooking time in your own slow cooker varies dramatically from those listed in this book, make a note of it to "calibrate" future recipes for your own slow cooker.

Tips for Slow-Cooking Success

Slow cooking is simple, but you can still make mistakes by not knowing some basic dos and don'ts. Follow these simple rules—and their exceptions—and you can transform what would have been so-so slow cooker meals into meals that are nothing short of sensational.

Try not to lift the lid when cooking. Doing so will reduce the cooking temperature considerably and cause your dish to take longer to cook. It is estimated that each time you lift the lid, you lose twenty minutes of cooking time. However, some rules are made to be broken, and sometimes you just need to lift the lid. Exceptions to this rule include the need to add certain ingredients before the end of cooking time or the need to stir a particular dish. For the most part, you should be able to check on what you're cooking by looking through the clear glass lid. If you do want to lift the lid to stir, check for doneness, or adjust seasonings, just do so as quickly as

5. If there's too much liquid left in the cooker at the end of cooking time, remove the lid and turn the heat to High to evaporate some of it. Conversely, if there's not enough liquid, add a little more and let it warm up and blend with the other flavors.

6. Hard vegetables, such as onions and carrots, added raw to soups and braises will soften just fine because of the amount of liquid they are cooking in. However, if these same vegetables are added raw to stews, they will remain hard long after the rest of the ingredients are cooked because there is not as much liquid for them to cook in. When using hard vegetables in a stew dish, it is best to sauté them first to soften them (or soften them in a covered bowl in a microwave).

7. The smaller or thinner you cut or slice ingredients, the more quickly they will cook.

8. For easy cleanup, consider using Reynolds Kitchens Slow Cooker Liners, made specifically for use in slow cookers on both High and Low settings.

9. With a few exceptions, you will achieve optimal results if the slow cooker is between one-half and three-quarters full. The majority of recipes in this book can be made in most medium-size to large slow cookers (4 to 6 quarts, or 3.8 o 5.7 L).

possible—and be aware that you may need to tack on a little extra cooking time.

Always fill your slow cooker at least half full. Avoid filling it more than three-quarters full to keep it from spilling over while simmering. Exceptions to this rule include recipes that call for "steam-baking," such as cheesecake on a trivet, stuffed vegetables, baked potatoes, or other such recipes. Special instructions are provided for recipes that require this step.

One size fits most. As a rule, most of these recipes can be made in 4- to 6-quart (3.8 to 5.7 L) slow cookers because they contain enough volume that they require no adjustment. For example, approximately 3 quarts (2.8 L) of total ingredient volume will fill a 4-quart (3.8 L) model three-quarters full (the maximum recommended volume), and the same amount of ingredients will fill a 6-quart (5.7 L) cooker one-half full (the minimum recommended volume).

Sometimes partial cooking is required. Some recipes call for partially cooking or browning some ingredients, such as onions and garlic, on the stovetop before placing them in the slow cooker. The short amount of time this extra step takes can make a big difference in the taste, texture, and appearance of the dish. In many cases, this step can be done in a microwave or even directly in the slow cooker, when the purpose is to bloom the flavor or soften the ingredients as opposed to browning them.

Save the best for last. Some recipes that use quick-cooking or delicate ingredients, such as fresh herbs or spinach, will call for these ingredients to be added at or near the end of the cooking time. This attention to detail will pay off when you taste the finished dish.

Adapt your own recipes. Because the lid remains on throughout most slow-cooked recipes, the liquids do not evaporate the way they do in similar stovetop recipes. Because of this, when converting your own recipes for the slow cooker, you may need to reduce the total amount of liquid called for. If you find that you have too much liquid near the end of the cooking time, remove the lid and cook on High for an additional thirty to forty minutes to reduce the excess liquid, or simply drain off some of the liquid before serving.

Always presoak dried beans. Soaking will help with digestibility and make your slow-cooked beans tender in less time. I also offer options for using canned beans in the recipes.

Dried beans prefer an "acid-free" zone. When cooking dried beans, don't add tomatoes or other acidic ingredients until after the beans have softened; otherwise they will take longer to cook and may remain tough. Once the beans are cooked, drain and discard the cooking liquid before using the beans in a recipe. This will improve their digestibility.

Add pasta or rice. There are two ways to add pasta or rice to slow-cooked recipes. You can either add dried pasta or raw rice during the final hour of cooking time, or cook the rice or pasta separately on the stovetop and add it to the dish just prior to serving. The latter is my preference because it gives you more control and assures the proper texture. Rice or pasta cooked directly in the slow cooker often turns out too mushy or starchy. In addition, cooking either one in the cooker will soak up much of the recipe's liquid and change the texture of the finished dish.

There are some recipes in this book that call for rice, but barley is my personal favorite grain to cook in a slow cooker.

The Microwave: An Optional Step for Extra Flavor

As I've mentioned, my recipes occasionally contain instructions to sauté some of the ingredients before adding them to the slow cooker. This is done for several reasons—usually to get the most flavor or most appealing color from certain ingredients or, in the case of particularly hard vegetables, to jump-start the cooking process. For that reason, you'll find that many recipes in this book begin with first sautéing onions (and other ingredients) in either a little water or oil for a few minutes for best results.

To me, that extra step and that extra pan to wash is a small price to pay for superior flavor. However, I understand that time is at a premium for many of you, and many people simply don't want to wash an extra pan when slow cooking. Rather than omit the step entirely, there is a compromise solution: Use your microwave!

Instead of sautéing onions and garlic and other ingredients in a skillet, you can simply "sweat" them in a covered microwave-safe bowl for a few minutes in the microwave to soften them and bring out their flavor. This also works for giving extra-hard ingredients, such as carrots, a head start so that they get done cooking at the same time as the softer vegetables in a recipe. The microwave option lets you avoid washing an extra pan, since you can then simply put the bowl in the dishwasher. Microwaving is also

a good choice if you wish to avoid the oil used when sautéing ingredients, as you can omit the oil and add a little water to the vegetables in the microwave. If you prefer not to use a microwave but want to avoid sautéing in oil, water-sauté the vegetables in a few tablespoons of water for a few minutes before adding to the slow cooker as suggested in many of the recipes.

Another way to give certain ingredients a head start is to place them in the slow cooker, cover, and turn it on High while you prep the rest of the ingredients. The amount of time this will take depends on the size and volume of the vegetables being used. For example, 1 tablespoon (10 g) of minced garlic may take only 15 minutes to soften and allow the flavor to bloom, while ½ cup (80 g) of chopped onion can take up to 30 minutes, so this shortcut is practical only if you plan to be in the kitchen doing other things anyway.

A final option is to simply skip all preliminary steps and just load the crock with the ingredients and let them cook in the slow cooker from start to finish. Remember, the smaller you cut the ingredients, the faster they will cook.

Note: If you plan to turn on the slow cooker in the morning before leaving the house, you can do any advance prep the night before to save time in the morning.

LAST-MINUTE ADDITIONS

The microwave can also come in handy near the end of cooking a recipe. You can use the microwave to cook delicate vegetables, such as spinach, for a last-minute addition to a slow-cooked dish. Just place washed spinach (or other delicate greens) in a microwave-safe bowl, cover, and wilt them in the microwave for a couple of minutes. Then drain off any liquid.

Other delicate ingredients are best added near the end of cooking, or at serving time, so that their flavors don't dissipate and they don't overcook. Cooked pasta or rice should be added close to the end of the cooking time so they do not become mushy. Fresh herbs are a good example of ingredients that lose their flavor if added too soon. Just as the flavor of fresh herbs dissipates if added at the beginning of the cooking time, the flavor of dried herbs can concentrate or turn bitter, so they need to be used in judicious quantities. You can always add more near the end of the cooking time, after checking the dish for flavor balance.

Cooking-Time Variables

Some slow-cooker brands and models cook a bit faster (hotter) than others, while others cook more slowly. For that reason, you may need to monitor the cooking times of the first recipes you try so that you can calibrate your particular slow cooker. Other cooking-time variables include the actual temperature of the food you start with—Is it at room temperature or cold from the refrigerator?—and the size of the pieces of food being cooked.

If you begin slow cooking with cold ingredients, they will take longer to cook than if they were at room temperature. If both the food and slow cooker insert are cold (as would be the case if you assemble your ingredients in the cooker insert the night before and refrigerate it until morning), the cooking time will be longer still. Be sure to factor in some extra time (thirty to forty-five minutes) for things to warm up when

estimating your cooking time. You can use this to your advantage if you will be away from home all day.

The original reason that slow cookers became so popular was because of their ability to cook dinner all day while we were at work. From that perspective, recipes that take about eight hours to cook have special appeal. For recipes to finish around the eight-hour mark, they will generally need to be cooked on Low (200°F). If you cook the same recipe on High (300°F), the food will be ready in about half the time.

Whenever possible, I cook on Low rather than High because I think that the slower, gentler cooking coaxes more flavor from the ingredients. Unless otherwise specified, most recipes in this book use the Low setting, although you may use the High setting if you're pressed for time or simply prefer your food to cook faster.

IF YOU NEED TO EXTEND THE COOKING TIME

For those with especially long workdays, having dinner ready when you get home is a dream come true. However, many slow-cooker recipes are done in six to eight hours, when you need it to be more like nine to ten hours. Here are three ways to extend the cooking time:

1. Choose a slow cooker that has a built-in timer to allow the cooker to turn on after you've gone to work. On the other end of the cooking time, it can also switch over to the Keep Warm setting, if needed.

2. A less expensive solution is to buy a small appliance kitchen timer (available at hardware stores). When you plug your cooker into a kitchen timer, you can set it to start up to two hours after you leave the house.

3. For a really low-tech solution, simply prepare your ingredients the night before and place them in the slow cooker insert, then refrigerate it overnight. Before you leave in the morning, place the cold insert in the cooker and turn it on Low. It will take an extra thirty to forty-five minutes for your recipe to cook from the cold state, so you can extend the cooking time that much further. If your cooker has an automatic Keep Warm setting, it will keep your dinner warm for you until you get home. (Remember not to leave food on this setting for longer than two hours.)

While some recipes require every bit of an eight-hour spread, many recipes will actually be quite ready to eat after about six hours, and some even less. Wherever possible, I've listed the cooking times in two-hour spreads, to compensate for the heat variables in individual slow cookers, and to indicate the particular time window when a recipe may be done. In many cases, if you're going to be a little later than the designated time, many recipes will hold just fine for a little while longer.

Some slow cookers have a built-in function that will allow them to cook for six or eight hours, for example, then automatically switch to the Keep Warm setting. This kind of cooker is great for people who don't arrive home at the same time each day. For food safety reasons, once your food is cooked, you should not let it sit on the Keep Warm setting for longer than two hours. If your schedule requires a longer time frame, I suggest you use an appliance timer with your cooker and set it to start cooking up to two hours after you leave the house.

Ways to Thicken Liquids

Because the food is essentially sealed inside the slow cooker while it is being cooked, there tends to be a lot of moisture produced that doesn't have an opportunity to evaporate, as in other cooking methods. In some cases, such as brothy soups, this extra liquid may be fine, but in some recipes, such as stews, you may prefer to thicken the liquid so it is more of a sauce. There are a number of ways to thicken the liquid in a slow-cooked dish. Here are the most common:

Mashed vegetables: After the food is cooked, mash a couple of chunks of cooked potato (you may want to add a few extra chunks to a recipe for this purpose) and stir it into the liquid. The addition of cooked rice can absorb some of the liquid as well.

Pureed vegetables: Scoop out a cup (or more; weight varies) of the cooked vegetables and puree them in a blender or food processor; then stir the puree back into the slow cooker.

SLOW–COOKER TIMING FACTORS

The amount of time it will take for food to cook in your slow cooker depends on more than just how long you cook it and whether you set it on High or Low. Here are some other factors that can affect the cooking time:

The type and model of slow cooker. One cooker's Low setting may be several degrees hotter than another cooker's Low setting. I have discovered that one of my slow cookers cooks "faster" (or hotter) than the others, and another cooks more slowly than normal, so I plan accordingly.

The temperature of the ingredients when you add them to the slow cooker. If your ingredients are at room temperature or hotter, they will cook faster than if the ingredients (or the entire ceramic cooking insert) just came out of the refrigerator.

The size of the pieces of vegetables and other ingredients you are using. This may be a no-brainer, but the smaller/thinner the pieces of your ingredients, the faster they will cook.

The amount of liquid in the pot and its temperature. Less liquid takes less time to heat up. In addition, if you use hot or boiling liquid, it will shorten the cooking time.

Cornstarch slurry: Blend 1 tablespoon (8 g) cornstarch with 2 tablespoons (30 ml) cold water (to thicken 1 cup, or 240 ml, of liquid). Set the slow cooker on High and stir the cornstarch mixture into the hot liquid. Put the lid back on the cooker and cook for about ten minutes longer.

Reduction: Set the slow cooker on High, remove the lid, and let the food simmer until the volume of liquid reduces.

Cashew sour cream or cream cheese: At the end of the cooking time, blend 2 tablespoons (28 g) Cashew Sour Cream (page 338) or Cashew Cream Cheese (22 g; page 339) with ½ cup (120 ml) of the hot liquid from the slow cooker to temper it and make it smooth. Stir the mixture back into the slow cooker liquid.

Arrowroot: Blend 1 tablespoon (8 g) arrowroot with 2 tablespoons (30 ml) cold water (to thicken 2 cups, or 480 ml, of liquid). Set the slow cooker on High and stir the arrowroot mixture into the hot liquid. Put the lid back on the cooker and cook for about ten minutes longer.

Roux: Melt 2 tablespoons (28 g) vegan butter in a small pan, then stir in 2 tablespoons (15.5 g) flour and stir for a minute or two. Pour in about ½ cup (120) of liquid from the slow cooker, then set the cooker on High and stir the roux mixture back into the hot liquid. Put the lid back on the cooker and cook for about ten minutes longer.

Tapioca starch: Blend 1 tablespoon (7.5 g) tapioca starch with 2 tablespoons (30 ml) cold water (to thicken 2 cups, or 480 ml, of liquid). Set the slow cooker on High and stir the tapioca mixture into the hot liquid. Put the lid back on the cooker and cook for about ten minutes longer.

Slow Cooking Plant-Based Ingredients

Since this is a plant-based cookbook, you obviously won't find the typical slow cooker recipes using cheap cuts of meat. Instead, you will find recipes that use a variety of beans, grains, and more vegetables than you ever imagined could be prepared in a slow cooker. In addition, there are recipes that use tofu, tempeh, seitan (also known as wheat meat), and other versatile ingredients. Here is a brief overview of the some of the ingredients used in this book.

TOFU

Tofu has become so mainstream that most people who use it are familiar with the two basic types and the various textures in which it can be purchased. "Regular" tofu, also known as "Chinese bean curd," is sold refrigerated in 14- to 16-ounce (395 to 455 g) tubs. "Silken" or "Japanese-style" tofu is most often sold in 12-ounce (340 g) aseptic containers. Both regular and silken tofu are available in varying textures, ranging from soft to extra-firm; the softer the tofu, the more water it contains. Generally, silken tofu is softer and creamier than regular tofu and is best suited to making sauces and desserts. Tofu in all its forms has come to be readily available in supermarkets these days, in addition to natural food and international grocery stores.

Because of the delicate texture of tofu, it does not usually hold up well in slow-cooker recipes unless added right at the end of the cooking time, although I have included recipes for braised tofu that allow for slabs of extra-firm tofu to cook in a small amount of liquid. Generally, however, tofu is most successful in slow-cooker recipes in which the tofu is mixed with other ingredients, as in a terrine, lasagna, stuffing, or dessert. Recipes calling for regular tofu will simply list "tofu" (usually firm or extra-firm). If silken tofu is required, it will be listed as such.

Regular tofu may be stored unopened in the refrigerator until you need it (in accordance with the expiration date on its package). Once tofu is opened, use it as soon as possible. It will keep for three to five days in the refrigerator if covered in fresh water in a tightly sealed container.

Because tofu is packed in water, it is important to drain it before using or it may add extra moisture into your recipe. After draining the tofu, you should blot it to remove even more moisture. To do this, cut the tofu into slabs and arrange them on a baking pan lined with two or three layers of paper towels. Cover the tofu with additional paper towels and blot.

If you wish to remove even more moisture from tofu, you can press it. Many people use a simple gadget called a tofu press to do this. If you don't have a tofu press, follow the steps for blotting tofu, then place a second baking pan on top of the top layer of paper towels. Place some heavy canned goods on top of the pan and allow the tofu to sit for an hour or so. Removing excess liquid will result in a firmer texture and allow the tofu to better absorb the surrounding flavors in your recipe.

TEMPEH

With its sturdy texture and ability to absorb surrounding flavors, tempeh is ideal for cooking in a slow cooker. Made from fermented soybeans that are compressed into a cake, tempeh has a chewy, meat-like texture and is especially suited to stews and braised dishes in the slow cooker. Tempeh can be sliced, diced, cubed, or grated. If you prefer a more mellow-flavored tempeh, you should steam it for at least fifteen minutes before using it in a recipe. To make it more visually appealing, you can sauté the tempeh in a little oil before adding it to the slow cooker to turn it a crisp golden brown, although that step is a personal choice.

Look for tempeh in the refrigerated or frozen section of natural food stores, Asian markets, and larger supermarkets, where it can be found in 8-ounce (225 g) packages. Increasingly, you can find versions made with a mix of soybeans and grains, or even from other beans such as black beans.

Tempeh can be stored in the refrigerator or freezer. If left unopened, tempeh will keep for several weeks or months (in accordance with the expiration date). Once opened, it is best to use it within four days.

SEITAN

Seitan (pronounced say-TAN) is made from the protein part of wheat known as gluten. The meaty texture and appearance of seitan make it a versatile ingredient that is ideal for slow cooking because it absorbs the surrounding flavors as it cooks and its texture holds up during long cooking. You can use diced seitan in stews and soups, shredded or ground seitan in chili, or sliced seitan braised in wine or vegetable stock. Larger pieces can be cooked as a roast.

Although precooked seitan is available in natural food stores and Asian markets, it is much more economical and versatile to make your own using vital wheat gluten, and it can typically be used from its raw, freshly made state. A recipe for homemade seitan can be found on page 154. It's best to make a large amount at once and freeze it in usable portions. If you do buy precooked commercial seitan, be sure to drain and rinse it before using, since it is often sold in a marinade that may not be compatible with your recipe.

PACKAGED MEAT ALTERNATIVES

Several varieties of packaged meat alternatives can be found in the frozen food department of natural food stores and well-stocked supermarkets. These products have the flavor and appearance of cooked meat and include plant-based sausage links and bacon. These products are convenient and versatile, and many have good flavor and texture. However, many people who follow a plant-based diet (especially a whole-foods plant-based diet) avoid such products because they can be highly processed.

To avoid processed foods as much as possible, I make my own plant-based sausage (page 174) and tempeh bacon (page 342). That way I know only wholesome ingredients are used. For those of you who would like to enjoy the flavors of such foods and don't have time to make your own, look for the least processed products you can find with easily recognizable ingredients.

SOY CURLS

Butler Soy Curls are similar to textured soy protein, but they are superior in texture and less processed. Soy curls are made from whole non-GMO soybeans. The product is high in fiber and protein and contains no additives or preservatives. It is very tender when reconstituted and ideal for adding to stews in the slow cooker. Soy curls are available online and in some natural food stores.

OTHER INGREDIENTS

Most of the ingredients used in this book can be found in well-stocked supermarkets. These days, many supermarkets have a good natural food section and international grocery aisles where you can find good-quality soy sauce, rice noodles, agave nectar, and so on, although a few ingredients, such as miso paste, nutritional yeast, and vital wheat gluten, may require a trip to a natural food store. If you can't find a particular ingredient where you live, do an online search and chances are you can easily find what you're looking for.

Plant milk, vegan cream cheese, vegan sour cream, and other dairy-free products are commonplace in many stores, but if you prefer to make your own, I have provided recipes for many of them including Cashew Cream Cheese (page 339), Cashew Sour Cream (page 338), and Cheesy Sauce (page 340).

Some ingredients are simply easier to buy ready-made, especially when you don't use it frequently. For me, one such ingredient is vegan butter. I rarely use it since I mostly avoid oils and fats in my cooking these days, but when only butter will do for a special meal or dessert, I use Miyoko's Cultured Vegan Butter because it is certified organic, non GMO, and made without palm oil. It also tastes great.

The chapter where you'll find these recipes, titled "Not from the Crock" (page 336), features recipes that are not prepared in a slow cooker but are called for in some of the recipes throughout the book.

Wide World of Beans

Because bean cooking was the intended use of the first slow cookers, it almost goes without saying that beans are a natural fit for the slow-cooking method. That said, however, there is a distinction to be made between "cooking beans" and "cooking with beans." Because beans take longer to cook than most vegetables, I prefer to use beans that have already been cooked in most of my recipes to avoid overcooking the vegetables. Another reason for using precooked beans in recipes is that it allows me to drain off the cooking liquid after cooking beans, making them more digestible.

In chapter 5 you will find a recipe for Basic Beans (page 114), along with variations. Cooking beans from the dried state in the slow cooker is both easy and economical. I like to cook large batches of different kinds of beans, portion them into containers, and freeze them to use later in recipes. If you prefer your beans firm rather than soft, you can slow cook your beans until they are just tender but still quite firm, and then allow them to cook the rest of the way in the various recipes you will be using them in.

While many of us enjoy cooking a variety of different beans, it's a safe bet that most of us have barely scratched the surface in terms of what types are available. Believe it or not, there are more than 13,000 different beans and legumes in the world—that's a lot of beans!

BEAN COOKING

There are some general guidelines to follow when cooking beans in a slow cooker. Bear in mind that dried beans expand when soaked and cooked. One cup of dried beans (weight varies) yields 2 to 3 cups (weight varies) cooked.

As a rule, you can cook 1 cup (weight varies) of presoaked beans in 4 cups (960 ml) of water. You should use 6 cups (1.4 L) of water for 2 cups (weight varies) of presoaked beans. For 1 pound (455 g) of dried beans, you will need 8 to 10 cups (1.9 to 2.4 L) of water. The beans should stay submerged in the water while cooking, so you should check on them about 1 hour before they are scheduled to be done and add some boiling water if needed. Otherwise, the beans that are not submerged may still be hard when the cooking time is over. Once cooked, the beans should cool in the slow cooker in their own liquid. You can then transfer the cooked beans into 1- to 2-cup (240 to 480 ml) containers, using a slotted spoon, then refrigerate or freeze until needed.

Most beans are done cooking in a slow cooker after three to four hours on High or eight to ten hours on Low, although some may take longer depending on the age and variety of bean, and others are done much sooner. With the exception of lentils and split peas, which do not require soaking, beans benefit from pre-soaking to shorten the cooking time and make them more digestible.

Note that uncooked kidney beans (including cannellini beans) contain a natural toxin (lectin phytohaemagglutinin) that must be destroyed by cooking. To do this, it is very important that you boil raw kidney beans in water for at least ten to fifteen minutes before cooking in the slow cooker, since the temperature of slow cooking alone may not be hot enough to destroy the toxin.

You may sometimes want to make a recipe using cooked beans but you don't happen to have any stashed in the freezer and there's no time to cook them from scratch. In those instances, let canned beans come to the rescue, which is another reason most recipes call for "cooked" beans—allowing you the choice of using cooked-from-scratch beans or canned beans. When a recipe calls for 1½ cups (425 g) of cooked beans, for example, you can use one

BEAN SLOW-COOKING TIMES

Here is a list of cooking times (on High) for presoaked dried beans. The times may vary depending on factors such as altitude and the age of the beans.

Black beans: 3 hours

Black-eyed peas: 3½ hours

Cannellini beans: 3 hours (boil 15 minutes before slow cooking)

Chickpeas: 4 hours

Great Northern beans: 2½ to 3 hours

Kidney beans: 3 hours (boil 15 minutes before slow cooking)

Lentils: 1½ to 2 hours (no need to presoak)

Navy beans: 2½ to 3 hours

Pinto beans: 3 hours

Split peas: 2½ hours (no need to presoak)

BEAN COOKING TIPS

- A convenient way to prepare dried beans to use in recipes is to cook the beans in your slow cooker overnight on Low. They will be done by morning and ready for you to use in recipes.

- A small piece of kombu sea vegetable added to the pot while the beans cook will help tenderize the beans while adding flavor and nutrients.

- Dried herbs should be added to beans during the final thirty minutes of cooking time. However, it is best to add fresh herbs after the beans are cooked for the best flavor.

- To keep cooked beans from drying out, cool them in their cooking liquid.

- For improved digestibility, be sure to drain the bean cooking liquid first before using the cooked beans in a recipe.

- For convenience, cook a large amount of beans, portion them into airtight containers, and store them in the refrigerator for up to one week or in the freezer for up to six months.

15-ounce (425 g) can of drained beans. Use two cans of beans when a recipe calls for 3 cups (750 g), and so on.

Here are some general ratios of dried, cooked, and canned beans to help you plan:

- 1 pound (455 g) dried beans = 2 cups (455 g) dried beans = 6 cups (1.5 kg) cooked beans = 4 (15-ounce, or 425 g) cans of beans

- ½ cup (125 g) dried beans = 1½ cups (425 g) cooked beans = 1 (15-ounce, or 425 g) can of beans

HOW TO SALT-SOAK BEANS

In recent years, many cooks have become enlightened about the relationship between beans and salt. Despite previous convictions to the contrary, it is now thought that "salt-soaking" your beans before cooking can actually help the beans cook faster.

Quick method: In a large pot or heatproof bowl, combine 1 pound (455 g) dried beans (rinsed and picked over), 2 tablespoons (36 g) salt, and 2 quarts (1.8 L) boiling water. Stir to dissolve the salt. Set aside at room temperature for one hour, then drain the beans, discard the soaking liquid, and rinse the beans before cooking.

Overnight method: In a large pot or bowl, combine 1 pound (455 g) dried beans (rinsed and picked over), 2 tablespoons (36 g) salt, and 4 quarts (3.8 L) cold water, stirring to dissolve the salt. Cover and set aside at room temperature for eight hours, then drain the beans, discard the soaking liquid, and rinse the beans before cooking.

Vegan versus Plant-Based versus Whole-Food Plant-Based

A vegan diet eliminates all animal products of all kinds, 100 percent of the time, often primarily for ethical reasons. In a plant-based diet, the majority of food comes from plants and is usually motivated by reasons of health. A whole-food plant-based diet consists of whole plant foods and avoids highly refined foods such as bleached flour, refined sugar, and most oil. It is possible (and common) to be both vegan and plant-based or whole-food plant-based.

About the Recipes

The recipes in this book are all vegan and plant-based, and many are also whole-food plant-based or have whole-food plant-based options.

With the exception of some of the desserts and a few other recipes, most of the recipes in this book are free of refined flours and processed ingredients. Many of them use little or no oil, or have an oil-free option.

In my home, I use very little oil, preferring to water-sauté, roast, or air-fry whenever possible.

The main reason oil is called for as a first choice in a few of the recipes is when it adds a particular nuance to a dish, such as browning, or when oil or vegan butter improves the flavor or texture of a cake or bread. Still, if you choose to eliminate all oil from your diet, feel free to eliminate it from those recipes as well, substituting water or broth, as needed. In the case of cake recipes, use applesauce in place of oil.

SOMETHING FOR EVERYONE

In the same way that I developed these recipes to be accessible to most types and sizes of slow cookers, I also wanted them to be accessible to as many people as possible, regardless of dietary restrictions.

Many of the recipes in this book are naturally low fat or even fat-free, while others are either gluten-free or soy-free, or both. Notes on the recipe pages indicate which recipes are gluten-free, oil-free, and/or soy-free, or can easily be made so.

Although there will invariably be exceptions that are not conducive to substitutions, if a particular recipe is not already in line with your food allergies or dietary preferences, here are some easy ways to make it so:

Gluten-free: Use wheat-free versions of ingredients such as soy sauce, pasta, and flours. For recipes that call for seitan, substitute tempeh or beans, depending on the type of recipe.

Oil-free: Some recipes call for a small amount of oil (usually 2 teaspoons) for advance sautéing of some ingredients. This use of oil in such recipes is optional to accommodate people who prefer to cook without oil. You can, instead, reduce the fat in recipes by spraying a skillet or pan with nonstick cooking spray or using a nonstick skillet. In many of these recipes you will find an oil-free option known as water-sauté, which means, simply, that you sauté the ingredients in water instead of oil.

If you prefer not to dirty a skillet (for either an oil or water-sauté) you can instead use a microwave: Place the ingredients and a few tablespoons of water in a covered microwave-safe bowl and microwave them for a couple of minutes instead of sautéing them.

To eliminate oil from cake or bread recipes, you can substitute any of the following for the oil in an equal volume: plant milk, unsweetened applesauce (or other pureed vegetable or fruit, depending on the recipe), ground flaxseed mixed with water, or pureed beans.

If and when you do use oil, try to use extra-virgin olive or avocado oil because they are the least processed oils.

Soy-free: Use almond milk instead of soy milk, and use soy-free vegan butter. For recipes that call for tofu or tempeh, substitute beans or seitan, depending on the type of recipe. And see the recipe on page 344 for a homemade Soy-Free Sauce you can use when soy sauce (or Worcestershire sauce) is called for in a recipe.

Also, if you have certain nut allergies, you can use a different type of nut or seed to replace the one you can't eat.

How to Use This Book

Some of the recipes in this book are inspired by traditional global recipes, while others are based on favorite recipes that I adapted for the slow cooker. I've been pleased to discover that, in addition to the usual soups, stews, bean dishes, and chili, the slow cooker can be used to braise vegetables, make risotto, "bake" breads and desserts, and cook delectable appetizers and snacks.

Many of the more foundational recipes, such as the basic bean cooking recipes, are similar to ones you may recall from my earlier cookbook, *Fresh from the Vegan Slow Cooker*. However, even within such basic recipes, you'll find new information, tips, and methods. And while most of the recipes themselves were in the previous book, they have been updated, revised, or otherwise improved.

The various sizes, shapes, and different heat levels of slow cookers make the standardizing of cooking directions somewhat challenging. However, to accommodate the broadest range of slow cookers, I've done my best to develop recipes that can be made in most slow cooker sizes. In each recipe, you will find the optimal size listed—that is, the best-size cooker for the

job—with many recipes calling for a size range of 4 to 6 quarts (3.8 to 5.7 L). In those instances, the ingredients should fit somewhere between the maximum recommended capacity for a 4-quart (3.8 L) cooker and the minimum recommended capacity for a 6-quart (5.7 L) cooker. Many recipes in this book specify a 4- to 6-quart (3.8 to 5.7 L) slow cooker, but in most cases, the recipe will also work fine in a 5-quart (4.8 L) or even a 7-quart (6.7 L) model, with little or no adjustment.

In terms of recipe yields, most recipes are designed to make four to six servings. Of course, a serving size can mean different things when you factor in big eaters, child-friendly portions, and second helpings. In my house, I purposely make large quantities of certain dishes so I can portion and freeze leftovers.

I can't stress enough that you need to get to know your slow cooker to familiarize yourself with how long different foods will actually take to cook in it. Once you do, you'll find that your slow cooker is the best kitchen helper you could ever want. I hope you enjoy preparing these recipes as much as I've enjoyed developing them.

Snacks and Appetizers

I f you've only used your slow cooker to make soup or chili, you may be excited to discover that it can also make snacks and appetizers, including dips, spreads, spiced nuts, and party mixes.

The versatile slow cooker can also double as a food warmer or chafing dish when you're having a get-together. Just set the food out in the cooker on the Keep Warm setting, and your guests can serve themselves. Larger slow cookers can even be employed as "steam cookers" to make luscious pâtés and terrines.

Featuring appetizer and snack recipes ranging from a luscious Savory Mediterranean Cheesecake to the crisp and crunchy Life of the Party Mix, this chapter can help you party hearty.

Spicy Tomato Queso Dip

MAKES ABOUT 2 CUPS (ABOUT 450 G)

SLOW COOKER SIZE: 1½- TO 2-QUART (1.4 TO 1.9 L) | COOK TIME: 2 HOURS ON LOW | GLUTEN-FREE | OIL-FREE | SOY-FREE

This is a quick and delicious dip that assembles easily. It also lends itself to variations. For example, you can add crumbled plant-based sausage or stir in some black beans. Serve with tortilla chips. To make it gluten-free, be sure to use certified gluten-free oat flour or substitute your favorite gluten-free flour.

1 (14.5-ounce, or 425 g) can diced tomatoes with green chilies, drained
½ cup (30 g) nutritional yeast
3 tablespoons (22.5 g) oat flour
1 teaspoon yellow mustard
1 teaspoon onion powder
1 teaspoon garlic powder
½ teaspoon ground cumin
½ teaspoon chili powder
½ teaspoon salt
1 cup (240 ml) plain unsweetened plant milk
1 tablespoon (15 ml) fresh lemon juice

1. Puree the tomatoes in a blender or food processor until smooth. Add the nutritional yeast, flour, mustard, onion and garlic powders, cumin, chili powder, and salt and blend until smooth.

2. Lightly coat the insert of the slow cooker with cooking spray and transfer the queso mixture to the cooker. Stir in the plant milk until well incorporated. Cover and cook on Low, stirring occasionally, for 2 hours, or until the mixture is thick and hot. If the mixture isn't thick after 2 hours, turn the setting to High, remove the lid, and cook for 20 to 30 minutes longer.

3. When ready to serve, spoon about ⅓ cup (75 g) of the queso into a small bowl, stir in the lemon juice, then stir the mixture back into the slow cooker. Taste and adjust the seasonings, if needed.

Warm and Creamy Artichoke-Spinach Dip

MAKES ABOUT 3½ CUPS (ABOUT 1 KG)

SLOW COOKER SIZE: 1½- TO 2-QUART (1.4 TO 1.9 L) | COOK TIME: 2 HOURS ON LOW | GLUTEN-FREE | OIL-FREE

Now you can enjoy a vegan version of the popular spinach and artichoke dip. This one is made with cashew cream cheese for a creamy, warm dip that can be cooked and served right from a small slow cooker. Serve this addictively delicious dip with your favorite crackers or lightly toasted baguette slices.

1 (10-ounce, or 280 g) package frozen chopped spinach, thawed and well drained

2 (8-ounce, or 225 g) jars marinated artichoke hearts, drained and chopped

1 cup (175 g) Cashew Cream Cheese (page 339), at room temperature

3 scallions, minced

⅓ cup (20 g) nutritional yeast

1 tablespoon (15 ml) fresh lemon juice

½ teaspoon Tabasco sauce

½ teaspoon salt

1. Lightly coat the slow cooker insert with cooking spray. Add all of the ingredients to the cooker and mix well to combine. Spread the mixture evenly in the cooker.

2. Cover and cook on Low for 2 hours. Serve warm from the slow cooker.

Smokin' Chipotle Bean Dip

MAKES ABOUT 3 CUPS (ABOUT 600 G)

SLOW COOKER SIZE: 1½- TO 2-QUART (1.4 TO 1.9 L) | COOK TIME: 3 TO 4 HOURS ON LOW | GLUTEN-FREE | OIL-FREE | SOY-FREE

This bean dip is smokin' hot thanks to the addition of chipotle chiles. This is a great dip for casual get-togethers because you can cook and serve it in the same small slow cooker. Serve with tortilla chips for dipping.

(continued)

1½ to 2 cups (258 to 344 g) cooked pinto beans (page 114), mashed,
    or 1 (15-ounce, or 425 g) can beans, rinsed, drained, and mashed

¾ cup (195 g) tomato salsa

¼ cup (60 ml) water

1 tablespoon (9 g) minced chipotle chiles in adobo, or to taste

1 teaspoon chili powder

½ cup (120 ml) Cheesy Sauce (page 340; optional)

Salt

1. Lightly coat the slow cooker insert with cooking spray. Combine the mashed beans, salsa, water, chipotle chiles, and chili powder in the slow cooker. Stir to mix well. Cover and cook on Low until the dip is hot and the flavors are well blended, 3 to 4 hours.

2. Just before serving, remove the lid and stir in the cheesy sauce (if using) and season to taste with salt. Serve warm from the slow cooker.

Golden Summer Caponata Bruschetta SERVES 6

SLOW COOKER SIZE: 4- TO 6-QUART (3.8 TO 5.7 L) | COOK TIME: 6 HOURS ON LOW | GLUTEN-FREE OPTION |
OIL-FREE | SOY-FREE

Reserve this version of caponata for late summer months, when fresh produce is plentiful and you want something delicious to enjoy with a glass of wine but don't want to heat up the kitchen. This caponata delivers the goods with a golden hue courtesy of yellow tomatoes and bell peppers. Enjoy it as a bruschetta as in this recipe, or serve it without bread as a side dish or a pasta topping. Best served at room temperature, caponata should be made well ahead of when you need it so that the flavors have a chance to meld. Use a gluten-free bread to make this gluten-free.

1 large yellow onion, minced

1 celery rib, minced

1 medium-size eggplant (about 1 pound, or 455 g),
    peeled and cut into ¼-inch (0.6 cm) cubes

1 yellow bell pepper, seeded and chopped

4 garlic cloves, chopped

3 large ripe yellow tomatoes, chopped

¼ cup (35 g) golden raisins

3 tablespoons (45 ml) white wine vinegar

1 teaspoon dried basil

½ teaspoon dried oregano

1 teaspoon salt

¼ teaspoon freshly ground black pepper

1 cup (100 g) green olives, pitted and coarsely chopped

1 to 2 tablespoons (9 to 18 g) capers, drained

2 tablespoons (8 g) chopped fresh flat-leaf parsley or basil

1 loaf French or Italian bread, cut into ½-inch (1 cm)-thick slices

1. Combine the onion, celery, eggplant, bell pepper, garlic, tomatoes, raisins, vinegar, basil, oregano, salt, and pepper in the slow cooker. Stir to mix well. Cover and cook on Low until the vegetables are soft but still hold some shape, about 6 hours.

2. Stir in the olives, capers, and parsley. Taste and adjust the seasonings. Transfer the caponata to a bowl and let cool to room temperature.

3. Preheat the broiler. Arrange the bread in a single layer on a baking sheet and broil until just toasted, watching carefully so the bread doesn't burn. Remove from the oven and turn the bread slices over, then return to the oven to lightly toast the other side. Serve the toasted bread immediately with the caponata.

Sherried Mushroom Crostini

SERVES 4 TO 6

SLOW COOKER SIZE: 4-QUART (3.8 L) | COOK TIME: 4 HOURS ON LOW | GLUTEN-FREE OPTION |
OIL-FREE OPTION | SOY-FREE

The fragrance of sherry and thyme signals the luscious flavor of these mushrooms. In addition to making a great crostini topping, the mushrooms are also delicious over cooked pasta. To make this gluten-free, use a gluten-free.

¼ cup (60 ml) water, or 2 teaspoons olive oil

3 large shallots, minced

1½ pounds (680 g) white or cremini mushrooms, sliced

3 tablespoons (45 ml) dry sherry

1½ teaspoons minced fresh thyme leaves, or ¾ teaspoon dried thyme

¼ cup (60 ml) vegetable broth

(continued)

Salt and freshly ground black pepper
1 French baguette, cut into ½-inch (1 cm) rounds
¼ cup (60 ml) plain unsweetened plant milk

1. Heat the water or oil in a small skillet over medium-high heat. Add the shallots and sauté until softened, about 3 minutes. Alternatively, place the shallots in a microwave-safe bowl with 2 tablespoons (30 ml) of water, cover, and microwave for 2 minutes to soften.

2. Transfer the shallots to the slow cooker. Add the mushrooms, 2 tablespoons (30 ml) of sherry, half the thyme, the broth, and salt and black pepper to taste. Cover and cook on Low until the mushrooms are soft, about 4 hours.

3. Preheat the broiler. Arrange the baguette rounds in a single layer on a baking sheet and broil until just toasted, watching carefully so the bread doesn't burn. Remove from the oven and turn the rounds over, then return to the oven to lightly toast the other side.

4. Use a slotted spoon to transfer the mushrooms to a serving bowl. Stir the plant milk into the cooker. Add the remaining 1 tablespoon (15 ml) of sherry and the remaining thyme. Taste and adjust the seasonings and pour over the mushrooms. Serve with the toasted bread rounds.

Savory Mediterranean Cheesecake SERVES 8 TO 12

SLOW COOKER SIZE: 6-QUART (5.7 L) | COOK TIME: 4 HOURS ON LOW | GLUTEN-FREE OPTION

The cheesecake takes a savory turn in this sophisticated appetizer made with cashew cream cheese and Mediterranean flavors, including sun-dried tomatoes and kalamata olives. It is at once cool and creamy, a bit tangy, a little garlicky, and deliciously herby. For the best flavor, serve and enjoy this at room temperature. Offer crackers or toasted bread rounds for spreading. To make this gluten-free, use gluten-free bread crumbs (or grind up gluten-free pretzels).

¼ cup (30 g) dried bread crumbs

1 cup (150 g) raw cashews, soaked overnight and well drained

3 garlic cloves, crushed

1 teaspoon salt

1 cup (175 g) Cashew Cream Cheese (page 339)

8 ounces (225 g) silken tofu

2 tablespoons (8 g) chopped oil-packed sun-dried tomatoes

2 tablespoons (23 g) chopped pitted kalamata olives

2 tablespoons (5 g) minced fresh basil

2 tablespoons (5 g) minced fresh flat-leaf parsley

1 tablespoon (8 g) cornstarch or tapioca starch

1 teaspoon minced fresh oregano or ½ teaspoon dried oregano

¼ teaspoon cayenne pepper

Crushed toasted pine nuts, minced fresh flat-leaf parsley or basil,
    and/or halved or quartered cherry tomatoes, for garnish

1. Lightly coat a 7-inch (18 cm) springform pan with cooking spray or line the bottom with parchment paper, cut to fit. Sprinkle the bread crumbs evenly in the bottom of the pan.

2. In a food processor, combine the cashews, garlic, and salt and process until it forms a paste. Add the cream cheese and tofu and process until smooth. Add the tomatoes, olives, basil, parsley, cornstarch, oregano, and cayenne and process until well combined. Scrape the mixture evenly into the prepared pan. Place the springform pan on of a sheet of aluminum foil and bring up the sides of the foil to prevent leakage. Cover the top of the springform pan tightly with aluminum foil, piercing the foil in several places on top to allow the steam to vent.

3. Place a rack, trivet, or a ring of crumpled aluminum foil in the bottom of the slow cooker insert. Pour about 1 inch (2.5 cm) of hot water into the bottom of the insert. Place the foil-covered springform pan on the rack, cover the cooker, and cook on Low for 4 hours.

4. Remove the pan from the cooker, take off the foil, and set aside to cool. When it is completely cool, cover and refrigerate for at least 3 hours or overnight. It should be completely chilled before removing from the pan.

5. To serve, remove the sides of the pan, using a knife to loosen it around the edges if necessary. Garnish with the pine nuts, minced herb, and/or cherry tomatoes.

Upcountry Pâté

SLOW COOKER SIZE: 6-QUART (5.7 L) | COOK TIME: 4 HOURS ON LOW | SOY-FREE OPTION

The hearty flavor of this country-style pâté improves if you make it ahead of time and refrigerate it overnight. The optional brandy adds a nice flavor, so try to include it if you can. This recipe requires a small loaf pan or springform pan that can fit inside your slow cooker. Crushed nuts and a fresh herb sprig make a nice garnish. For a soy-free version, omit the soy sauce and use Soy-Free Sauce (page 344), or coconut aminos, or add some soy-free vegetable broth base or additional salt.

1 cup (133 g) unsalted sunflower seeds, soaked overnight and well drained
¾ cup (90 g) walnut pieces
1 small yellow onion, chopped
3 garlic cloves, chopped
1 small Yukon Gold potato (5 to 6 ounces, or 150 to 170 g), peeled and chopped
1½ cups (288 g) cooked brown lentils, well drained
½ cup (30 g) nutritional yeast
⅓ cup (85 g) whole-grain flour
2 tablespoons (8 g) vital wheat gluten
1 tablespoon (15 ml) olive oil
2 tablespoons (30 ml) soy sauce
2 tablespoons (30 ml) brandy (optional)
2 tablespoons (8 g) chopped fresh flat-leaf parsley
1 teaspoon sweet paprika
1 teaspoon dried thyme
1 teaspoon salt
½ teaspoon freshly ground black pepper
½ teaspoon ground sage
⅛ teaspoon ground allspice
⅛ teaspoon cayenne pepper

1. Combine the sunflower seeds and walnuts in a food processor and blend until smooth. Sauté the onion and garlic in a skillet in a small amount of water or oil until softened, or combine them in a microwave-safe bowl, cover, and microwave for 2 minutes. Transfer the onion and garlic to the food processor along with the potato and lentils. Pulse a few times until just combined.

2. Add all of the remaining ingredients to the food processor and process until just combined. Do not overprocess. Taste and adjust the seasonings, adding more salt if needed.

3. Lightly coat a small loaf pan or 7-inch (18 cm) springform pan with cooking spray, depending on the shape of your slow cooker. Fill the pan with the mixture, packing it evenly and smoothing the top. If using a springform pan, place the pan on a sheet of aluminum foil and bring up the sides of the foil to prevent leakage. Cover tightly with aluminum foil, piercing the foil in several places to allow the steam to vent.

4. Place a rack, trivet, or a ring of crumpled aluminum foil in the bottom of the cooker insert. Pour about 1 inch (2.5 cm) of hot water into the bottom of the cooker. Place the foil-covered pan on the rack, cover the cooker, and cook on Low for 4 hours.

5. Remove the pan from the slow cooker, take off the foil, and set aside to cool. When it is completely cool, cover and refrigerate for at least 3 hours or overnight.

6. To serve, run a knife around the edge of the pan to loosen, then transfer to a serving plate. Serve cool or at room temperature.

Chickpea, Artichoke, and Mushroom Pâté

SERVES 6 TO 8

SLOW COOKER SIZE: 6-QUART (5.7 L) | COOK TIME: 4 TO 5 HOURS ON LOW | GLUTEN-FREE | OIL-FREE OPTION

This recipe calls for a small loaf pan or springform pan—whichever will fit inside your slow cooker. The pâté can be served as is with crackers for spreading or sliced and plated as a first course.

¼ cup (60 ml) water, or 2 teaspoons olive oil
3 garlic cloves, chopped
1 cup (70 g) chopped mushrooms of your choice
2 cups (600 g) canned or frozen artichoke hearts, thawed, drained
½ cup (75 g) raw cashews, soaked overnight and drained
1 cup (200 g) crumbled extra-firm tofu
1½ cups (247.5 g) cooked chickpeas (page 114)
    or 1 (15-ounce, or 425 g) can chickpeas, rinsed and drained
1 tablespoon (15 ml) fresh lemon juice

(continued)

1 tablespoon (4 g) minced fresh basil or 1 teaspoon dried basil
Salt and freshly ground black pepper
Paprika, for garnish
Shredded fresh basil leaves, for garnish

1. Heat the water or oil in a large skillet over medium heat. Add the garlic and cook, stirring, until fragrant, about 30 seconds. Add the mushrooms and cook until softened, about 3 minutes. Stir in the artichokes and cook until the moisture evaporates.

2. In a food processor, combine the drained cashews and tofu and process until smooth and well blended. Add the artichoke mixture, chickpeas, lemon juice, basil, and salt and black pepper to taste. Process until smooth. Taste and adjust the seasonings, if needed.

3. Lightly coat a small loaf pan or 7-inch (18 cm) springform pan (depending on the shape of your slow cooker) with cooking spray. Spoon the pâté mixture inside, packing it evenly and smoothing the top. If using a springform pan, place the pan on of a sheet of aluminum foil and bring up the sides of the foil to prevent leakage. Cover tightly with aluminum foil, piercing the foil in several places to allow the steam to vent.

4. Place a rack, trivet, or a ring of crumpled aluminum foil in the bottom of the cooker insert. Pour about 1 inch (2.5 cm) of hot water into the bottom of the cooker. Place the foil-covered pan on the rack, cover the cooker, and cook on Low until firm, 4 to 5 hours.

5. Remove the pan from the slow cooker, take off the foil, and set aside to cool. When it is completely cool, cover and refrigerate for at least 3 hours or overnight.

6. To serve, run a knife around the edge of the pan to loosen, then transfer the pâté to a serving plate. Garnish by sprinkling the top with paprika and mounding some basil in the center. Serve cool or at room temperature.

Artisanal Sweet and Spicy Wiener Balls

SERVES 4 TO 6

SLOW COOKER SIZE: 4-QUART (3.8 L) | COOK TIME: 3 HOURS ON LOW | OIL-FREE | SOY-FREE

Remember the first time you tried one of those little smokies or mini hot dogs simmered in a "mystery" sweet and sour sauce, and then found out the sauce was made with grape jelly and chili sauce? This version improves upon the original with homemade ketchup and marmalade and tasty vegan wiener balls. For a shortcut version, use purchased marmalade and ketchup and your favorite plant-based sausage links, cut into 1-inch (2.5 cm) pieces.

1 cup (256 g) cooked white beans (page 114) or canned beans, rinsed and drained
¼ cup (60 ml) water or vegetable broth
¾ teaspoon liquid smoke
1 teaspoon smoked paprika
½ teaspoon onion powder
¼ teaspoon garlic powder
½ teaspoon salt
¼ teaspoon freshly ground black pepper
1 cup (120 g) vital wheat gluten
3 tablespoons (11.25 g) nutritional yeast
1 cup (240 g) Handcrafted Ketchup (page 259)
1 cup (320 g) Orange Marmalade with a Twist of Lemon (page 258)
1 tablespoon (15 ml) rice vinegar
1 chipotle chile in adobo, minced

1. Process the beans in a food processor until smooth. Add the water, liquid smoke, paprika, onion and garlic powders, salt, and pepper and process until smooth. Add the vital wheat gluten and nutritional yeast and process to form a stiff dough. (If the dough is too dry, add up to 3 tablespoons, or 45 ml, additional water.) Transfer to a work surface and knead for 2 minutes.

2. In the slow cooker insert, stir together the ketchup, marmalade, vinegar, and chipotle chile. Turn the cooker on Low. Pinch off a small piece of the dough and roll it between your palms to make a ¾-inch (2 cm) sphere, then add it to the mixture in the slow cooker. Repeat until all the wiener mixture is used up. Stir gently to coat the wiener balls with the sauce, cover, and cook on Low for about 3 hours. Serve hot from the slow cooker.

Southern-Style Sugar and Spice Pecans

MAKES ABOUT 4 CUPS (ABOUT 455 G)

SLOW COOKER SIZE: 4-QUART (3.8 L) | COOK TIME: 30 MINUTES ON HIGH, PLUS 2 HOURS ON LOW |
GLUTEN-FREE | SOY-FREE OPTION

A popular treat in the South, a mixture of crunchy pecans coated with brown sugar, cinnamon, and other spices is wonderful, especially around the holidays. They make a great gift, too. When Terri Merritts tested this recipe for me she had to make it twice—it was such a huge hit with her family that they ate the entire first batch before she could photograph it. In her words, "The pecans turned out beautifully and taste divine. The recipe is perfect." Terri always lines the slow cooker crock with a Reynolds Slow Cooker Liner for easy cleanup. Use a soy-free vegan butter to make this soy-free.

⅓ cup (75 g) vegan butter
1 pound (455 g; about 4 cups) unsalted pecan halves
½ cup (75 g) light brown sugar
1½ teaspoons ground cinnamon
¼ teaspoon ground allspice
¼ teaspoon ground ginger
⅛ teaspoon ground nutmeg or cloves

1. Melt the butter in the slow cooker on High for 15 minutes. Add the pecans, stirring to coat. In a small bowl, combine the sugar and spices, then sprinkle the mixture over the pecans, stirring to coat evenly. Cover and cook on High for 15 minutes.

2. Reduce the setting to Low, remove the lid, and cook, stirring occasionally, until the pecans are nicely glazed, about 2 hours.

3. Spread the nut mixture in a single layer on a baking sheet and set aside to cool. Serve warm or at room temperature. If not serving right away, cool the nuts completely, then transfer to an airtight container and store in the refrigerator for up to 4 weeks or in the freezer for up to 3 months.

Seven-Spice Cashews

SLOW COOKER SIZE: 4-QUART (3.8 L) | COOK TIME: 15 MINUTES ON HIGH, PLUS 2 HOURS ON LOW |
GLUTEN-FREE | OIL-FREE | SOY-FREE

Spiced nuts are delicious, but they can be expensive to purchase. So why not make your own? It's easy to do and, best of all, you can season them just the way you like. This recipe combines sweet and savory spices for cashews that can be used to top salads or stir-fries, or just eaten out of hand. This flavor combination is also good with almonds.

¼ cup (80 g) maple syrup
2 tablespoons (30 g) light brown sugar
1¼ teaspoons ground cumin
1 teaspoon ground coriander
1 teaspoon ground cinnamon
½ teaspoon salt
¼ teaspoon sweet paprika
¼ teaspoon cayenne pepper
¼ teaspoon ground ginger
¼ teaspoon ground allspice
1 pound (455 g; about 4 cups) unsalted cashews

1. Lightly coat the slow cooker insert with cooking spray. Combine all of the ingredients except the cashews in a small bowl and mix well. Place the cashews in the slow cooker, then add the spice mixture, stirring to coat. Cover and cook on High for 15 minutes.

2. Reduce the setting to Low, remove the lid, and cook, stirring occasionally, for 2 hours.

3. Spread the nut mixture in a single layer on a baking sheet and set aside to cool. Serve at room temperature. If not serving right away, cool the nuts completely, then transfer to an airtight container and store in the refrigerator for up to 4 weeks or in the freezer for up to 3 months.

Life of the Party Mix

SLOW COOKER SIZE: 4- TO 6-QUART (3.8 TO 5.7 L) | COOK TIME: 2 HOURS AND 15 MINUTES ON HIGH, PLUS 2 HOURS ON LOW | GLUTEN-FREE OPTION | SOY-FREE OPTION

Some things never get old, like the retro appeal of party mix. Use your slow cooker to make a batch of this favorite snack food without worrying about it burning on top of the stove. A larger, shallow slow cooker works best for this recipe, as it allows you to stir the ingredients together much more easily. If you don't want a spicy mix, leave out the Tabasco and cayenne.

¼ cup (56 g) vegan butter
2 tablespoons (30 ml) vegan Worcestershire sauce
½ teaspoon Tabasco sauce
5 cups (150 g) Rice Chex cereal (or similar cereal)
1½ cups (60 g) small pretzel sticks or other small pretzels
1 cup (145 g) unsalted roasted peanuts or almonds
1 cup (150 g) unsalted roasted cashews
½ teaspoon seasoned salt
½ teaspoon onion powder
¼ teaspoon cayenne pepper (optional)

1. Melt the butter in the slow cooker on High for 15 minutes. Stir in the Worcestershire sauce and Tabasco, then add all of the remaining ingredients and mix gently to combine and coat.

2. Cook uncovered on High for 2 hours, stirring every 30 minutes. Reduce the heat to Low and cook for another 2 hours, stirring occasionally.

3. Spread the mixture in a single layer on a baking sheet and set aside to cool completely. Store in an airtight container until ready to use. The party mix will keep for several weeks.

NOTE: If using salted nuts, omit the seasoned salt. For gluten-free, use gluten-free pretzels; for soy-free, use a soy-free vegan butter, and omit the Worcestershire sauce and use Soy-Free Sauce (page 344) or coconut aminos or add some soy-free vegetable broth base or additional salt.

Oregon Trail Mix

SLOW COOKER SIZE: 4-QUART (3.8 L) | COOK TIME: 2½ HOURS ON LOW | GLUTEN-FREE OPTION | SOY-FREE OPTION

Who hasn't bought a bag of trail mix and wished there were more of one ingredient and less of another? Now you can blaze new trails by making your own customized mix. This recipe includes some of my favorite ingredients, but you can use it as a guideline to make a personalized trail mix, perhaps substituting your favorite dry cereal for some of the nuts, or using a different combination of dried fruit. For a gluten-free version, use gluten-free pretzels; for a soy-free version, use a soy-free vegan butter.

2 cups (290 g) unsalted almonds or cashews
1½ cups (185 g) walnut halves
½ cup (67 g) unsalted sunflower seeds
2½ cups (100 g) pretzel sticks or other small pretzels
½ cup (60 g) dried cranberries
½ cup (80 g) dried blueberries
½ cup (65 g) dried mangos or apricots, cut into ½-inch (1 cm) pieces
⅓ cup (67 g) granulated natural sugar
¼ cup (56 g) vegan butter, melted
3 tablespoons (45 ml) water
1 teaspoon pure vanilla extract

1. Combine the almonds, walnuts, sunflower seeds, pretzels, cranberries, blueberries, and mangos in the slow cooker. Stir to mix.

2. In a small bowl, combine the sugar, melted butter, water, and vanilla and stir to mix. Pour the wet mixture over the dry mixture, stirring gently to coat evenly. Cook, uncovered, on High, stirring occasionally, for 2½ hours. (If your cooker runs hot, check the mixture at 2 hours to make sure it isn't sticking or burning.)

3. Spread the mixture in a single layer on a baking sheet and set aside to cool completely. Store in an airtight container until ready to use. The trail mix will keep for several weeks.

Soups that Satisfy

O f all the recipes one can make in a slow cooker, soups seem to be the most popular—and with good reason. Homemade soup is one of those soul-satisfying foods that everyone loves. A pot of soup is healthful, restorative, and delicious. When made in a slow cooker, it's also easy and convenient. Even those of us with busy schedules and hectic lifestyles can enjoy the simple pleasure of a bowl of hot, freshly made soup.

It's also fair to say that soups are the most flexible recipes that can be made in a slow cooker. You can add, increase, or eliminate various ingredients to suit your taste. You can even leave them cooking (or keeping warm) after they're done, and they'll still taste great.

Because soups usually contain more liquid than other recipes, I prefer to make them in a larger slow cooker; they need a few inches of space at the top so they can bubble up when cooking without spilling over.

Simple Slow-Simmered Vegetable Broth

MAKES ABOUT 8 CUPS (1.9 L)

SLOW COOKER SIZE: 4- TO 6-QUART (3.8 TO 5.7 L) | COOK TIME: 8 HOURS ON LOW | GLUTEN-FREE | OIL-FREE | SOY-FREE OPTION

Just toss some ingredients in the slow cooker, set it, and forget it. A few hours later, you'll have a pot full of flavorful and nutritious broth to use in soups, stews, and sauces. A large cooker is best so that you can make a big batch of broth. If you use a smaller cooker, just cut back proportionately on the amounts of the ingredients used. You can leave the peels on the vegetables as long as they're organic and well washed. The dried mushrooms add depth to the overall flavor in this medium-strength broth. The color is fairly dark, but the flavor is milder than you might assume. To make this broth soy-free, omit the soy sauce and use Soy-Free Sauce (page 344), or coconut aminos, or add some soy-free vegetable broth base or additional salt.

1 large yellow onion, thickly sliced
2 large carrots, cut into 1-inch (2.5 cm) chunks
1 large russet potato, peeled and cut into 1-inch (2.5 cm) chunks
1 celery rib, cut into 1-inch (2.5 cm) pieces
3 garlic cloves, crushed
⅓ cup (8 g) coarsely chopped fresh flat-leaf parsley leaves
2 bay leaves
½ teaspoon peppercorns
8 cups (1.9 L) water
1 tablespoon (15 ml) soy sauce
½ teaspoon salt
3 dried shiitake or porcini mushrooms (optional)

1. Combine the onion, carrots, potato, celery, garlic, parsley, bay leaves, and peppercorns in the slow cooker. Add the water, soy sauce, salt, and dried mushrooms (if using). Cover and cook on Low for 8 hours.

2. Let the soup cool slightly, then strain through a fine-mesh sieve into a pot or bowl, pressing the vegetables against the sieve to release their juices. Portion the cooled broth into airtight containers and store in the refrigerator for up to 5 days or in the freezer for up to 3 months.

VEGETABLE BROTH OPTIONS

Vegetable broth is a foundational ingredient in many of the recipes in this book. If you want to make your own broth, the recipe (opposite) makes it quick and easy for you to put on a pot of broth to simmer all day unattended. I like to make a large quantity of this broth and then portion and freeze it to use in other recipes.

If you don't have homemade broth on hand, there are other options. You could purchase one of the many ready-made vegetable broths on the market. The various brands differ widely in flavor and sodium content, so be sure to do a taste test before using any purchased broth in recipes. Some are so strong that they need to be diluted by as much as half with water. This can also be an expensive option, and I have yet to find a brand that I like enough to recommend.

What I do recommend, however, is to use vegetable base (paste, cubes, or powder) combined with water. My favorite brand of vegetable base is Superior Touch "Better Than Bouillon," which comes in the form of a highly concentrated paste. It is available in three vegan-certified flavors: no beef, no chicken, and vegetable. (Note: Their mushroom base is not vegan, as it contains whey.) I also recommend Massel vegetable "Ultracubes," as well as their vegetable stock powder.

Because every vegetable broth and broth product has a different degree of inherent saltiness, most of the recipes in this book that call for vegetable broth will also call for salt "to taste" so that you can decide how much salt is needed.

Thai Coconut Soup

SERVES 4 TO 6

SLOW COOKER SIZE: 4- TO 6-QUART (3.8 TO 5.7 L) | COOK TIME: 6 TO 8 HOURS ON LOW | GLUTEN-FREE | OIL-FREE

The flavorful Thai soup known as *tom kha* is easy to make at home in a slow cooker. Look for galangal, which is similar to ginger, and lemongrass at well-stocked supermarkets or Asian markets. The optional curry paste adds an extra flavor boost, but the soup is also delicious without it.

(continued)

1 small yellow onion, thinly sliced

4 thin slices galangal or 1 tablespoon (6 g) minced peeled fresh ginger

2 tablespoons (10 g) chopped lemongrass (tender inner part only)

2 garlic cloves, minced

3 cups (720 ml) vegetable broth

2 tablespoons (30 ml) tamari

1 large carrot, thinly sliced

1 small red bell pepper, seeded and diced

8 ounces (225 g) small white mushrooms, trimmed and quartered or sliced

1 or 2 Thai chiles or other small chiles, stemmed and seeded, thinly sliced

1 cup (150 g) grape tomatoes or cherry tomatoes, halved

1 teaspoon coconut sugar

Salt, to taste

1 tablespoon (15 g) Thai red curry paste (optional)

12 to 16 ounces (340 to 455 g) extra-firm tofu, cut into ½-inch (1 cm) dice

2 (14-ounce, or 395 ml) cans full-fat coconut milk

3 tablespoons (3 g) chopped fresh cilantro

Juice of 2 limes

Zest of 2 limes

Cooked jasmine rice, for serving

1. In a large slow cooker, combine the onion, galangal, lemongrass, garlic, broth, and tamari. Add the carrot, bell pepper, mushrooms, chiles, tomatoes, sugar, and salt to taste. If adding the curry paste, blend it in a small bowl with about ¼ cup (60 ml) of hot water, stirring until well blended, then add the curry mixture to the slow cooker.

2. Cover, and cook on Low for 6 to 8 hours.

3. Shortly before serving time, stir in the tofu, coconut milk, cilantro, and lime juice and zest. Taste and adjust the seasonings, if needed. Remove and discard the galangal. Serve hot with rice on the side to add as desired.

Red Bean Gumbo

SERVES 4

SLOW COOKER SIZE: 4- TO 6-QUART (3.8 TO 5.7 L) | COOK TIME: 6 TO 8 HOURS ON LOW | GLUTEN-FREE | OIL-FREE | SOY-FREE

Long, gentle cooking in a slow cooker is a great way to bring out the flavors in a gumbo, in which okra and filé powder are natural thickeners. For a heartier gumbo, add some sliced and sautéed plant-based sausage just before serving. This recipe is gluten-free (without the optional plant-based sausage), soy-free, and oil-free if you water-sauté the vegetables.

1 large yellow onion, finely chopped

2 celery ribs, finely chopped

3 garlic cloves, minced

4 cups (960 ml) vegetable broth

1 (14-ounce, or 395 g) can diced fire-roasted tomatoes, with their juices

3 cups (770 g) cooked dark red kidney beans or other red beans (page 114) or 2 (15-ounce, or 425 g) cans beans, rinsed and drained

1 small green bell pepper, seeded and chopped

1 cup (300 g) sliced fresh or frozen okra, thawed

1 teaspoon dried thyme

1 teaspoon filé powder (optional)

Salt and freshly ground black pepper

½ recipe Plant-Based Sausage Links (page 174), sliced (optional)

1 teaspoon Tabasco sauce, or to taste

½ teaspoon liquid smoke

3 cups (600 g) cooked brown rice, for serving

1. Combine the onion, celery, and garlic in the slow cooker. Add the broth, tomatoes and their juices, beans, bell pepper, okra, thyme, filé powder (if using), and salt and pepper to taste. Cover and cook on Low for 6 to 8 hours or until the vegetables are tender.

2. Meanwhile, sauté the sausage (if using), and set aside.

3. Taste and adjust the seasonings. Just before serving, stir in the Tabasco and liquid smoke. If the gumbo isn't thick enough, turn the cooker to High and cook uncovered for 20 minutes, stirring frequently, until the broth thickens. Add the sautéed sausage (if using). To serve, spoon some cooked rice into bowls and ladle the hot gumbo on top.

Smoky Split Pea Soup

SLOW COOKER SIZE: 4- TO 6-QUART (3.8 TO 5.7 L) | COOK TIME: 7 TO 8 HOURS ON LOW | GLUTEN-FREE |
OIL-FREE | SOY-FREE

Split peas don't need to be soaked before going into the slow cooker. Just pick them over to remove any small stones and rinse them before using. The addition of liquid smoke and the optional vegan bacon provide that smoky flavor synonymous with split pea soup. This recipe is soy-free and gluten-free, depending on whether you use the optional vegan bacon and what it's made from.

1 medium-size yellow onion, chopped
1 carrot, chopped
1 celery rib, chopped
1 medium-size Yukon Gold potato, peeled and diced
1 pound (455 g) green split peas, rinsed and picked over
7 cups (1.6 L) vegetable broth or water
1 bay leaf
1 teaspoon salt
1 teaspoon ground coriander
½ teaspoon ground cumin
¼ teaspoon freshly ground black pepper
1 teaspoon liquid smoke
4 slices vegan bacon, cooked and chopped, for garnish (optional)
Minced fresh flat-leaf parsley, for garnish

1. Combine the onion, carrot, and celery in the slow cooker. Add the potato, split peas, broth, bay leaf, salt, coriander, cumin, and pepper. Cover and cook on Low for 7 to 8 hours.

2. Just before serving, stir in the liquid smoke. Taste and adjust the seasonings. Serve hot, garnished with the vegan bacon (if using) and parsley.

Ribollita

SLOW COOKER SIZE: 4- TO 6-QUART (3.8 TO 5.7 L) | COOK TIME: 6 TO 8 HOURS ON LOW |
GLUTEN-FREE OPTION | OIL-FREE | SOY-FREE

This soup is a fine example of Italian peasant food—hearty, healthful, and inexpensive. I like it very thick. My mother made this when I was growing up, and I had the pleasure of enjoying it again in Tuscany a few years ago. Now I make it at home in my slow cooker. This soup is even better the next day. To make it gluten-free, use a gluten-free bread.

1 large yellow onion, chopped

3 carrots, chopped

2 celery ribs, chopped

4 or 5 garlic cloves, minced

6 cups (540 g) chopped cabbage or kale

1 russet potato, peeled and chopped

3 cups (540 g) cooked cannellini beans (page 114)
    or 2 (15-ounce, or 425 g) cans beans, rinsed and drained

1 (28-ounce, or 794 g) can Italian plum tomatoes, chopped, juices reserved

5 cups (1.2 L) vegetable broth

½ teaspoon dried basil

½ teaspoon dried marjoram

¼ teaspoon red pepper flakes

Salt and freshly ground black pepper

2 cups (70 g) Italian bread cubes, crusts removed

½ cup (20 g) chopped fresh basil leaves

¼ cup (33.5 g) Almond Parmesan (page 341; optional)

1. Combine the onion, carrots, celery, and garlic in the slow cooker. Add the cabbage, potato, beans, tomatoes and their juices, broth, dried basil, marjoram, red pepper flakes, and salt and black pepper to taste. Cover and cook on Low until the vegetables are tender, 6 to 8 hours.

2. If you prefer a smoother-textured soup, use an immersion blender to puree a portion of the soup right in the cooker, or transfer 2 to 3 cups (weight varies) of the soup to a food processor or blender, puree it, then stir it back into the soup. Stir in the bread cubes, cover, and cook for 10 minutes longer. Just before serving, stir in the fresh basil. Taste and adjust the seasonings, if needed. Serve hot, sprinkled with Almond Parmesan (if using).

Summer Vegetable Soup

SERVES 4 TO 6

SLOW COOKER SIZE: 4- TO 6-QUART (3.8 TO 5.7 L) | COOK TIME: 5 HOURS ON LOW, PLUS 1 HOUR ON HIGH |
GLUTEN-FREE | OIL-FREE | SOY-FREE

This vegetable-packed soup is inspired by the abundance of vegetables that seem to take over my kitchen and my menus every summer, especially after my weekly trip to the farmers' market. You can vary the vegetables according to personal preference and what's on hand or in season. Add some red pepper flakes if you like a little heat.

1 carrot, thinly sliced

2 garlic cloves, minced

3 small red potatoes, scrubbed and diced

1 yellow bell pepper, seeded and chopped

6 cups (1.4 L) vegetable broth

Salt and freshly ground black pepper

4 ounces (115 g) asparagus, ends trimmed, cut into 1-inch (2.5 cm) pieces

2 small zucchini or yellow squash, diced

4 scallions, chopped

1½ cups (270 g) cooked cannellini or other white beans (page 114)
    or 1 (15-ounce, or 425 g) can beans, rinsed and drained

1½ cups (300 g) cherry or grape tomatoes, halved

3 cups (110 g) chopped chard, kale, or spinach

2 tablespoons (8 g) chopped fresh flat-leaf parsley

2 tablespoons (8 g) chopped fresh basil

1 tablespoon (4 g) minced fresh dill or tarragon (optional)

1. Combine the carrot, garlic, and potatoes in the slow cooker. Add the bell pepper and broth. Season to taste with salt and pepper. Cover and cook on Low for 5 hours.

2. Add the asparagus, zucchini, scallions, cannellini beans, tomatoes, and chard. Cover and cook on High for 1 hour, or until all the vegetables are tender.

3. Just before serving, stir in the parsley, basil, and dill (if using). Taste and adjust the seasonings, if needed. Serve hot.

Grandmom Gennaro's Minestre

SERVES 4 TO 6

SLOW COOKER SIZE: 4- TO 6-QUART (3.8 TO 5.7 L) | COOK TIME: 6 TO 7 HOURS ON LOW, PLUS 30 MINUTES ON HIGH | GLUTEN-FREE OPTION | OIL-FREE | SOY-FREE

My grandmother always had a pot of minestrone soup—or minestre, as my family called it—on the stove. Like most of what my grandmother cooked, there was no recipe, just a little of this and some of that—and it was always delicious. I still make this long-cooking, full-flavored vegetable soup, only I use a slow cooker to get that rich flavor.

Note that the amount of vegetables listed here will fill a 4-quart (3.8 L) cooker to within 2 inches (5 cm) of the top and will fill a 6-quart (5.7 L) cooker a little over halfway. If using a 6-quart (5.7 L) cooker, you can add extra vegetables and another cup (240 ml) of broth to make more servings. Use gluten-free pasta to make this gluten-free.

1 large yellow onion, minced

2 carrots, chopped

3 garlic cloves, minced

1 cup (100 g) chopped celery

1½ cups (247.5 g) cooked chickpeas (page 114)
  or 1 (15-ounce, or 425 g) can chickpeas, rinsed and drained

2 small zucchini, diced

1 (28-ounce, or 794 g) can diced tomatoes, with their juices

4 cups (960 ml) vegetable broth

½ teaspoon dried basil

½ teaspoon dried marjoram

1 bay leaf

Salt and freshly ground black pepper

⅓ cup (67 g) dried stelline or other small soup pasta

¼ cup (16 g) chopped fresh flat-leaf parsley

¼ cup (16 g) chopped fresh basil

1. Combine the onion, carrots, and garlic in the slow cooker. Add the celery, chickpeas, zucchini, tomatoes and their juices, and broth. Stir in the dried basil, marjoram, bay leaf, and salt and black pepper to taste. Cover and cook on Low for 6 to 7 hours.

2. Add the stelline to the slow cooker, cover, and cook on High until the pasta is tender, about 30 minutes. Just before serving, stir in the parsley and fresh basil. Taste and adjust the seasonings, if needed. Serve hot.

Root Vegetable Bisque with Herbes de Provence

SERVES 4 TO 6

SLOW COOKER SIZE: 4- TO 6-QUART (3.8 TO 5.7 L) | COOK TIME: 6 TO 8 HOURS ON LOW | GLUTEN-FREE | OIL-FREE | SOY-FREE

Traditional bisques are often thickened with rice, so I've added some to this recipe. The soup is pureed after cooking and then returned to the pot to serve. If you prefer a chunky rather than creamy soup, you can omit the pureeing step—just don't call it a bisque!

1 medium-size yellow onion, chopped

3 garlic cloves, chopped

2 carrots, coarsely chopped

2 medium-size parsnips, peeled and coarsely chopped

1 small turnip, peeled and diced

1 medium-size Yukon Gold potato, peeled and diced

⅓ cup (63 g) raw brown rice

1 (14-ounce, or 395 g) can diced tomatoes, drained

4 cups (960 ml) vegetable broth

2 teaspoons dried herbes de Provence

Salt and freshly ground black pepper

2 tablespoons (8 g) chopped fresh flat-leaf parsley, for garnish

1. Combine the onion and garlic in the slow cooker. Add the carrots, parsnips, turnip, potato, and rice. Stir in the tomatoes, broth, herbes de Provence, and salt and pepper to taste. Cover and cook on Low until the vegetables are tender, 6 to 8 hours.

2. Use an immersion blender to puree the soup right in the pot or transfer the soup, in batches, to a high-powered blender or food processor and puree until smooth, then return to the pot. Taste and adjust the seasonings, if needed. Serve hot, sprinkled with the parsley.

Baked Potato Soup

SLOW COOKER SIZE: 4- TO 6-QUART (3.8 TO 5.7 L) | COOK TIME: 6 TO 8 HOURS ON LOW |
GLUTEN-FREE OPTION | OIL-FREE | SOY-FREE OPTION

If you enjoy "loaded" baked potatoes, then you'll love this creamy soup, which has all of those same great flavors. As with its namesake, you can pile on as many toppings as you like: tempeh bacon, sour cream, and a cheesy sauce, plus minced chives or scallions. This recipe can be made gluten- or soy-free by choosing gluten- or soy-free toppings.

4 or 5 large (about 3 pounds, 1.3 kg) russet potatoes,
    peeled and cut into 1-inch (2.5 cm) dice
4 cups (960 ml) vegetable broth, plus more if needed
1 teaspoon garlic powder
1 teaspoon onion powder
1 to 2 teaspoons salt
½ teaspoon freshly ground black pepper
2 tablespoons (9 g) nutritional yeast
1 cup (240 ml) plain unsweetened plant milk, plus more if needed
½ cup (115 g) Cashew Sour Cream (page 338), for garnish (optional)
½ cup (120 ml) Cheesy Sauce (page 340), for garnish (optional)
¼ cup (16 g) chopped fresh chives or finely minced scallions, for garnish
4 slices Tempeh Bacon (page 342), cooked and chopped, for garnish

1. Combine the potatoes, broth, garlic powder, onion powder, 1 teaspoon salt, and pepper in the slow cooker. Cover and cook on Low until the potatoes are soft, 6 to 8 hours.

2. Use a potato masher to mash the potatoes right in the slow cooker, adding the nutritional yeast and the plant milk a little at a time. Taste and adjust the seasonings, adding up to 1 teaspoon of additional salt, if needed, depending on the saltiness of your broth. If the soup is too thick, add additional broth or plant milk.

3. Ladle the soup into bowls and top with as many of the garnishes as desired. Serve hot.

Chipotle Corn Chowder

SERVES 4

SLOW COOKER SIZE: 4- TO 6-QUART (3.8 TO 5.7 L) | COOK TIME: 6 HOURS ON LOW | GLUTEN-FREE |
OIL-FREE OPTION | SOY-FREE

Creamy and rich, this chowder can be made with either fresh or frozen corn kernels. For less heat, use only one chipotle chile instead of two. Pureeing a portion of the chowder helps thicken the broth and bring out the flavor of the corn.

¼ cup (60 ml) water, or 2 teaspoons olive oil
1 medium-size yellow onion, chopped
1 celery rib, chopped
1 large Yukon Gold potato, peeled and cut into ¼-inch (0.6 cm) dice
4 cups (620 g) fresh or (660 g) frozen corn kernels, thawed
4 cups (960 ml) vegetable broth
1 or 2 chipotle chiles in adobo, minced
Salt and freshly ground black pepper
2 tablespoons (8 g) minced fresh cilantro or flat-leaf parsley, for garnish

1. Heat the water or oil in a medium-size skillet over medium-high heat. Add the onion and celery and sauté until softened, about 5 minutes. Alternatively, place them in a microwave-safe bowl with 2 tablespoons of water, cover, and microwave for 2 minutes to soften.

2. Transfer the vegetables to the slow cooker. Add the potato, corn, broth, and chipotles. Season to taste with salt and black pepper, cover, and cook on Low for 6 hours.

3. Use an immersion blender to blend a portion of the soup right in the pot, or ladle 2 cups (weight varies) of the soup solids into a food processor or blender and process until smooth, then stir the puree back into the chowder. Taste and adjust the seasonings, if needed. Ladle the soup into bowls and garnish with the cilantro.

Caramelized Onion Soup

SERVES 4 TO 6

SLOW COOKER SIZE: 4- TO 6-QUART (3.8 TO 5.7 L) | COOK TIME: 8½ HOURS ON LOW |
GLUTEN-FREE OPTION | SOY-FREE OPTION

Long, slow cooking is the secret to perfect caramelized onions, and a slow cooker is a great way to get the job done. Use the first part of the recipe to make just the caramelized onions to use in other recipes, or add the broth and other ingredients to make a rich-tasting onion soup. Use a gluten-free bread to make this recipe gluten-free. To make this recipe soy-free, omit the Worcestershire sauce and use Soy-Free Sauce (page 344) or coconut aminos, or add some soy-free vegetable broth base or additional salt, and use a soy-free vegan cheese.

2 tablespoons (30 ml) plus 1 teaspoon olive oil
4 or 5 medium-size yellow onions, thinly sliced
5 cups (1.2 L) vegetable broth
⅓ cup (80 ml) brandy, dry red wine, or sherry (optional)
1 teaspoon vegan Worcestershire sauce
½ teaspoon dried thyme
Salt and freshly ground black pepper
4 slices French or Italian bread, cut into 1-inch (2.5 cm) cubes
Smoked paprika
Almond Parmesan, for garnish (page 341)

1. Spread 2 tablespoons of the oil in the slow cooker and add the onions, spreading evenly. Cover and cook on Low until the onions are very soft and well caramelized, about 8 hours.

2. Stir in the broth, brandy (if using), Worcestershire sauce, and thyme and season to taste with salt and black pepper. Cover and cook until hot, 30 to 45 minutes.

3. Preheat the oven to 400°F (200°C).

4. In a bowl, combine the bread cubes, the remaining 1 teaspoon of oil, and salt and black pepper to taste, along with a few shakes of smoked paprika. Spread in a single layer on a baking sheet and bake until toasted, turning occasionally, 15 to 20 minutes. Remove from the oven and sprinkle with Almond Parmesan. Ladle the soup into bowls and top with a few of the croutons. Serve immediately.

Callaloo Soup

SLOW COOKER SIZE: 4- TO 6-QUART (3.8 TO 5.7 L) | COOK TIME: 6 HOURS ON LOW | GLUTEN-FREE | OIL-FREE OPTION | SOY-FREE

Because this recipe uses spinach instead of actual callaloo, it's more correct to say that it's a callaloo-inspired soup. The traditional Jamaican recipe uses callaloo leaves (aka taro leaves), which taste like a cross between spinach and cabbage, but they're not available to most people. If you can find actual callaloo leaves at an Asian market, then by all means use them instead of the spinach for a more authentic soup. You can also use chard, if you prefer. Either way, this is a delicious change from the usual vegetable soup, with its subtle heat and light coconut broth. If you use medium-size vegetables, the soup ingredients will fit in a 4-quart (3.8 L) slow cooker. If you increase the vegetable sizes to large, you will need a 6-quart (5.7 L) slow cooker.

1 medium-size yellow onion, minced

3 garlic cloves, minced

2 medium-size sweet potatoes, peeled and diced (2 cups)

1 medium-size red bell pepper, seeded and chopped

1 or 2 jalapeño chiles or other hot chiles, seeded and minced

1 (14.5-ounce, or 410 g) can diced tomatoes, drained

1½ cups (384 g) cooked dark red kidney beans or other red beans (page 114)
    or 1 (15-ounce, or 425 g) can beans, rinsed and drained

4 cups (960 ml) vegetable broth

½ teaspoon fresh or dried thyme

¼ teaspoon ground allspice

Salt and freshly ground black pepper

8 ounces (225 g) baby spinach

1 (13.5-ounce, or 405 ml) can unsweetened coconut milk

1. Combine the onion and garlic in the slow cooker. Add the sweet potatoes, bell pepper, jalapeño, tomatoes, and beans. Stir in the broth, thyme, and allspice and season to taste with salt and pepper.

2. Cover and cook on Low for 5½ hours, or until the vegetables are tender.

3. Stir in the spinach and coconut milk. Taste and adjust the seasonings. Cover and cook until the spinach is wilted, about 30 minutes longer. Serve hot.

Cabbage and Yellow Beet Borscht

SERVES 6

SLOW COOKER SIZE: 4- TO 6-QUART (3.8 TO 5.7 L) | COOK TIME: 8 HOURS ON LOW | GLUTEN-FREE | OIL-FREE | SOY-FREE OPTION

Yellow beets provide a new look to this satisfying borscht (although it can be made with red beets instead, if you prefer). To cut down on prep time, you can shred, rather than chop, the vegetables. This will change the texture of the soup, but some people prefer it this way. The beets and the potato will begin to darken if not submerged in liquid right away. So, as soon as you cut or shred them, add them to the slow cooker along with the broth. This can be soy-free if you use a soy-free cashew sour cream.

5 cups (1.2 L) vegetable broth

4 medium-size yellow beets, peeled and minced or shredded (3½ to 4 cups, or 788 to 900 g)

1 large yellow onion, minced

1 large carrot, minced or shredded

1 large russet potato, peeled and minced

3 cups (270 g) shredded cabbage

1 teaspoon granulated natural sugar

1 teaspoon dried thyme

¼ cup (16 g) minced fresh dill, or 1 tablespoon dried dill weed

½ teaspoon caraway seeds

Salt and freshly ground black pepper

2 tablespoons (30 ml) fresh lemon juice

½ cup (115 g) Cashew Sour Cream (page 338), for garnish

1. Combine the broth, beets, onion, carrot, potato, and cabbage in the slow cooker. Add the sugar, thyme, half of the dill, and the caraway seeds. Cover and cook on Low for 8 hours.

2. Season to taste with salt and black pepper. Stir in the lemon juice, then taste and adjust the seasonings, if needed.

3. Serve hot, or set aside to cool and then refrigerate until well chilled and serve cold. Garnish each serving with a spoonful of cashew sour cream and a sprinkling of the remaining dill.

Spicy Tortilla Soup

SLOW COOKER SIZE: 4- TO 6-QUART (3.8 TO 5.7 L) | COOK TIME: 6 HOURS ON LOW | GLUTEN-FREE OPTION |
OIL-FREE | SOY-FREE

While you can certainly make your own strips of crispy tortillas for this soup, this recipe opts for the convenience of lightly crushed tortilla chips. This is one spicy and delicious soup. If you prefer less heat, cut back on the amount of chipotles used and be sure to remove the jalapeño ribs. If you use gluten-free tortilla chips, this recipe can be gluten-free.

1 medium-size yellow onion, minced

3 garlic cloves, minced

1 jalapeño chile, seeded and minced

2 tablespoons (32 g) tomato paste

2 to 3 teaspoons (17 g) chipotle chiles in adobo, minced

1 teaspoon ground cumin

1 (14-ounce, or 395 g) can diced tomatoes, with their juices

3 cups (758 g) cooked black beans (page 114)
  or 2 (15-ounce, or 425 g) cans beans, rinsed and drained

5 cups (1.2 L) vegetable broth

Salt and freshly ground black pepper

1 cup (155 g) fresh or (165 g) frozen corn kernels, thawed

½ cup (8 g) chopped fresh cilantro leaves

3 cups (189 g) lightly crushed tortilla chips

½ cup (115 g) Cashew Sour Cream (page 338), for garnish

1 ripe Hass avocado, pitted, peeled, and diced, for garnish

2 tablespoons (16 g) toasted pepitas (green pumpkin seeds), for garnish

Lime wedges, for serving

1. In the slow cooker, combine the onion, garlic, jalapeño, tomato paste, chipotles, and cumin, stirring to mix. Stir in the tomatoes and their juices, black beans, and broth and season to taste with salt and pepper. Cover and cook on Low for 6 hours.

2. Shortly before serving time, stir in the corn kernels and ¼ cup (4 g) of cilantro. Taste and adjust the seasonings.

3. Divide the tortilla chips among 4 soup bowls. Ladle the soup over the tortilla chips and top each serving with a spoonful of sour cream, some avocado, a sprinkling of pepitas, and the remaining cilantro. Serve hot, with the lime wedges.

Four-Way Tomato Soup

SLOW COOKER SIZE: 4- TO 6-QUART (3.8 TO 5.7 L) | COOK TIME: 6 HOURS ON LOW | GLUTEN-FREE | OIL-FREE OPTION | SOY-FREE

This is nothing like the canned tomato soup you had as a child. Four kinds of tomatoes—fresh, sun-dried, crushed, and paste—contribute to the layers of flavor. Fresh yellow tomatoes are added at the end for contrast, but red tomatoes may be used if yellow are unavailable. For added flavor, substitute fire-roasted tomatoes for all or part of the diced plum tomatoes. Some roasted red pepper makes a good addition as well.

If adding the optional plant milk, choose one that is soy-free to make this a soy-free soup. Instead of adding the optional plant milk, you could stir in some soy creamer, or maybe a little cashew sour cream or even vegan cream cheese (blended in a bowl first with a bit of the hot broth).

¼ cup (60 ml) water, or 2 teaspoons olive oil
1 large yellow onion, chopped
2 garlic cloves, minced
2 tablespoons (32 g) tomato paste
1 teaspoon granulated natural sugar
1 teaspoon dried basil
1 teaspoon dried marjoram
1 cup (240 ml) vegetable broth
1 (28-ounce, or 794 g) can whole or diced Italian plum tomatoes, with their juices
1 (14-ounce, or 395 g) can crushed tomatoes
¼ cup (29 g) oil-packed sun-dried tomatoes, chopped
Salt and freshly ground black pepper
½ cup (120 ml) plain unsweetened plant milk (optional)
2 tablespoons (8 g) chopped fresh basil leaves, for garnish
1 cup (150 g) yellow grape or cherry tomatoes, quartered, for garnish

1. Heat the water or oil in a medium-size skillet over medium-high heat. Add the onion and sauté until softened, about 5 minutes. Add the garlic and cook for 1 minute longer. Alternatively, place the onion and garlic in a microwave-safe bowl with 2 tablespoons of water, cover, and microwave for 2 minutes to soften.

(continued)

2. Transfer the onion mixture to the slow cooker. Stir in the tomato paste, sugar, dried basil, marjoram, broth, plum tomatoes and their juices, crushed tomatoes, sun-dried tomatoes, and salt and black pepper to taste. Cover and cook on Low for 6 hours.

3. Puree the soup in a food processor or blender, or use an immersion blender to puree it directly in the slow cooker. Taste and adjust the seasonings. For a creamier soup, stir in the plant milk. Ladle the hot soup into bowls and top each serving with fresh basil and yellow tomatoes.

Wild Mushroom Soup with Barley   SERVES 4 TO 6

SLOW COOKER SIZE: 4- TO 6-QUART (3.8 TO 5.7 L) | COOK TIME: 6 HOURS ON LOW | OIL-FREE OPTION |
SOY-FREE OPTION

The combination of barley and mushrooms is an Eastern European favorite, and this soup makes the best of both ingredients by layering the flavor with three kinds of mushrooms. Be sure to use pearl barley for the best results. For a soy-free version, omit the soy sauce and use Soy-Free Sauce (page 344) or coconut aminos, or add some soy-free vegetable broth base or additional salt.

½ ounce (14 g) dried porcini mushrooms, rinsed
¼ cup (60 ml) water, or 2 teaspoons olive oil
1 large yellow onion, chopped
1 large carrot, chopped
½ cup (50 g) raw pearl barley
8 ounces (225 g) cremini mushrooms, sliced
4 ounces (115 g) shiitake mushrooms, stemmed and sliced
5 cups (1.2 L) vegetable broth
1 (14-ounce, or 395 g) can crushed tomatoes
2 tablespoons (30 ml) soy sauce
1 teaspoon dried thyme
Salt and freshly ground black pepper
3 tablespoons (12 g) minced fresh flat-leaf parsley or dill, for garnish

1 cup (16 g) fresh cilantro leaves, for garnish
½ cup (50 g) fresh bean sprouts, for garnish
2 scallions, thinly sliced, for garnish
1 small green chile, seeded and thinly sliced, for garnish
Lime wedges, for serving

1. Place the star anise, cloves, and ginger in the center of a small piece of cheesecloth. Gather the ends of the cheesecloth to enclose the spices and tie it closed with a piece of kitchen twine. Set aside.

2. Combine the onion and garlic in the slow cooker. Add the spice bag, broth, soy sauce, hoisin sauce, and miso mixture. Cover and cook on Low for 6 hours.

3. Stir in the seitan and rice noodles. Cover and cook until the noodles are tender, about 30 minutes longer.

4. Add the lime juice and taste and adjust the seasonings, if needed. Ladle the soup into bowls and garnish with the cilantro, bean sprouts, scallions, and chile. Serve with the lime wedges.

Indonesian-Inspired Noodle Soup

SERVES 4

SLOW COOKER SIZE: 4- TO 6-QUART (3.8 TO 5.7 L) | COOK TIME: 6 HOURS PLUS 30 MINUTES ON LOW |
GLUTEN-FREE | OIL-FREE OPTION

This luscious soup is inspired by the Indonesian soup known as laksa. It features rice noodles, tofu, and coconut milk, and is at once spicy hot and refreshing.

¼ cup (60 ml) water or 2 teaspoons avocado oil
1 medium-size yellow onion, chopped
2 teaspoons grated peeled fresh ginger
2 to 3 teaspoons (6 g) curry powder
2 teaspoons ground coriander
½ teaspoon paprika
1 teaspoon granulated natural sugar
1 teaspoon salt
¼ teaspoon ground turmeric
¼ teaspoon cayenne pepper
¼ teaspoon freshly ground black pepper
1 teaspoon Asian chili paste
4 cups (960 ml) vegetable broth
6 ounces (170 g) dried rice noodles
8 ounces (225 g) extra-firm tofu, cut into ½-inch (1 cm) dice
3 scallions, chopped
1 (14-ounce, or 395 g) can unsweetened coconut milk
1 tablespoon (15 ml) fresh lime juice
1 teaspoon sriracha sauce (optional)
½ English cucumber, peeled and chopped, for garnish
1 cup (150 g) cherry tomatoes, quartered, for garnish
1 bunch fresh cilantro, chopped, for garnish
Lime wedges, for serving

1. Heat the water or oil in a medium-size skillet over medium-high heat. Add the onion, ginger, curry powder, coriander, paprika, and sugar and sauté for about 4 minutes to soften the onion and bloom the flavor of the spices. Sprinkle on a little more water, if needed, so the mixture doesn't burn.

2. Transfer the onion mixture to the slow cooker. Add the salt, turmeric, cayenne, black pepper, and chili paste. Stir in the broth, cover, and cook on Low for 6 hours.

3. Stir in the noodles, tofu, scallions, and coconut milk. Cover and continue to cook until the noodles are tender, about 30 minutes.

4. Just before serving, stir in the lime juice. Taste and adjust the seasonings, adding the sriracha (if using) for more heat. Ladle the soup into bowls and garnish with the cucumber, tomatoes, and cilantro. Serve with the lime wedges.

Miso Potato Soup

SERVES 4

SLOW COOKER SIZE: 4- TO 6-QUART (3.8 TO 5.7 L) | COOK TIME: 6 HOURS ON LOW | GLUTEN-FREE | OIL-FREE

I'd always enjoyed miso soup and potato soup as two separate entities until my neighbor Seung Hee Han served me a delicious soup that combines them both. Now I'm hooked.

1 small yellow onion, minced
2 large russet potatoes, peeled and cut into ¼-inch (0.6 cm) dice
4 cups (360 g) chopped napa cabbage
1 (2-inch, or 5 cm) piece kombu sea vegetable (optional)
6 cups (1.4 L) water
3 tablespoons (45 ml) soy sauce, plus more as needed
½ teaspoon salt, plus more as needed
¼ teaspoon freshly ground black pepper
¼ cup (63 g) white miso paste, plus more as needed
¼ cup (25 g) chopped scallions

1. Combine the onion, potatoes, cabbage, kombu (if using), water, and soy sauce in the slow cooker. Add the salt and pepper. Cover and cook on Low until the vegetables are tender, about 6 hours.

2. Spoon the miso paste into a bowl and add about 1 cup (240 ml) of the hot broth, stirring to blend and thin the miso. Scrape the miso mixture into the slow cooker and add the scallions. Taste and adjust the seasonings, adding more miso, soy sauce, or salt, if needed. Remove and discard the kombu (if using). Serve hot.

Stews and Chili

The slow cooker is a great way to cook a stew or chili. The long simmering brings out the flavors as it allows the various ingredients a chance to mingle. Once it's done cooking, you can serve it right from the cooker for a hearty meal that's ready when you are.

The selection of stew recipes runs the gamut from an all-American Farm Stand Stew to the international flavors of a Moroccan tagine, an Indian curry, and a Mexican posole. There are also several kinds of chili made with a variety of beans and vegetables. There's even a chili topped with corn bread that cooks right in the slow cooker.

For the best flavor and texture, onions and certain other ingredients should be sautéed in a skillet before adding them to the slow cooker, or at least cooked in the microwave for a few minutes, as directed in the recipes. This extra step will infuse your stew or chili with more flavor, and it will also help ensure that the vegetables become tender. If you skip this step, it may result in some of the ingredients being too hard or crunchy when the rest of the dish is ready to eat, and the overall flavor may not be as rich. That said, you may prefer to skip that step and simply "load the crock."

Oyster Mushroom Bouillabaisse

SERVES 4 TO 6

SLOW COOKER SIZE: 4- TO 6-QUART (3.8 TO 5.7 L) | COOK TIME: 6 HOURS ON LOW | GLUTEN-FREE | SOY-FREE OPTION

While traditional bouillabaisse is made with fish, this hearty version sacrifices nothing in terms of flavor by instead featuring mushrooms. To make this soy-free, use coconut aminos instead of tamari and omit the rouille. Serve with a loaf of crusty grilled bread to soak up the delicious broth.

1 fennel bulb, trimmed and chopped

1 leek, white and light green parts only, thinly sliced crosswise

4 small red potatoes, quartered

2 cups (600 g) frozen artichoke hearts, thawed, halved or quartered

3 large scallions, coarsely chopped

3 plum tomatoes, cored and diced

1 teaspoon dried thyme leaves

¼ teaspoon ground turmeric

1 tablespoon (6 g) lemon or orange zest

1 bay leaf

2 tablespoons (30 ml) tamari or coconut aminos

6 cups (1.4 L) vegetable broth

1 tablespoon (15 ml) olive oil

12 ounces (340 g) oyster mushrooms, caps cut into large dice, stems cut into rounds

2 garlic cloves, minced

2 tablespoons (32 g) tomato paste

½ cup (120 ml) dry white wine (optional)

Salt and freshly ground black pepper

Rouille (opposite), for serving (optional)

1. In a large slow cooker, combine the fennel, leek, potatoes, artichoke hearts, scallions, tomatoes, thyme, turmeric, lemon zest, and bay leaf. Stir in the tamari and the broth. Cover and cook on Low for 4 hours.

2. Heat the oil in a large skillet over medium heat. Add the mushrooms and garlic and cook, stirring until the mushrooms are lightly browned, about 5 minutes. Stir in the tomato paste and the wine (if using). Season with salt and black pepper.

3. Stir the mushroom mixture into the slow cooker. Cover and cook on Low for an additional 2 hours. Taste and adjust seasonings, adding more salt and black pepper if needed.

4. Serve hot in bowls with rouille on the side to add to the soup (if using).

ROUILLE

. . . .

2 large garlic cloves, crushed
½ jarred roasted red bell pepper, seeded and coarsely chopped
2 teaspoons fresh lemon juice
Small pinch of saffron threads or ground turmeric
¼ cup (60 g) vegan mayonnaise
Salt and freshly ground black pepper

1. In a food processor, combine the garlic, red pepper, lemon juice, and saffron. Pulse until smooth, then add the mayo and process until smooth and well blended. Season with salt and pepper to taste.

2. Transfer to a small bowl, cover, and refrigerate until needed.

Three-Bean Spezzatino

SLOW COOKER SIZE: 4- TO 6-QUART (3.8 TO 5.7 L) | COOK TIME: 6 TO 8 HOURS ON LOW |
GLUTEN-FREE OPTION | OIL-FREE | SOY-FREE

This hearty Italian stew is especially delicious served over freshly cooked noodles. For a gluten-free option, use gluten-free flour.

1 medium-size onion, finely chopped

2 carrots, finely chopped or thinly sliced

½ cup (50 g) finely chopped celery

1 Yukon Gold potato, diced

1 red or yellow bell pepper, seeded and chopped

1 tablespoon (10 g) minced garlic

3 tablespoons (23.25 g) all-purpose flour

½ cup (120 ml) dry red wine or vegetable broth

1 (12-ounce, or 340 g) package cremini mushrooms, trimmed and quartered

1 (28-ounce, or 794 g) can diced fire-roasted tomatoes, undrained

1½ cups (270 g) cooked cannellini beans (page 114)
   or 1 (15-ounce, or 425 g) can cannellini beans, drained and rinsed

1½ cups (247.5 g) cooked chickpeas (page 114)
   or 1 (15-ounce, or 425 g) can chickpeas, drained and rinsed

1½ cups (258 g) cooked black beans (page 114)
   or 1 (15-ounce, or 425 g) can black beans, drained and rinsed

1 cup (240 ml) vegetable broth

2 teaspoons chopped fresh oregano, or 1 teaspoon dried

2 teaspoons chopped fresh thyme, or 1 teaspoon dried

1 teaspoon ground fennel seed

1 teaspoon onion powder

1 bay leaf

Salt and freshly ground black pepper

2 tablespoons (5 g) chopped fresh basil or (8 g) parsley

Balsamic Reduction (page 345), for serving (optional)

1. Combine the onion, carrot, and celery in the slow cooker. Add the potato, bell pepper, and garlic, then sprinkle with the flour. Stir in the wine.

2. Add the mushrooms, tomatoes, all the beans, broth, oregano, thyme, fennel, onion powder, and bay leaf. Season with salt and black pepper to taste and stir to combine.

3. Cover and cook on Low for 6 to 8 hours. Taste and adjust the seasonings, if needed. Serve hot, garnished with fresh basil or parsley and a drizzle of the balsamic reduction (if using).

Brunswick Bean Stew

SERVES 6

SLOW COOKER SIZE: 4- TO 6-QUART (3.8 TO 5.7 L) | COOK TIME: 8 HOURS ON LOW | GLUTEN-FREE | OIL-FREE | SOY-FREE OPTION

Like the classic Southern stew, this vegan version contains corn and limas and a rich smoky flavor, but it leaves out the wild game in favor of two kinds of beans. Seitan and plant-based sausage are also good additions for an even heartier stew. For soy-free, omit the Worcestershire or soy sauce and use Soy-Free Sauce (page 344) or coconut aminos or add some soy-free vegetable broth base or additional salt.

1 large yellow onion, minced
1 celery rib, chopped
2 carrots, thinly sliced
4 garlic cloves, minced
2 teaspoons grated peeled fresh ginger
1 green bell pepper, seeded and chopped
1½ cups (249 g) frozen lima beans, thawed
1½ cups (384 g) cooked dark red kidney beans (page 114)
   or 1 (15-ounce, or 425 g) can beans, rinsed and drained
1½ cups (258 g) cooked pinto beans (page 114)
   or 1 (15-ounce, or 425 g) can beans, rinsed and drained
1 (14.5-ounce, or 410 g) can diced tomatoes, with their juices
1 tablespoon (15 ml) vegan Worcestershire sauce or soy sauce
2 teaspoons brown mustard
1 teaspoon brown sugar
3½ cups (840 ml) vegetable broth

(continued)

Salt and freshly ground black pepper

1 cup (155 g) fresh or (165 g) frozen corn kernels, thawed

1 teaspoon liquid smoke

2 tablespoons (8 g) minced fresh flat-leaf parsley, for garnish

1. In the slow cooker, combine the onion, celery, carrots, garlic, and ginger. Add the bell pepper, lima beans, kidney beans, pinto beans, and tomatoes and their juices.

2. In a small bowl, combine the Worcestershire sauce, mustard, and brown sugar, stirring to blend. Stir in about ¼ cup (60 ml) of broth, then add the mixture to the slow cooker, along with the remaining broth and salt and black pepper to taste. Cover and cook on Low for 8 hours.

3. Stir in the corn and liquid smoke and cook, uncovered, for about 10 minutes to let the corn heat up. Taste and adjust the seasonings, if needed. For a thicker stew, puree a small amount of the stew right in the slow cooker using an immersion blender or scoop out 1 to 2 cups (weight varies) of stew and puree it in a blender or food processor, then stir the puree back into the rest of the stew in the cooker. Serve hot, sprinkled with the parsley.

Jackfruit Posole

SERVES 6

SLOW COOKER SIZE: 4- TO 6-QUART (3.8 TO 5.7 L) | COOK TIME: 6 TO 8 HOURS ON LOW |
GLUTEN-FREE | OIL-FREE | SOY-FREE OPTION

This vegan version of a traditional Mexican stew is fragrant, fun, and delicious enough to serve company. I like to make it in a large slow cooker and set it out with warm tortillas and bowls of accompaniments for everyone to add according to their own taste. My favorite garnishes are avocado, cilantro, and pepitas, but you can also put out bowls of salsa, shredded lettuce, sliced radishes, and Cashew Sour Cream (page 338). If you don't have jackfruit on hand, you can instead use chopped seitan, Soy Curls (see page 27), or just add extra pinto beans. This recipe can be made soy-free by omitting the soy sauce and using Soy-Free Sauce (page 344), or coconut aminos, or adding some soy-free vegetable broth base or additional salt.

1 (20-ounce, or 560 g) can young green jackfruit in water or brine (not syrup)

1 large yellow onion, finely chopped

1 carrot, thinly sliced

4 garlic cloves, minced

2 tablespoons (32 g) tomato paste

2 teaspoons chili powder

1 teaspoon dried oregano

½ teaspoon ground coriander

½ teaspoon ground cumin

1 red bell pepper, seeded and cut into ½-inch (1 cm) dice

1 (4-ounce, or 115 g) can chopped (hot or mild) green chilies, drained

1 (14.5-ounce, or 410 g) can diced tomatoes, drained

2 (15-ounce, or 425 g) cans hominy, rinsed and drained

3 cups (516 g) cooked pinto beans (page 114)
  or 2 (15-ounce, or 425 g) cans beans, rinsed and drained

2 tablespoons (30 ml) soy sauce

3 cups (720 ml) vegetable broth

Salt and freshly ground black pepper

Diced avocado, chopped fresh cilantro, and pepitas
  (green pumpkin seeds; optional), for garnish

Lime wedges, for serving

1. Rinse and drain the jackfruit, then coarsely chop it, discarding the seeds, if desired. Alternatively, place the jackfruit in a food processor and pulse it a few times until it breaks up into smaller shredded pieces.

2. Transfer the jackfruit to the slow cooker. Add the onion, carrot, and garlic. Stir in the tomato paste, chili powder, oregano, coriander, and cumin.

3. Add the bell pepper, chilies, tomatoes, hominy, pinto beans, soy sauce, and broth. Season to taste with salt and black pepper. Cover and cook on Low for 6 to 8 hours.

4. When ready to serve, taste and adjust the seasonings, if needed. If you desire a thicker stew, remove the lid and cook for 20 minutes longer on High. Ladle into bowls and garnish with the avocado, cilantro, and pepitas (if using). Serve with lime wedges on the side.

Split Pea and Barley Stew

SLOW COOKER SIZE: 4- TO 6-QUART (3.8 TO 5.7 L) | COOK TIME: 8 HOURS ON LOW | OIL-FREE |
SOY-FREE OPTION

This savory stew can be assembled quickly and benefits from long, slow cooking, making it ideal for putting on before work to cook all day. Do the chopping and load the crock the night before, refrigerate overnight, and it will be ready to go the next morning. This golden stew was adapted from a recipe shared with me by Nancy and Jonathan Shanes. For a soy-free version, omit the soy sauce and use Soy-Free Sauce (page 344) or coconut aminos, or add some soy-free vegetable broth base or additional salt.

1 large yellow onion, chopped

1½ pounds (680 g) sweet potatoes, peeled and cut into 1½-inch (3.5 cm) chunks

3 medium-size carrots, cut into ½-inch (1 cm) chunks

1 cup (225 g) dried split peas, rinsed and picked over

⅔ cup (133 g) raw pearl barley

1 (28-ounce, or 794 g) can diced tomatoes, with their juices

4 cups (960 ml) vegetable broth, plus more as needed

1 tablespoon (15 ml) soy sauce

1 teaspoon salt, plus more as needed

¼ teaspoon freshly ground black pepper

1 teaspoon liquid smoke (optional)

1. Combine the onion, sweet potatoes, carrots, split peas, barley, tomatoes and their juices, broth, soy sauce, salt, and pepper in the slow cooker. Cover and cook on Low until the ingredients are tender, about 8 hours.

2. Just before serving, stir in the liquid smoke (if using). Taste and adjust the seasonings, if needed; depending on the saltiness of your broth, you may need to add up to 1 more teaspoon of salt. If the stew is too dry, stir in up to 1 cup (240 ml) more of broth.

Farm Stand Stew

SERVES 4 TO 6

SLOW COOKER SIZE: 4- TO 6-QUART (3.8 TO 5.7 L) | COOK TIME: 6 TO 8 HOURS ON LOW | GLUTEN-FREE | OIL-FREE | SOY-FREE OPTION

Mix and match vegetables—for example, if you don't like fennel, leave it out and add more green beans, or include some bok choy or kale, or maybe some fresh corn kernels. If adding a more delicate vegetable, such as a leafy green or corn, add it about 1 hour before serving time so that it doesn't overcook. For soy-free, omit the soy sauce and use Soy-Free Sauce (page 344), or coconut aminos, or add some soy-free vegetable broth base or additional salt.

1 red onion, finely chopped

1 medium-size carrot, thinly sliced

4 ounces (115 g) green beans, cut into 1-inch (2.5 cm) pieces

1 red or yellow bell pepper, seeded and chopped

8 ounces (225 g) small red or white potatoes, scrubbed and left whole if about 1 inch (2.5 cm) in diameter, halved or quartered if larger

1 medium-size fennel bulb, trimmed and coarsely chopped

3 cups (540 g) cooked cannellini or other white beans (page 114) or 2 (15-ounce, or 425 g) cans beans, rinsed and drained

2 small zucchini, cut into ½-inch (1 cm) pieces

4 cups (960 ml) vegetable broth

¼ cup (60 ml) dry white wine

2 tablespoons (30 ml) soy sauce

1 teaspoon dried basil

1 teaspoon dried marjoram or thyme

1 teaspoon onion powder

½ teaspoon garlic powder

1 bay leaf

Salt and freshly ground black pepper

1 large ripe tomato, cut into 1-inch (2.5 cm) dice

¼ cup (16 g) chopped fresh flat-leaf parsley or (10 g) basil

(continued)

1. In the slow cooker, combine the onion, carrot, green beans, and bell pepper. Add the potatoes, fennel, cannellini beans, zucchini, broth, wine, soy sauce, dried basil, marjoram, onion powder, garlic powder, and bay leaf. Season to taste with salt and pepper.

2. Cover and cook on Low for 6 hours.

3. Just before serving, taste and adjust the seasonings, if needed, then gently stir in the tomato and parsley. Remove the bay leaf and serve hot.

Chickpea and Mushroom Tagine   SERVES 4 TO 6

SLOW COOKER SIZE: 4- TO 6-QUART (3.8 TO 5.7 L) | COOK TIME: 6 TO 7 HOURS PLUS 30 MINUTES ON LOW | GLUTEN-FREE | OIL-FREE OPTION | SOY-FREE

A tagine is a Moroccan stew cooked slowly in an earthenware pot that is also called a tagine. Happily, a tagine also cooks well in a slow cooker! Serve this fragrant stew over freshly cooked couscous or rice.

¼ cup (60 ml) water, or 2 teaspoons olive oil

1 large yellow onion, chopped

3 garlic cloves, minced

1 teaspoon grated peeled fresh ginger

2 teaspoons ground coriander

1 teaspoon sweet paprika

½ teaspoon ground cumin

½ teaspoon ground turmeric

¼ teaspoon cayenne pepper

1 large red bell pepper, seeded and chopped

3 cups (495 g) cooked chickpeas (page 114)
    or 2 (15-ounce, or 425 g) cans chickpeas, rinsed and drained

8 ounces (225 g) portobello mushroom caps, gills scraped out and discarded, cut into 1-inch (2.5 cm) dice

1 (14.5-ounce, or 410 g) can diced tomatoes, drained

6 dried apricots, quartered

1½ cups (360 ml) vegetable broth

Salt and freshly ground black pepper

1 (9-ounce, or 255 g) can artichoke hearts, drained and quartered

½ cup (65 g) frozen green peas, thawed

¼ cup (35 g) golden raisins
1 tablespoon (15 ml) fresh lemon juice
2 tablespoons (32 g) almond butter
¼ cup (39 g) pitted green olives (preferably imported), halved
Freshly cooked couscous or rice, for serving
2 tablespoons (8 g) minced fresh flat-leaf parsley or (2 g) cilantro, for garnish
¼ cup (23 g) toasted sliced almonds, for garnish

1. Heat the water or oil in a medium-size skillet over medium-high heat. Add the onion and sauté until softened, about 5 minutes. Alternatively, place the onion in a microwave-safe bowl with 2 tablespoons of water, cover, and microwave for 2 minutes to soften. Stir in the garlic, ginger, coriander, paprika, cumin, turmeric, and cayenne.

2. Transfer the onion mixture to the slow cooker. Add the bell pepper, chickpeas, mushrooms, tomatoes, apricots, and broth. Season to taste with salt and black pepper. Cover and cook on Low for 6 to 7 hours.

3. Add the artichoke hearts, peas, raisins, and lemon juice. Ladle about ½ cup (120 ml) of broth into a cup and whisk in the almond butter until smooth, then stir the mixture back into the stew in the cooker. Cover and cook for 30 minutes longer.

4. When ready to serve, stir in the olives. Taste and adjust the seasonings, if needed. Serve over couscous and sprinkle with the parsley and almonds.

Creole-Style Jambalaya

Just as different areas of the country have different ideas of barbecue sauce, there are regional variations on jambalaya. Tempeh and red beans are used here, although a good spicy plant-based sausage (sliced, sautéed, and added at the end of the cooking time) would be a wonderful inclusion. Serve over your favorite freshly cooked rice, passing more hot sauce at the table.

2 teaspoons olive oil

8 ounces (225 g) tempeh, cut into 1-inch (2.5 cm) pieces

1 large yellow onion, chopped

1 medium-size green bell pepper, seeded and chopped

1 celery rib, chopped

4 garlic cloves, minced

3 cups (768 g) cooked dark red kidney beans (page 114)
    or 2 (15-ounce, or 425 g) cans beans, rinsed and drained

1 (15-ounce, or 425 g) can crushed tomatoes

1 (14.5-ounce, or 410 g) can fire-roasted tomatoes, drained

1 cup (240 ml) vegetable broth

1 teaspoon filé powder (optional)

1 teaspoon dried thyme

½ teaspoon smoked paprika

¼ teaspoon cayenne pepper

2 large bay leaves

½ teaspoon Old Bay Seasoning

Salt and freshly ground black pepper

1 teaspoon Tabasco or Texas Pete hot sauce, plus more for serving

½ teaspoon liquid smoke

Freshly cooked rice, for serving

1. Heat the oil in a large skillet over medium-high heat. Add the tempeh and cook until browned, about 5 minutes. Transfer the tempeh to a plate and set aside. To the same skillet, add the onion, bell pepper, celery, and garlic; cover and cook until softened, about 5 minutes, adding a little water to sauté the vegetables so they don't stick.

2. Transfer the vegetable mixture to the slow cooker. Add the beans, both tomatoes, broth, filé powder (if using), thyme, paprika, cayenne, bay leaves, and Old Bay and season to taste with salt and black pepper—you'll need to start with at least 1 teaspoon of salt. Add the tempeh, cover, and cook on Low until the vegetables are tender, about 6 hours.

3. Just before serving, add the Tabasco and liquid smoke, then taste and adjust the seasonings, if needed. Serve over rice.

Italian-Style Vegetable Stew

SERVES 4

SLOW COOKER SIZE: 4- TO 6-QUART (3.8 TO 5.7 L) | COOK TIME: 6 TO 8 HOURS ON LOW | GLUTEN-FREE |
OIL-FREE | SOY-FREE

This recipe was inspired by a chicken dish my mother used to make. When I was a child, I remember enjoying everything about it—except for the chicken. Now I can have it my way, with delicious vegetables and herbs simmered in a luscious broth. I like to serve this over freshly cooked noodles, but it's also good with warm crusty bread for dunking.

1 yellow onion, minced

3 garlic cloves, minced

2 tablespoons (32 g) tomato paste

1 teaspoon dried oregano

1 teaspoon dried basil

1 teaspoon fresh or dried rosemary

3 carrots, thinly sliced

1 celery rib, chopped

2 medium-size Yukon gold potatoes, peeled and diced

1 red bell pepper, seeded and chopped

3 cups (495 g) cooked chickpeas (page 114)
    or 2 (15-ounce, or 425 g) cans chickpeas, rinsed and drained

1 (14.5-ounce, or 410 g) can diced tomatoes, with their juices

½ cup (120 ml) dry white wine

1 cup (240 ml) vegetable broth

¼ cup (15 g) nutritional yeast

2 bay leaves

Salt and freshly ground black pepper

(continued)

1. In the slow cooker, combine the onion, garlic, tomato paste, oregano, basil, and rosemary, stirring to mix.

2. Add the carrots, celery, potatoes, bell pepper, chickpeas, tomatoes and their juices, and wine. Stir in the broth, nutritional yeast, and bay leaves and season to taste with salt and pepper. Cover and cook on Low until the vegetables are tender, 6 to 8 hours.

3. Taste and adjust the seasonings, if needed. Remove and discard the bay leaves before serving.

African-Inspired Peanut Stew

SERVES 6

SLOW COOKER SIZE: 4- TO 6-QUART (3.8 TO 5.7 L) | COOK TIME: 6 HOURS ON LOW | GLUTEN-FREE | OIL-FREE OPTION | SOY-FREE

This colorful stew has a deep, rich flavor owing to the peanut butter and spices, and it's so easy to make. Crunchy peanut butter works especially well in this dish, adding an extra layer of texture. Serve over rice, couscous, or quinoa.

¼ cup (60 ml) water, or 2 teaspoons olive oil

1 medium-size yellow onion, minced

3 garlic cloves, minced

2 teaspoons grated peeled fresh ginger (optional)

1 teaspoon ground coriander

1 teaspoon ground cumin

1 teaspoon curry powder

¼ teaspoon cayenne pepper

2 medium-size sweet potatoes, peeled and cut into ½-inch (1 cm) dice

1 green bell pepper, seeded and cut into ½-inch (1 cm) dice

3 cups (768 g) cooked kidney beans (page 114)
    or 2 (15-ounce, or 425 g) cans beans, rinsed and drained

1 (14.5-ounce, or 410 g) can diced tomatoes, with their juices

1½ cups (360 ml) vegetable broth

⅓ cup (87 g) peanut butter, preferably crunchy

Salt and freshly ground black pepper

6 cups (180 g) coarsely chopped fresh spinach or Swiss chard

1. Heat the water or oil in a medium-size skillet over medium-high heat. Add the onion and sauté until softened, about 5 minutes. Add the garlic and cook for 1 minute longer, then stir in the ginger (if using), coriander, cumin, curry powder, and cayenne. Alternatively, place the onion and garlic in a microwave-safe bowl with 2 tablespoons of water, cover, and microwave for 2 minutes to soften, then stir in the ginger and spices.

2. Transfer the onion mixture to the slow cooker. Stir in the sweet potatoes, bell pepper, beans, and tomatoes and their juices.

3. Combine about ½ cup (120 ml) of the broth in a small bowl with the peanut butter, stirring to blend, then scrape the mixture into the slow cooker along with the remaining broth. Season to taste with salt and black pepper. Cover and cook on Low for 6 hours.

4. Just before serving time, stir in the spinach and continue cooking for a few minutes until the spinach is wilted.

Lentil and Chickpea Curry   SERVES 4

SLOW COOKER SIZE: 4- TO 6-QUART (3.8 TO 5.7 L) | COOK TIME: 6 TO 8 HOURS ON LOW | GLUTEN-FREE |
OIL-FREE | SOY-FREE

Both chickpeas and lentils are popular in Indian cooking, as are cauliflower and potatoes. Put them all in the same pot and you have one delicious dish. The slow cooker is an ideal way to cook curries, because it allows the aromatic spices to permeate the other ingredients.

1 large yellow onion, minced
3 garlic cloves, minced
1 teaspoon grated peeled fresh ginger
¼ cup (64 g) tomato paste
2 cups (480 ml) water, divided
1 tablespoon (6 g) curry powder
1 teaspoon ground coriander
1 teaspoon dried thyme
½ teaspoon ground cumin
¼ teaspoon cayenne pepper
¼ teaspoon ground turmeric
½ cup (98.5 g) dried brown lentils
1 large green bell pepper, seeded and chopped

(continued)

3 cups (300 g) small cauliflower florets

1 large russet potato, peeled and diced

3 cups (495 g) cooked chickpeas (page 114)
   or 2 (15-ounce, or 425 g) cans chickpeas, rinsed and drained

Salt and freshly ground black pepper

2 tablespoons (40 g) lime marmalade or minced mango chutney

1 tablespoon (15 ml) white wine vinegar

½ cup (65 g) frozen green peas, thawed

1 cup (240 ml) unsweetened coconut milk (optional)

2 tablespoons (8 g) minced fresh flat-leaf parsley or cilantro, for garnish

1. In the slow cooker, combine the onion, garlic, ginger, tomato paste, and ¼ cup (60 ml) of water, stirring to blend. Stir in the curry powder, coriander, thyme, cumin, cayenne, and turmeric.

2. Add the lentils, bell pepper, cauliflower, potato, chickpeas, and remaining 1¾ cups (420 ml) of water. Season to taste with salt and black pepper, cover, and cook on Low until the vegetables are tender, 6 to 8 hours.

3. Blend the marmalade and vinegar in a small bowl and stir it into the curry, along with the peas. For a thicker curry, puree 1 to 2 cups (weight varies) of the stew in a blender or food processor, then stir the puree back into the rest of the stew. Alternatively, use an immersion blender to puree some of the curry right in the cooker, then stir to mix. For a saucier stew, stir in 1 cup (240 ml) of coconut milk and let it heat up for a few minutes. Taste and adjust the seasonings, if needed. Serve hot, sprinkled with the parsley.

Portobello and White Bean Goulash

SERVES 4

SLOW COOKER SIZE: 4- TO 6-QUART (3.8 TO 5.7 L) | COOK TIME: 6 HOURS ON LOW |
GLUTEN-FREE OPTION | OIL-FREE | SOY-FREE

Because mushrooms, sauerkraut, and white beans have a natural affinity for one another, they are a harmonious flavor combination for this goulash, seasoned with caraway and paprika. Serve over wide egg-free noodles or gluten-free noodles, if desired.

1 large yellow onion, minced

3 garlic cloves, minced

2 tablespoons (32 g) tomato paste

2 tablespoons (16 g) sweet Hungarian paprika

1 teaspoon caraway seeds

1½ cups (360 ml) vegetable broth

1 (14.5-ounce, or 410 g) can diced tomatoes, drained

1 cup (142 g) sauerkraut, rinsed and drained

3 cups (516 g) cooked white beans (page 114)
    or 2 (15-ounce, or 425 g) cans beans, rinsed and drained

¼ cup (60 ml) dry white wine

2 bay leaves

5 large portobello mushroom caps, gills scraped out and discarded,
    cut into 1-inch (2.5 cm) dice

Salt and freshly ground black pepper

½ cup (115 g) Cashew Sour Cream (page 338)

Cooked wide noodles, for serving

2 tablespoons (8 g) minced fresh flat-leaf parsley or dill

1. In the slow cooker, combine the onion, garlic, the tomato paste, paprika, caraway seeds, and ½ cup (120 ml) of broth, stirring to blend.

2. Stir in the tomatoes, sauerkraut, beans, wine, bay leaves, mushrooms, and the remaining 1 cup (240 ml) of broth. Season to taste with salt and black pepper and stir to combine. Cover and cook on Low for 6 hours.

3. Just before serving, ladle ½ cup (120 ml) of broth into a small bowl and stir in the cashew sour cream. Stir this mixture back into the goulash, taste to adjust the seasonings, and serve at once over the noodles, garnished with the parsley.

Seitan Stroganoff

SLOW COOKER SIZE: 4- TO 6-QUART (3.8 TO 5.7 L) | COOK TIME: 6 TO 8 HOURS ON LOW, PLUS 20 MINUTES ON HIGH | GLUTEN-FREE OPTION | SOY-FREE OPTION

The seitan cooks right in the slow cooker, absorbing all of the delicious flavors of the surrounding ingredients as it cooks. For a gluten-free stroganoff, omit the seitan instructions and add more mushrooms along with some Soy Curls (see page 27) or tempeh, and use a gluten-free flour to help thicken the sauce. For soy-free, omit the soy sauce and use Soy-Free Sauce (page 344), or coconut aminos.

SEITAN

1½ cups (180 g) vital wheat gluten

2 tablespoons (15 g) tapioca starch

2 tablespoons (7.5 g) nutritional yeast

1 teaspoon garlic powder

1 teaspoon onion powder

¼ teaspoon salt

2 tablespoons (30 ml) soy sauce

1 tablespoon (15 g) ketchup

1 tablespoon (30 ml) olive oil

½ teaspoon vegan gravy browner (such as Kitchen Bouquet; optional)

1 cup (240 ml) water

STROGANOFF

2 teaspoons olive oil, or ¼ cup (60 ml) water

2 large yellow onions, chopped

3 garlic cloves, minced

2 tablespoons (32 g) tomato paste

1 tablespoon (8 g) sweet Hungarian paprika

1 teaspoon dried thyme

1 teaspoon Dijon mustard

¼ cup (60 ml) soy sauce

⅓ cup (80 ml) dry red wine

2 tablespoons (15.5 g) all-purpose flour

8 ounces (225 g) mushrooms (any kind), sliced

2 cups (480 ml) vegetable broth

1 bay leaf
Salt and freshly ground black pepper
½ cup (115 g) Cashew Sour Cream (page 338)
1 tablespoon (4 g) minced fresh dill, for garnish

1. To make the seitan: In a large bowl, combine the vital wheat gluten, tapioca starch, nutritional yeast, garlic and onion powders, and salt. In a separate bowl, combine the soy sauce, ketchup, oil, and gravy browner (if using). Stir in the water to blend, then pour the wet mixture into the dry mixture, stirring to form a stiff dough. Transfer the dough to a flat work surface and knead the dough for about 2 minutes. Flatten the dough and cut it into 1-inch (2.5 cm) pieces. Set aside.

2. To make the stroganoff: For the best flavor, heat the oil in a large skillet over medium-high heat. Add the onions and sauté until softened, about 5 minutes. Add the garlic and cook for 1 minute longer. Stir in the tomato paste, paprika, thyme, mustard, soy sauce, and wine and blend until smooth. Alternatively, omit the oil and sauté these ingredients in a few tablespoons of water or combine them in a microwave-safe bowl with a little water, cover, and microwave for 2 minutes.

3. Transfer the onion mixture to the slow cooker. Sprinkle with the flour, stirring to coat. Stir in the mushrooms, broth, and bay leaf and season to taste with salt and black pepper. Place the seitan pieces in the cooker, submerging them as much as possible and arranging them so they don't touch. Cover and cook on Low for 6 to 8 hours.

4. Remove the lid and cook on High for 20 minutes. Remove the bay leaf. Ladle about 1 cup (240 ml) of broth into a bowl and slowly stir in the cashew sour cream, then stir the mixture back into the stew. Serve at once, garnished with the dill.

Three-Bean Cholent

SLOW COOKER SIZE: 4- TO 6-QUART (3.8 TO 5.7 L) | COOK TIME: 8 TO 11 HOURS ON LOW |
GLUTEN-FREE OPTION | OIL-FREE | SOY-FREE OPTION

Because cholent, a traditional Sabbath dish, requires long, slow cooking, it's ideal for the slow cooker. This is one of the few recipes in this book that begins with dried beans and takes longer than 8 hours to cook. Because this recipe requires a long cooking time, if you are planning to cook and serve it on the same day, consider prepping the vegetables the night before and combining them with the canned tomatoes in a covered bowl in the refrigerator overnight— the tomatoes will keep the potatoes from browning. Combine the other ingredients in another refrigerated bowl. Then, in the morning, simply combine the drained soaked beans, vegetables, and other ingredients in the slow cooker and turn it on. This recipe can be made soy-free by omitting the soy sauce and Worcestershire sauce and using Soy-Free Sauce (page 344) or coconut aminos, or adding some soy-free vegetable broth base or additional salt. For gluten-free, omit the seitan.

½ cup (125 g) dried black beans, rinsed and picked over

½ cup (89 g) dried lima beans, rinsed and picked over

½ cup (96.5 g) dried pinto beans, rinsed and picked over

1 large yellow onion, chopped

2 celery ribs, chopped

4 garlic cloves, minced

1½ pounds (680 g) small red-skinned potatoes, scrubbed and cut into 1-inch (2.5 cm) chunks

2 carrots, cut into ¼-inch (0.6 cm) slices

½ cup (100 g) raw pearl barley

1 (14.5-ounce, or 410 g) can diced tomatoes, with their juices

2 tablespoons (32 g) tomato paste

1 teaspoon Dijon mustard

1 teaspoon granulated natural sugar

3 cups (720 ml) vegetable broth

1 tablespoon (15 ml) soy sauce

1 teaspoon vegan Worcestershire sauce

1 teaspoon smoked paprika

1 teaspoon salt

¼ teaspoon freshly ground black pepper

8 ounces (225 g) seitan (page 154), cut into 1-inch (2.5 m) pieces (optional)

1. Combine the beans in a bowl and add enough water to cover the beans by 2 inches (5 cm). Leave the beans to soak overnight.

2. Drain the beans and add them to the slow cooker. Add the onion, celery, garlic, potatoes, carrots, barley, and tomatoes and their juices.

3. In a small bowl, combine the tomato paste, mustard, and sugar. Add about ½ cup (120 ml) of broth and blend until smooth, then add to the slow cooker. Add the remaining broth, soy sauce, Worcestershire, paprika, salt, and pepper. Cover and cook on Low until the beans and vegetables are tender, 8 to 11 hours.

4. Add the seitan (if using), cover, and cook for 20 minutes longer. Taste and adjust the seasonings, if needed, and serve.

Jackfruit and Black Bean Chili

SERVES 4

SLOW COOKER SIZE: 4- TO 6-QUART (3.8 TO 5.7 L) | COOK TIME: 6 TO 8 HOURS ON LOW | GLUTEN-FREE |
OIL-FREE | SOY-FREE OPTION

Jackfruit combines with black beans to make a hearty chili made even better by slow cooking. Use hot or mild green chilies, according to your own taste. To make this soy-free, use coconut aminos instead of tamari.

1 (20-ounce, or 560 g) can young green jackfruit in water or brine (not syrup)

1 small yellow onion, minced

1 small red bell pepper, seeded and chopped

4 garlic cloves, minced

2 (14.5-ounce, or 410 g) cans crushed tomatoes

1 (4-ounce, or 115 g) can diced (mild or hot) green chilies, drained

3 tablespoons (48 g) tomato paste

1 tablespoon (20 g) maple syrup

1 tablespoon (15 ml) tamari or coconut aminos

(continued)

3 cups (516 g) cooked black beans (page 114)
      or 2 (15-ounce, or 425 g) cans black beans, rinsed and drained

1 cup (240 ml) vegetable broth

2 tablespoons (15 g) chili powder, or to taste

1 teaspoon ground cumin

1 teaspoon ground coriander

1 teaspoon dried oregano

1 teaspoon onion powder

1 teaspoon smoked paprika

Salt and freshly ground black pepper

Optional toppings: chopped scallions, diced avocado, Cashew Sour Cream
      (page 338), vegan cheese shreds

1. Rinse and drain the jackfruit, then coarsely chop it, discarding the seeds, if desired. Alternatively, place the jackfruit in a food processor and pulse it a few times until it breaks up into smaller shredded pieces.

2. Transfer the jackfruit to the slow cooker. Add the onion, bell pepper, garlic, crushed tomatoes, and chilies. In a small bowl combine the tomato paste, maple syrup, and tamari and blend until smooth.

3. Stir the tomato paste mixture into the slow cooker. Add the beans, broth, chili powder, cumin, coriander, oregano, onion powder, and paprika. Season with salt and black pepper to taste. Cover and cook on Low for 6 to 8 hours, or until the vegetables are tender and the flavors are well developed.

4. Taste and adjust the seasonings, if needed. If the chili isn't thick enough, stir well, and cook uncovered for 30 minutes longer. Serve hot, garnished with your favorite toppings.

Two-Lentil Chili

SLOW COOKER SIZE: 4- TO 6-QUART (3.8 TO 5.7 L) | COOK TIME: 6 TO 8 HOURS ON LOW | GLUTEN-FREE |
OIL-FREE | SOY-FREE OPTION

Two kinds of lentils give this chili a great texture—the red lentils cook down and thicken while the brown lentils hold their shape. Make it as spicy as you want by adjusting the amounts of jalapeño and chili powder. I like to serve this chili over cooked brown rice or quinoa. For a soy-free chili, omit the soy sauce and use Soy-Free Sauce (page 344), or coconut aminos, or add some soy-free vegetable broth base or additional salt, and choose soy-free toppings.

1 medium-size yellow onion, chopped

4 garlic cloves, minced

1 or 2 jalapeño chiles, seeded and minced

1 bell pepper (any color), seeded and chopped

3 tablespoons (22.5 g) chili powder

1 teaspoon dried oregano

1 teaspoon ground cumin

1 cup (197 g) dried brown lentils, rinsed and picked over

1 cup (197 g) dried red lentils, rinsed and picked over

1 (28-ounce, or 794 g) can crushed tomatoes

1 tablespoon (15 ml) soy sauce

1 teaspoon granulated natural sugar

1 teaspoon unsweetened cocoa powder

Salt and freshly ground black pepper

4 cups (960 ml) water

Diced avocado, minced onion, Cashew Sour Cream (page 338), and/or chopped fresh cilantro, for garnish

1. Combine the onion, garlic, chiles, and bell pepper in the slow cooker. Stir in chili powder, oregano, and cumin.

2. Add both lentils, the tomatoes, soy sauce, sugar, cocoa, and salt and black pepper to taste. (You may need to add up to 2 teaspoons of salt.) Stir in the water, cover, and cook on Low until the lentils and vegetables are tender, 6 to 8 hours.

3. Taste and adjust the seasonings, if needed. Serve hot, garnished with your favorite chili toppings.

The White Chili

SLOW COOKER SIZE: 4- TO 6-QUART (3.8 TO 5.7 L) | COOK TIME: 6 TO 8 HOURS ON LOW | GLUTEN-FREE | OIL-FREE | SOY-FREE

No collection of chili recipes is complete without a white version. So here it is, made with white beans, potato, and hominy—and not a tomato in sight. Canned hominy is available in well-stocked supermarkets. Be sure to rinse it well before using. To make this chili soy-free, use a soy-free cashew sour cream.

1 large yellow onion, chopped

4 garlic cloves, minced

2 teaspoons ground cumin

2 teaspoons ground coriander

1 teaspoon dried marjoram

1 large russet potato, peeled and chopped

4 cups (720 g) cooked cannellini or other white beans (page 114) or 3 (15-ounce, or 425 g) cans beans, rinsed and drained

1 (16-ounce, or 455 g) can hominy, rinsed and drained

1 (4-ounce, or 115 g) can (hot or mild) minced green chilies, drained

2 cups (480 ml) vegetable broth or water

1 teaspoon salt

¼ teaspoon ground white pepper

Cashew Sour Cream (page 338), diced avocado, lime wedges, minced scallions, and/or chopped fresh cilantro, for garnish

1. Combine the onion, garlic, cumin, coriander, and marjoram in the slow cooker. Stir in the potato, beans, hominy, chilies, broth, salt, and white pepper.

2. Cover and cook on Low for 6 to 8 hours.

3. Taste and adjust the seasonings, if needed. Serve hot, garnished with desired toppings.

Chipotle Black Bean Chili with Winter Squash

SERVES 6

SLOW COOKER SIZE: 4- TO 6-QUART (3.8 TO 5.7 L) | COOK TIME: 6 TO 8 HOURS ON LOW | GLUTEN-FREE | OIL-FREE | SOY-FREE

The sweetness of the butternut squash is a good foil for the smoky heat of the chipotle in this hearty black bean chili. Use more or less chipotles and/or chili powder, depending on your heat tolerance. You can always add some chipotles and chili powder early on and then add more later if desired, as slow cooking can dissipate the flavor of spices.

1 yellow onion, finely chopped

4 garlic cloves, minced

2 tablespoons (32 g) tomato paste

1 (14.5-ounce, or 410 g) can crushed tomatoes, with their juices

1 tablespoon (17 g) minced chipotle chile in adobo

2 tablespoons (15 g) chili powder, or to taste

1 teaspoon ground cumin

1 teaspoon ground coriander

½ teaspoon dried oregano

1 small butternut squash, peeled, seeded, and cut into ½-inch (1 cm) dice (about 3 cups, or 420 g)

1 small red bell pepper, seeded and chopped

4 cups (688 g) cooked black beans (page 114) or 3 (15-ounce, or 425 g) cans beans, rinsed and drained

1½ cups (360 ml) water

Salt and freshly ground black pepper

Diced avocado, minced onion, Cashew Sour Cream (page 338), shredded vegan cheese, and/or chopped fresh cilantro, for garnish

1. Combine the onion, garlic, and tomato paste in the slow cooker. Stir in the tomatoes and their juice, chipotles, chili powder, cumin, coriander, and oregano.

2. Add the squash, bell pepper, beans, and water. Season to taste with salt and black pepper, cover, and cook on Low for 6 to 8 hours.

3. Taste and adjust the seasonings, if needed. If the chili isn't thick enough, stir well, and cook uncovered for 30 minutes longer. Serve hot, garnished with your favorite chili toppings.

Indian-Spiced Chickpea-Potato Chili

SERVES 4 TO 6

SLOW COOKER SIZE: 4- TO 6-QUART (3.8 TO 5.7 L) | COOK TIME: 6 TO 8 HOURS ON LOW | GLUTEN-FREE | OIL-FREE | SOY-FREE OPTION

The pairing of chickpeas and potatoes is popular in Indian cooking, and the combination is especially good in this chili-type dish seasoned with ginger, coriander, cumin, and other spices. For a soy-free version, use a soy-free vegan yogurt.

1 yellow onion, minced

3 garlic cloves, minced

1½ teaspoons grated peeled fresh ginger

1 tablespoon (6 g) curry powder

1 teaspoon ground coriander

1 teaspoon ground cumin

¼ teaspoon cayenne pepper

2 Yukon Gold potatoes, cut into ½-inch (1 cm) dice

1 (14.5-ounce, or 410 g) can crushed tomatoes

1 (4-ounce, or 115 g) can (hot or mild) minced green chilies, drained

4 cups (660 g) cooked chickpeas (page 114)
    or 3 (15-ounce, or 425 g) cans chickpeas, rinsed and drained

1 cup (240 ml) water

Salt

¾ cup (97.5 g) frozen baby green peas, thawed

½ cup (115 g) plain vegan yogurt

⅓ cup (5 g) minced fresh cilantro leaves

1. In the slow cooker, combine the onion, garlic, and ginger. Stir in the curry powder, coriander, cumin, and cayenne.

2. Add the potatoes, tomatoes, chiles, chickpeas, and water. Season with salt.

3. Cover and cook on Low for 6 to 8 hours. About 15 minutes before you're ready to serve, stir in the peas.

4. Stir the yogurt and the cilantro into the chili, then taste and adjust the seasonings, if needed. Serve hot.

Happy New Year Chili

SLOW COOKER SIZE: 4- TO 6-QUART (3.8 TO 5.7 L) | COOK TIME: 4 TO 6 HOURS ON LOW | GLUTEN-FREE |
OIL-FREE OPTION | SOY-FREE OPTION

Inspired by two Southern specialties, dirty rice and Hoppin' John, this chili is a great way to begin the New Year. It's ideal accompanied by the collards on page 221. To mellow the flavor of the tempeh, steam it for 15 minutes before using it in the recipe. Instead of tempeh, you may substitute 1 to 2 cups (255 to 510 g) finely chopped seitan (which would make the chili soy-free) or sliced Plant-Based Sausage Links (page 174).

¼ cup (60 ml) water, or 2 teaspoons olive oil

1 large yellow onion, chopped

5 garlic cloves, minced

1 celery rib, chopped

1 fresh hot chile, seeded and minced (optional)

2 tablespoons (32 g) tomato paste

1 small green bell pepper, seeded and chopped

8 ounces (225 g) tempeh, chopped or crumbled

2 tablespoons (15 g) chili powder

1 teaspoon ground cumin

1 teaspoon dried thyme

½ cup (97.5 g) raw long-grain brown rice

3 cups (510 g) cooked black-eyed peas (page 114)
    or 2 (15-ounce, or 425 g) cans black-eyed peas, rinsed and drained

1 (28-ounce, or 794 g) can diced tomatoes, with their juices

2 cups (480 ml) vegetable broth or water

Salt and freshly ground black pepper

Cashew Sour Cream (page 338), for serving

Tabasco sauce, for serving

1. Heat the water or oil in a medium-size skillet over medium-high heat. Add the onion, garlic, celery, and chile (if using) and sauté until softened, about 5 minutes. Stir in the tomato paste, bell pepper, tempeh, chili powder, cumin, and thyme and cook for 2 minutes longer.

(continued)

2. Transfer the onion mixture to the slow cooker. Add the rice, black-eyed peas, tomatoes and their juices, and broth. Season to taste with salt and black pepper. Cover and cook on Low for 4 to 6 hours.

3. Taste and adjust the seasonings, if needed. Serve hot, offering cashew sour cream and Tabasco at the table.

Pantry Raid Chili

SERVES 4

SLOW COOKER SIZE: 4-QUART (3.8 TO 5.7 L) | COOK TIME: 6 HOURS ON LOW | GLUTEN-FREE | OIL-FREE | SOY-FREE OPTION

Even when you're too busy to cook, this easy-to-assemble chili requires very little prep, so you can literally toss it together with just a few items from your pantry. Hint: If you cook this recipe on High, it can be ready to eat in about 3 hours. For a soy-free version, omit the soy sauce and use Soy-Free Sauce (page 344), or coconut aminos, or add some soy-free vegetable broth base or additional salt.

1 (24-ounce, or 675 g) jar fire-roasted chunky tomato salsa
2 tablespoons (15 g) chili powder
1 teaspoon dried marjoram
½ teaspoon ground cumin
1 cup (240 ml) water
3 cups (516 g) cooked pinto beans (page 114)
    or 2 (15-ounce, or 425 g) cans beans, rinsed and drained
1 tablespoon (15 ml) soy sauce
Salt and freshly ground black pepper
2 cups (310 g) fresh or (330 g) frozen corn kernels, thawed
Diced avocado, minced onion, Cashew Sour Cream (page 338),
    shredded vegan cheese, and/or chopped fresh cilantro, for garnish

1. Combine the salsa, chili powder, marjoram, cumin, and water in the slow cooker and stir to combine. Add the beans and soy sauce and season to taste with salt and pepper. Cover and cook on Low for 4 to 6 hours.

2. Stir in the corn kernels and cook, uncovered, for 10 minutes longer to let the corn get hot. Serve hot, garnished with your favorite chili toppings.

Holy Mole Red Bean Chili

SERVES 4 TO 6

SLOW COOKER SIZE: 4- TO 6-QUART (3.8 TO 5.7 L) | COOK TIME: 6 TO 8 HOURS ON LOW |
GLUTEN-FREE OPTION | OIL-FREE | SOY-FREE

The rich depth of flavor from the mole sauce elevates a humble chili to new heights. I especially like the addition of chopped seitan in this chili, but you may substitute Soy Curls (see page 27), tempeh, or jackfruit, if you prefer.

1 large yellow onion, chopped

4 garlic cloves, minced

½ small green bell pepper, seeded and chopped

3 tablespoons (48 g) tomato paste

2 tablespoons (10 g) unsweetened cocoa powder

2 tablespoons (32 g) almond butter

2 to 3 tablespoons (15 to 22.5 g) chili powder

1 tablespoon (17 g) minced chipotle chiles in adobo

½ teaspoon ground cinnamon

1 (14.5-ounce, or 410 g) can diced fire-roasted tomatoes, drained and juices reserved

1 (14-ounce, or 395 g) can crushed tomatoes

3 cups (768 g) cooked dark red kidney beans (page 114) or 2 (15-ounce, or 425 g) cans beans, rinsed and drained

8 ounces (225 g) seitan (page 154), chopped

2 cups (480 ml) water

1 teaspoon salt

¼ teaspoon freshly ground black pepper

Diced avocado, pepitas (green pumpkin seeds), chopped scallions, and/or chopped fresh cilantro, for garnish

1. In the slow cooker combine the onion, garlic, and bell pepper. Stir in the tomato paste, cocoa, almond butter, chili powder, chipotles, cinnamon, and the juices from the diced tomatoes, stirring to blend.

2. Stir in the diced tomatoes, crushed tomatoes, beans, seitan, water, salt, and pepper. Cover and cook on Low for 6 to 8 hours.

3. Taste and adjust the seasonings, if needed. Serve hot, garnished with desired toppings.

Corn Bread–Topped Chili

SLOW COOKER SIZE: 4- TO 6-QUART (3.8 TO 5.7 L) | COOK TIME: 5 TO 6 HOURS ON LOW, PLUS 1 HOUR ON HIGH | GLUTEN-FREE | SOY-FREE OPTION

The steamy heat of the slow cooker allows the corn bread to cook right on top of the simmering vegetables. Spooning the corn bread batter onto the vegetables gives it a rustic look. You can make this chili as mild or as spicy as you like, depending on the heat of the chili powder you use and the addition of your choice of mild or hot green chilies. For soy-free, omit the soy sauce and use Soy-Free Sauce (page 344) or coconut aminos or add some soy-free vegetable broth base or additional salt.

¼ cup (60 ml) water, or 2 teaspoons olive oil

1 large yellow onion, minced

3 garlic cloves, minced

3 tablespoons (22.5 g) chili powder

1 teaspoon ground coriander

1 teaspoon ground cumin

1 small bell pepper (any color), seeded and chopped

4 cups (1 kg) cooked dark red kidney beans, black beans, or pinto beans, or a combination (page 114) or 3 (15-ounce, or 425 g) cans beans, rinsed and drained

1 cup (155 g) fresh or (165 g) frozen corn kernels, thawed

1 (4-ounce, or 115 g) can (mild or hot) chopped green chilies, drained

1 (14-ounce, or 395 g) can crushed tomatoes

½ cup (120 ml) water

1 tablespoon (15 ml) soy sauce

1 tablespoon (1 g) minced fresh cilantro leaves

Salt and freshly ground black pepper

1 cup (140 g) medium-ground cornmeal

2 teaspoons baking powder

½ teaspoon baking soda

½ cup (120 ml) plain unsweetened plant milk

2 tablespoons (30 ml) olive oil

1. Lightly coat the insert of the slow cooker with nonstick cooking spray. Heat the water or oil in a medium-size skillet over medium-high heat. Add the onion and sauté until softened, about 5 minutes. Stir in the garlic, chili powder, coriander, and cumin and cook for 30 seconds longer.

2. Transfer the onion mixture to the prepared slow cooker and add the bell pepper, beans, corn, and chilies. Stir in the tomatoes, water, soy sauce, and cilantro. Season to taste with salt and black pepper. Cover and cook on Low for 5 to 6 hours.

3. In a large bowl, combine the cornmeal, baking powder, baking soda, and ½ teaspoon salt. Add the plant milk and oil and stir to blend.

4. Drop the corn bread batter by the spoonful onto the simmering chili, then turn the heat setting to High. Cover and cook until the topping is cooked through, about 1 hour. For best results, serve within 15 minutes after the corn bread is finished cooking.

Beans and Grains

Beans and slow cookers were made for each other, since beans take a notoriously long time to cook and in fact benefit from long, slow cooking. Because beans are rich in protein, fiber, and nutrients, they are key ingredients in many vegan recipes. While beans are used in recipes throughout this book, it's in this chapter that they play a starring role, with recipes such as Smoky Molasses-Maple Baked Beans, Burgundy Red Beans, and Crockery Cassoulet.

Because beans are often paired with grains, there are several grain-based recipes in this chapter as well. It's important to note that some grains can be difficult to prepare in a slow cooker. Of the various types of rice, converted rice cooks the best in a slow cooker, when added during the last hour of cooking. Risotto, with its creamy texture, can be made well in a slow cooker. Most grains, however, are best when cooked separately on top of the stove or in a rice cooker and either added to the slow cooker just before serving or enjoyed alongside of (or under) what you've cooked in the slow cooker.

The first recipe in this chapter is called Basic Beans; it provides basic proportions and timing for cooking dried beans in a slow cooker. For additional information about beans, including cooking guidelines and soaking methods, see the section "Wide World of Beans" (page 28) in chapter 1.

BEAN BASICS

It's important to note that most of the recipes using beans in this book call for cooked beans. This is done for four basic reasons:

Digestibility: Cooking the beans first, then draining off the cooking liquid, makes the beans easier to digest.

Timing: Starting with cooked beans helps ensure that everything in the slow cooker will be done at the same time, thus making your cooking time more reliable.

Flexibility: Calling for cooked beans allows you the option of using canned beans or beans that you've previously cooked and frozen.

Convenience: Using cooked beans encourages you to cook a large batch of dried beans in the slow cooker and then portion and freeze them for later use. For economy and flavor, portioning and freezing home-cooked beans gives you the same convenience as canned beans. If you use frozen beans, thaw them first. If you use canned beans, they should be rinsed and drained. Either way, the resulting bean dishes prepared in the slow cooker will be delicious and full of flavor.

Basic Beans

MAKES 6 TO 7 CUPS (1 KG TO 1.2 KG)

SLOW COOKER SIZE: 4- TO 6-QUART (3.8 TO 5.7 L) | COOK TIME: 6 TO 8 HOURS ON HIGH | GLUTEN-FREE | OIL-FREE | SOY-FREE

This is a basic recipe for slow cooking dried beans such as pintos, kidneys, cannellinis, chickpeas, and black-eyed peas. To add some flavor to the beans, include the optional onion, garlic, and bay leaves. If you prefer them unseasoned, just cook them in water and you will have beans that are ready to use in any kind of recipe calling for cooked beans.

    1 pound (455 g) dried beans, rinsed and picked over
    1 large yellow onion, quartered (optional)
    2 garlic cloves, crushed (optional)
    2 bay leaves (optional)

1. Salt-soak the beans according to one of the methods described on page 30.

2. Place the beans in the slow cooker. (If cooking kidney beans or cannellini beans, boil them for 10 minutes on top of the stove before adding to the slow cooker.) Add the onion, garlic, and bay leaves (if using), and enough water to cover. Cover and cook on High until tender, 6 to 8 hours, depending on the type of bean.

VARIATIONS ON A BEAN

Jazz up plain cooked beans with a variety of global flavors in these variations on a (bean) theme! To make the beans more digestible, drain the Basic Beans after cooking, then proceed with the desired variation.

SOUTHWEST BEANS

MAKES 6 TO 7 CUPS (1 KG TO 1.2 KG)

GLUTEN-FREE | OIL-FREE | SOY-FREE

1 recipe Basic Beans (page 114)
1 (4-ounce, or 115 g) can chopped mild green chilies, drained
1 teaspoon ground cumin
1 teaspoon smoked paprika
½ teaspoon dried oregano
Salt and freshly ground black pepper
Water or vegetable broth, as needed (optional)

Drain off any remaining cooking liquid from the beans, if desired, then stir in the chilies, cumin, paprika, and oregano, and season to taste with salt and pepper. Reduce the heat to Low, cover, and cook for 30 minutes to blend the flavors. For a more saucy consistency, add up to 1 cup (240 ml) water or broth.

ASIAN BEANS

MAKES 6 TO 7 CUPS (1 KG TO 1.2 KG)

GLUTEN-FREE | SOY-FREE OPTION

1 recipe Basic Beans (page 114)
2 tablespoons (30 ml) soy sauce or Soy-Free Sauce (page 344) or coconut aminos
1 teaspoon grated peeled fresh ginger (optional)
2 scallions, minced
2 teaspoons toasted sesame oil

Drain off any remaining cooking liquid from the beans, if desired, then stir in the soy sauce, ginger (if using), scallions, and sesame oil.

MEDITERRANEAN BEANS

MAKES 6 TO 7 CUPS (1 KG TO 1.2 KG)

GLUTEN-FREE | SOY-FREE

2 teaspoons olive oil, or ¼ cup (60 ml) water
3 garlic cloves, minced
¼ cup (29 g) oil-packed sun-dried tomatoes, chopped
1 teaspoon dried basil
½ teaspoon dried oregano
¼ to ½ teaspoon red pepper flakes
1 recipe Basic Beans (page 114)
Salt and freshly ground black pepper

For the best flavor, heat the oil in a small skillet over medium-high heat. Add the garlic and cook until fragrant, about 30 seconds. Stir in the tomatoes, basil, oregano, and red pepper flakes. Alternatively, omit the oil and sauté these ingredients in a few tablespoons of water or combine them in a microwave-safe bowl with a little water, cover, and microwave for 1 minute. Rewarm the beans if necessary, drain them, and then stir the seasoning mixture into the beans. Season to taste with salt and pepper.

Smoky Molasses–Maple Baked Beans

SLOW COOKER SIZE: 4-QUART (3.8 L) | COOK TIME: 6 TO 7 HOURS ON LOW | GLUTEN-FREE |
OIL-FREE OPTION | SOY-FREE

These baked beans have a rich depth of flavor thanks to two kinds of natural sweeteners, chipotle chiles, and long slow cooking.

¼ cup (60 ml) water, or 2 teaspoons olive oil

1 medium-size yellow onion, minced

5 to 6 cups (860 g to 1 kg) cooked navy beans (page 114)
    or 4 (15-ounce, or 425 g) cans beans, rinsed and drained

¼ cup (80 g) maple syrup

¼ cup (85 g) light molasses (not blackstrap)

3 tablespoons (48 g) tomato paste

1 tablespoon (17 g) minced chipotle chiles in adobo

2 teaspoons stoneground mustard

1 teaspoon rice vinegar

½ teaspoon salt

¼ teaspoon freshly ground black pepper

1 teaspoon liquid smoke

1. Heat the water or oil in a small skillet over medium-high heat. Add the onion and sauté until softened, about 5 minutes. Alternatively, place the onion in a microwave-safe bowl with 2 tablespoons (30 ml) of water, cover, and microwave for 2 minutes to soften.

2. Transfer the onion to the slow cooker. Add the beans and set the heat to Low.

3. In a medium-size bowl, combine the maple syrup, molasses, tomato paste, chipotles, mustard, vinegar, salt, and pepper. Add ¼ cup (60 ml) of water, stirring until blended, then add the mixture to the slow cooker.

4. Cover and cook on Low for 6 hours. Just before serving, stir in the liquid smoke. If the sauce is too thick, add a little more water. If the sauce is too thin, remove the lid, turn the slow cooker to High, and cook for 30 minutes longer, or until any extra liquid evaporates. Taste and adjust the seasonings, if needed.

Barbecue Beans
with Coffee and Bourbon

SERVES 4 TO 6

SLOW COOKER SIZE: 4- TO 6-QUART (3.8 TO 5.7 L) | COOK TIME: 6 HOURS ON LOW | GLUTEN-FREE |
OIL-FREE OPTION | SOY-FREE OPTION

Let the slow cooker be the star of your next cookout instead of the grill with these flavorful beans that are slow-simmered in a zesty barbecue sauce made with coffee, bourbon, and maple syrup. Whoever coined the phrase "lip-smackin' good" surely had these beans in mind. For soy-free, omit the soy sauce and use Soy-Free Sauce (page 344), or coconut aminos, or add some soy-free vegetable broth base or additional salt.

¼ cup (60 ml) water, or 2 teaspoons olive oil

1 large yellow onion, minced

3 garlic cloves, minced

⅓ cup (80 g) ketchup or barbecue sauce

⅓ cup (80 ml) strong brewed coffee

¼ cup (60 ml) bourbon

¼ cup (50 g) granulated natural sugar

2 tablespoons (40 g) maple syrup or molasses (not blackstrap)

1 tablespoon (15 g) stoneground mustard

1 tablespoon (15 ml) soy sauce

5 to 6 cups (860 g to 1 kg) cooked navy beans (page 114)
    or 4 (15-ounce, or 425 g) cans beans, rinsed and drained

1. Heat the water or oil in a medium-size skillet over medium-high heat. Add the onion and sauté until softened, about 5 minutes. Add the garlic and cook for 1 minute longer. Alternatively, place the onion in a microwave-safe bowl with 2 tablespoons (30 ml) of water, cover, and microwave for 2 minutes to soften.

2. Transfer the onion mixture to the slow cooker. Stir in the ketchup, coffee, and bourbon and set the heat to Low.

3. In a bowl, combine the sugar, maple syrup, mustard, soy sauce, and ½ cup (120 ml) of water. Stir until well blended, then add to the slow cooker. Stir in the beans. Cover and cook on Low for 6 hours.

Burgundy Red Beans

SLOW COOKER SIZE: 4- TO 6-QUART (3.8 TO 5.7 L) | COOK TIME: 4 TO 6 HOURS ON LOW | GLUTEN-FREE | OIL-FREE OPTION | SOY-FREE

The Burgundy wine region of France is the inspiration for this hearty bean dish. Cremini mushrooms add to the texture and flavor, although seitan makes a good addition as well. Serve over mashed potatoes or cooked noodles (gluten-free, if desired), with a green vegetable alongside. If this turns out more brothy than you'd like, just stir 1 tablespoon (8 g) of cornstarch blended with 2 tablespoons (30 ml) of water into the hot liquid just before serving time (with the slow cooker turned to High). Or use an immersion blender to puree a small amount of the mixture right in the cooker, then stir to thicken.

¼ cup (60 ml) water, or 2 teaspoons olive oil

1 large yellow onion, minced

2 large carrots, thinly sliced

4 garlic cloves, minced

2 tablespoons (32 g) tomato paste

1 teaspoon dried thyme

½ teaspoon dried marjoram

2 bay leaves

8 ounces (225 g) cremini mushrooms, quartered or sliced

6 cups (1.5 kg) cooked dark red kidney beans (page 114)
    or 4 (15-ounce, or 425 g) cans beans, rinsed and drained

1 cup (240 ml) vegetable broth

2 tablespoons (15 g) tapioca starch or cornstarch

½ cup (120 ml) dry red wine

Salt and freshly ground black pepper

1 teaspoon vegan gravy browner (such as Kitchen Bouquet; optional)

Cooked noodles or mashed potatoes, for serving

2 tablespoons (8 g) minced fresh flat-leaf parsley, for garnish

1. Heat the water or oil in a large skillet over medium-high heat. Add the onion and carrots and sauté until softened, about 5 minutes. Alternatively, place the onion and carrot in a microwave-safe bowl with 2 tablespoons (30 ml) of water, cover, and microwave for 2 minutes to soften. Stir in the garlic, tomato paste, thyme, and marjoram.

(continued)

2. Transfer the onion mixture to the slow cooker. Add the bay leaves, mushrooms, beans, and broth. Place the tapioca starch in a small bowl and stir in the wine until smooth, then add to the pot, season to taste with salt and black pepper, and stir gently to combine. Cover and cook on Low until the vegetables are tender, 4 to 6 hours.

3. Just before serving, remove the bay leaves and stir in the gravy browner (if using). Taste and adjust the seasonings, if needed. Serve hot over noodles or mashed potatoes, sprinkled with the parsley.

Greek-Style Beans with Tomatoes and Spinach

SERVES 4 TO 6

SLOW COOKER SIZE: 4- TO 6-QUART (3.8 TO 5.7 L) | COOK TIME: 6 HOURS ON LOW | GLUTEN-FREE | OIL-FREE OPTION | SOY-FREE

Greek gigante beans or large butter beans work best for this wholesome dish and are easiest to find in a dried state. As with most bean dishes in this book, this recipe starts with beans that have already been cooked, so be sure to plan ahead so that you can get your beans cooked before making this recipe.

¼ cup (60 ml) water, or 2 teaspoons olive oil
1 large yellow onion, minced
5 garlic cloves, minced
4 cups (720 g) cooked gigante beans or large butter beans (page 114) or 3 (15-ounce, or 425 g) cans beans, rinsed and drained
1 (28-ounce, or 794 g) can diced tomatoes, with their juices
1 teaspoon dried marjoram
1 teaspoon dried basil
Salt and freshly ground black pepper
5 cups (150 g) chopped baby spinach
1 teaspoon lemon zest (optional)

1. Heat the water or oil in a medium-size skillet over medium-high heat. Add the onion and sauté until softened, about 5 minutes. Add the garlic and cook for 1 minute longer. Alternatively, place the onion and garlic in a microwave-safe bowl with 2 tablespoons (30 ml) of water, cover, and microwave for 2 minutes to soften.

2. Transfer the onion mixture to the slow cooker and add the beans, tomatoes and their juices, marjoram, basil, and salt and black pepper to taste. Stir to combine.

3. Cover and cook on Low for 6 hours. About 5 minutes before serving, stir in the spinach and lemon zest (if using). Taste and adjust the seasonings, if needed. Serve hot.

Crockery Cassoulet

SERVES 4 TO 6

SLOW COOKER SIZE: 4- TO 6-QUART (3.8 TO 5.7 L) | COOK TIME: 6 TO 8 HOURS ON LOW

White beans are an essential part of any classic French cassoulet, and here they take center stage as they slowly simmer with vegetables and herbs. The addition of plant-based sausage at the end of the cooking time provides added texture and flavor. If you eliminate the oil and the plant-based sausage links, this recipe will be oil-free, soy-free, and gluten-free. Serve with crusty French bread.

2 teaspoons olive oil (1 teaspoon optional for ¼ cup, or 60 ml, water)
1 large yellow onion, minced
2 large carrots, thinly sliced
5 garlic cloves, minced
1½ tablespoons (24 g) tomato paste
4½ cups (810 g) cooked Great Northern, cannellini, or other white beans (page 114) or 3 (15-ounce, or 425 g) cans beans, rinsed and drained
1 (14-ounce, or 395 g) can diced tomatoes, drained
½ cup (120 ml) vegetable broth
⅓ cup (80 ml) white wine
1 teaspoon dried thyme
¼ teaspoon dried marjoram
2 bay leaves
Salt and freshly ground black pepper
⅓ cup (33 g) panko or (38 g) plain dry bread crumbs
½ recipe Plant-Based Sausage Links (page 174), sliced
½ to 1 teaspoon liquid smoke
2 tablespoons (8 g) minced fresh flat-leaf parsley, for garnish

(continued)

1. Heat 1 teaspoon of oil or ¼ cup (60 ml) of water in a large skillet over medium-high heat. Add the onion and sauté until softened, about 5 minutes, adding a little extra water, if needed, to keep it from burning. Add the carrots, garlic, and tomato paste and cook for 2 minutes longer.

2. Transfer the onion mixture to the slow cooker. Add the beans, tomatoes, broth, wine, thyme, marjoram, and bay leaves. Season to taste with salt and black pepper, cover, and cook on Low for 6 to 8 hours.

3. While the cassoulet is cooking, lightly toast the panko in a small dry skillet until lightly browned. Set aside.

4. Heat the remaining 1 teaspoon oil in a medium-size skillet over medium-high heat. Add the sausage and cook until browned on both sides.

5. When the cassoulet is ready to serve, remove and discard the bay leaves and stir in the sausage and liquid smoke. Taste and adjust the seasonings, if needed. Top with the reserved bread crumbs and the parsley. Serve hot.

Two-Lentil Dal

SERVES 4 TO 6

SLOW COOKER SIZE: 4-QUART (3.8 L) | COOK TIME: 8 HOURS ON LOW | GLUTEN-FREE | OIL-FREE | SOY-FREE

Aromatic spices turn everyday beans and lentils into an exotic dish with the flavors of India. If a smoother texture is desired, use an immersion blender to puree a portion of the dal right in the slow cooker, or transfer about 2 cups (400 g) of the cooked dal to a blender or food processor and puree it, then stir the puree back into the pot. Serve over freshly cooked basmati rice.

1 large yellow onion, minced
1½ teaspoons grated peeled fresh ginger
1 teaspoon ground cumin
1 teaspoon ground coriander
½ teaspoon ground turmeric
½ teaspoon dry mustard
¼ teaspoon ground cardamom
¼ teaspoon cayenne pepper

1 cup (197 g) dried red lentils, rinsed and picked over
1 cup (197 g) dried brown lentils, rinsed and picked over
4 cups (960 ml) water
Salt and freshly ground black pepper
Freshly cooked basmati rice, for serving
3 tablespoons (3 g) minced fresh cilantro or (12 g) flat-leaf parsley, for garnish

1. In the slow cooker, combine the onion, ginger, cumin, coriander, turmeric, mustard, cardamom, and cayenne, stirring to mix.

2. Add the red and brown lentils, water, and salt and black pepper to taste. Cover and cook on Low for 8 hours. Taste and adjust the seasonings, if needed. Serve over rice, with a sprinkling of cilantro.

Slow and Spicy Sloppy Joes

SERVES 6 TO 8

SLOW COOKER SIZE: 4- TO 6-QUART (3.8 TO 5.7 L) | COOK TIME: 6 HOURS ON LOW | GLUTEN-FREE OPTION |
OIL-FREE OPTION | SOY-FREE OPTION

Sloppy Joes are a favorite in my house, so I like to make a big pot and then portion and freeze it for quick meals. In this recipe, the "meatiness" comes from a combination of lentils, seitan, and mushrooms. If you're not a fan of any one of them, just leave it out and add an extra amount of the others. Serve in split burger rolls with slaw on the side. For gluten-free, use chopped tempeh or jackfruit instead of seitan and use gluten-free rolls; for soy-free, omit the soy sauce and use Soy-Free Sauce (page 344), or coconut aminos, or add some soy-free vegetable broth base or additional salt.

¼ cup (60 ml) water, or 2 teaspoons olive oil
1 large yellow onion, minced
3 garlic cloves, minced
1 small red or green bell pepper, seeded and minced
2 teaspoons chili powder
1 cup (197 g) dried brown lentils, rinsed and picked over
1 cup (242 g) canned crushed tomatoes
½ cup (120 g) ketchup

(continued)

8 ounces (225 g) finely chopped seitan (page 154), tempeh, or jackfruit
8 ounces (225 g) chopped mushrooms (any kind)
2 tablespoons (30 ml) soy sauce
1 tablespoon (17 g) minced chipotle chiles in adobo
1 tablespoon (11 g) yellow or brown mustard
1 tablespoon (12.5 g) granulated natural sugar
1 teaspoon salt
Freshly ground black pepper
1 teaspoon liquid smoke
Toasted rolls, for serving

1. Heat the water or oil in a medium-size skillet over medium-high heat. Add the onion and sauté until softened, about 5 minutes. Add the garlic, bell pepper, and chili powder, stirring to coat. Cook for 30 seconds longer. Alternatively, combine the ingredients in a microwave-safe bowl with 2 tablespoons (30 ml) of water, cover, and microwave for 2 minutes to soften.

2. Transfer the onion mixture to the slow cooker and add the lentils, tomatoes, ketchup, seitan, mushrooms, and 2 cups (480 ml) of water.

3. In a bowl, combine the soy sauce, chipotle chiles, mustard, sugar, salt, and pepper to taste and stir to combine. Add to the slow cooker, cover, and cook on Low for 6 hours. Stir in the liquid smoke, then taste and adjust the seasonings, if needed, adding a bit more water if the mixture is too dry. Serve hot, spooned into the toasted rolls.

Ful Medames

SLOW COOKER SIZE: 4- TO 6-QUART (3.8 TO 5.7 L) | COOK TIME: 7 TO 8 HOURS ON LOW | GLUTEN-FREE |
OIL-FREE | SOY-FREE

Slow-cooked fava beans, known as *ful medames*, is a popular breakfast in Egypt. If dried fava beans are unavailable, substitute dried butter beans, broad beans, or large limas.

12 ounces (340 g) dried fava beans, washed and picked over
1 yellow onion, finely chopped
3 garlic cloves, minced
⅓ cup (66 g) dried red lentils
1 teaspoon ground cumin
½ teaspoon paprika
½ teaspoon dried oregano
Salt and freshly ground black pepper
1 (14-ounce, or 395 g) can fire-roasted diced tomatoes, undrained
1 tablespoon (15 ml) fresh lemon juice
½ cup (70 g) chopped cucumber, ½ cup (90 g) chopped ripe tomato, and ¼ cup (16 g) finely chopped parsley, for garnish

1. Soak the beans overnight in enough water to cover. Drain the beans and add them to the slow cooker.

2. Add the onion, garlic, lentils, cumin, paprika, oregano, and salt and black pepper to taste. Add 6 cups (1.4 L) of water or enough water to cover the ingredients. Cover and cook on Low for 7 hours, or until the beans are tender.

3. Stir in the tomatoes. If the water has been absorbed and the beans are still too firm, add a little more water, put the lid back on, and continue to cook for 1 more hour, or until the beans are soft.

4. Stir in the lemon juice, and serve hot, topped with chopped cucumber, tomato, and parsley.

Sorghum and Butternut Squash with Beans and Greens

SERVES 4

SLOW COOKER SIZE: 4- TO 6-QUART (3.8 TO 5.7 L) | COOK TIME: 6 TO 8 HOURS ON LOW | GLUTEN-FREE | OIL-FREE | SOY-FREE

This hearty stick-to-your-ribs dish is ideal for a cold winter night. Best of all, it's a one-dish meal and leftovers are delicious, too. Sorghum is rich in protein and iron and gluten-free. It's great to cook in a slow cooker because it retains a good texture, even after a long cooking time. Look for sorghum in well-stocked supermarkets or online.

1 cup (192 g) whole-grain sorghum, soaked overnight, then drained

3½ cups (840 ml) vegetable broth or water

3 cups (420 g) diced butternut squash

1 teaspoon salt

½ teaspoon freshly ground black pepper

1½ cups (384 g) cooked dark red kidney beans (page 114)
    or 1 (15-ounce, or 425 g) can beans, drained and rinsed

6 cups (180 g) chopped spinach or arugula

2 tablespoons (30 ml) apple cider vinegar

2 tablespoons (40 g) maple syrup

1 tablespoon (15 ml) water

2 teaspoons nutritional yeast

2 teaspoons Dijon mustard

1 teaspoon onion powder

1 teaspoon smoked paprika

1. Combine the drained sorghum and broth in the slow cooker. Add the butternut squash, salt, and pepper.

2. Cover and cook on Low for 6 to 8 hours or until the sorghum and squash are tender. If any water remains, drain it off or turn the slow cooker to High and cook uncovered for 30 minutes.

3. Close to serving time, stir in the beans and spinach and cook a few minutes to heat the beans and wilt the spinach.

4. In a small bowl, combine the vinegar, maple syrup, water, nutritional yeast, mustard, onion powder, and smoked paprika. Stir until well blended.

5. When ready to serve, drizzle the sauce on top and serve hot.

N'awlins Red Beans and Rice

SERVES 4

SLOW COOKER SIZE: 4- TO 6-QUART (3.8 TO 5.7 L) | COOK TIME: 6 HOURS ON LOW | GLUTEN-FREE OPTION |
OIL-FREE OPTION | SOY-FREE OPTION

Red beans and rice is a Louisiana Creole dish traditionally made and served on Mondays. You can spoon the red beans over the cooked rice, but I prefer to add my rice to the cooking red beans to give the rice extra flavor. Most types of rice tend to get mushy when cooked directly in a slow cooker, so I add cooked brown rice to this recipe near the end of the cooking time. If you prefer to cook your rice right in the slow cooker, you will get the best results by adding ¾ cup (141 g) converted white rice about an hour before the end of cooking time and increasing the water by ¾ cup (180 ml). For gluten-free and soy-free, omit the soy sauce and use Soy-Free Sauce (page 344) or coconut aminos, or add some soy-free vegetable broth base or additional salt, and omit the optional chorizo or use soy-free.

¼ cup (60 ml) water, or 2 teaspoons olive oil
1 large yellow onion, minced
1 celery rib, minced
4 garlic cloves, minced
1 teaspoon smoked paprika
½ teaspoon dried thyme
¼ teaspoon cayenne pepper
1 green bell pepper, seeded and chopped
3 cups (768 g) cooked dark red kidney beans (page 114)
    or 2 (15-ounce, or 425 g) cans beans, rinsed and drained
1 (14.5-ounce, or 410 g) can diced tomatoes, drained

(continued)

1 large bay leaf
1½ cups (360 ml) water or vegetable broth
1 tablespoon (15 ml) soy sauce
Salt and freshly ground black pepper
3 cups (600 g) cooked brown rice
2 scallions, minced
1 cup (192 g) Tofu Chorizo (page 343; optional)
½ teaspoon liquid smoke (optional)

1. Heat the water or oil in a medium-size skillet over medium-high heat. Add the onion and celery and sauté until softened, about 5 minutes. Add the garlic, paprika, thyme, and cayenne and cook, stirring, for 1 minute longer. Alternatively, combine the ingredients and 2 tablespoons (30 ml) of water in a microwave-safe bowl and microwave for 2 minutes.

2. Transfer the onion mixture to the slow cooker. Add the bell pepper, beans, tomatoes, bay leaf, water, and soy sauce. Season to taste with salt and black pepper, cover, and cook on Low for 5½ hours. Stir in the rice and scallions, cover, and cook for 30 minutes longer.

3. Just before serving, stir in the sausage and/or liquid smoke (if using). Taste and adjust the seasonings, if needed. Remove the bay leaf and serve hot.

"Dirty John" Quinoa

SERVES 4 TO 6

SLOW COOKER SIZE: 4-QUART (3.8 L) | COOK TIME: 2 HOURS ON HIGH | GLUTEN-FREE |
OIL-FREE OPTION | SOY-FREE

In this new spin on two Southern classics, dirty rice and hoppin' John, quinoa replaces rice and combines with black-eyed peas to create the same great taste and stick-to-your-ribs goodness of both dishes. If you prefer to use rice instead of quinoa, you have two options: (1) use raw brown basmati rice and cook for 3½ to 4 hours on High, or (2) cook your brown rice separately and add it to the slow cooker just before serving time. If you like, you may substitute another variety of cooked beans for the black-eyed peas. For an even heartier dish, add some cooked crumbled or chopped plant-based sausage just before serving time. To make this dish soy-free, omit the Worcestershire sauce and use Soy-Free Sauce (page 344), or coconut aminos, or add some soy-free vegetable broth base or additional salt.

¼ cup (60 ml) water, or 2 teaspoons olive oil

1 small yellow onion, minced

2 garlic cloves, minced

1 teaspoon dried thyme

1 cup (184 g) quinoa, rinsed and drained

1 cup (70 g) chopped mushrooms of your choice

3 cups (510 g) cooked black-eyed peas (page 114)
or 2 (15-ounce, or 425 g) cans black-eyed peas, rinsed and drained

1 (14.5-ounce, or 410 g) can diced tomatoes, drained and finely chopped

1 (4-ounce, or 115 g) can diced mild green chilies, drained and finely chopped

1 teaspoon vegan Worcestershire sauce

1 teaspoon smoked paprika

1½ cups (360 ml) vegetable broth

Salt and freshly ground black pepper

Hot sauce, for serving

1. Heat the water or oil in a medium-size skillet over medium-high heat. Add the onion and sauté until softened, about 5 minutes. Add the garlic and thyme and cook for 30 seconds longer. Alternatively, combine the onion and garlic in a microwave-safe bowl with 2 tablespoons (30 ml) of water, cover, and microwave for 2 minutes to soften. Stir in the thyme.

2. Transfer the onion mixture to the slow cooker. Add the quinoa, mushrooms, black-eyed peas, tomatoes, chilies, Worcestershire sauce, paprika, and broth. Season to taste with salt and black pepper. Cover and cook on High until the quinoa is tender, about 2 hours. If your slow cooker runs "hot," check it after 1½ hours.

3. Taste and adjust the seasonings, if needed. Serve hot, passing the hot sauce at the table.

Artichoke Risotto

SLOW COOKER SIZE: 4-QUART (3.8 L) | COOK TIME: 2 HOURS ON HIGH | GLUTEN-FREE | OIL-FREE OPTION | SOY-FREE

In order to achieve the right texture and flavor, this risotto requires a few minutes of skillet time before combining in the slow cooker. It's not a bad trade-off when compared to all of the hands-on stirring involved in making conventional risotto. Using nutritional yeast makes this soy-free, although you can substitute a soy-free vegan Parmesan instead.

¼ cup (60 ml) water, or 2 teaspoons olive oil

1 small yellow onion or 2 shallots, minced

¼ cup (60 ml) dry white wine

1¼ cups (237.5 g) Arborio rice

3½ cups (840 ml) vegetable broth, plus more if needed

2 teaspoons chopped fresh thyme leaves, or 1 teaspoon dried thyme

½ teaspoon salt

2 cups (600 g) canned or frozen artichoke hearts, thawed, chopped

2 tablespoons (7.5 g) nutritional yeast, or ¼ cup (33.5 g)
    Almond Parmesan (page 341)

2 teaspoons fresh lemon juice

Freshly ground black pepper

¼ cup (30 g) chopped toasted walnuts, for garnish

2 tablespoons (6 g) snipped fresh chives, for garnish

1. Heat the water or oil in a medium-size skillet over medium-high heat. Add the onion and sauté until softened, about 5 minutes. Stir in the wine and cook for 30 seconds, then add the rice and cook, stirring, for 2 minutes.

2. Transfer the rice mixture to the slow cooker. Add the broth, thyme, and salt, cover, and cook on High until all of the liquid is absorbed and the rice is just tender, about 2 hours.

3. Stir in the artichokes, nutritional yeast, lemon juice, and pepper to taste. Taste and adjust the seasonings, if needed. If the mixture is too dry, stir in a little more hot broth as needed.

4. Serve hot, spooned into shallow bowls. Sprinkle each serving with the toasted walnuts and chives.

Creamy Polenta
with Mushroom Ragu

SERVES 4 TO 6

SLOW COOKER SIZE: 4- TO 6-QUART (3.8 TO 5.7 L) | COOK TIME: 4 TO 6 HOURS ON LOW | GLUTEN-FREE | OIL-FREE OPTION | SOY-FREE OPTION

Making polenta in the slow cooker is easy because it doesn't require all of the stirring and close watching that is necessary in the stovetop method. If you use water instead of broth, you will need about ½ teaspoon additional salt. You could also use half broth and half water, if you prefer. Instead of topping with the mushroom ragu, the polenta may be enjoyed as is with a pat of vegan butter or a drizzle of olive oil and freshly cracked pepper, or with any of the following topping variations: fresh chopped basil or sage, grated vegan Parmesan, shredded vegan mozzarella, sautéed sliced plant-based sausage, sautéed broccoli rabe and garlic. Alternatively, you may cool the polenta, refrigerate it to firm up, and then slice it and fry it. Fried polenta may be topped with any of the same toppings as well. Use a soy-free vegan butter to make this soy-free.

7 cups (1.7 L) boiling vegetable broth or water
1 teaspoon salt
1½ cups (210 g) coarse-ground polenta
¼ cup (60 ml) water, or 2 teaspoons olive oil
3 garlic cloves, minced
1 pound (455 g) cremini mushrooms, sliced
Salt and freshly ground black pepper
2 tablespoons (30 ml) dry red wine (optional)
3 cups (750 g) marinara sauce or your favorite tomato sauce for pasta

1. Coat the slow cooker insert with nonstick cooking spray and set the cooker on High. Carefully pour in the boiling broth, add the salt, then slowly whisk in the polenta, stirring until blended. Cover and cook on Low, stirring occasionally, if possible, until the polenta has thickened, 4 to 6 hours. If the polenta is too thin, remove the lid and cook for 30 minutes longer.

(continued)

2. Heat the water or oil in a large skillet over medium heat. Add the garlic and cook until fragrant and slightly softened, about 1 minute. Add the mushrooms and cook until softened. Season to taste with salt and black pepper. Add the wine (if using) then stir in the marinara sauce and heat until hot.

3. Taste the polenta and adjust the seasonings, if needed. Top with bits of vegan butter (if using) and several grinds of black pepper. Spoon the polenta into shallow bowls and top with a spoonful of the mushroom ragu. Serve hot.

Barley Orzotto with White Beans and Vegetables

SERVES 4

SLOW COOKER SIZE: 4- TO 6-QUART (3.8 TO 5.7 L) | COOK TIME: 2½ TO 3 HOURS ON HIGH |
OIL-FREE OPTION | SOY-FREE

Similar to risotto, orzotto is made with pearl barley and is prepared in regions of northern Italy. Like risotto, it cooks up thick and creamy. The addition of white beans and a variety of vegetables makes this a satisfying one-dish meal.

¼ cup (60 ml) water, or 2 teaspoons olive oil

1 medium-size yellow onion, minced

1 large carrot, minced

1 small celery rib, minced

3 garlic cloves, minced

1 teaspoon minced fresh thyme, or ½ teaspoon dried thyme

¼ cup (60 ml) dry white wine

1 cup (200 g) raw pearl barley

½ small red bell pepper, seeded and minced

6 ounces (170 g) mushrooms of your choice, chopped

1½ cups (270 g) cooked cannellini beans (page 114)
    or 1 (15-ounce, or 425 g) can beans, rinsed and drained

3 cups (720 ml) vegetable broth

Salt and freshly ground black pepper

¾ cup (112.5 g) fresh or (97.5 g) frozen green peas, thawed

1. Heat the water or oil in a medium-size skillet over medium-high heat. Add the onion, carrot, and celery and sauté until softened, about 5 minutes. Stir in the garlic, thyme, and wine and cook for 1 minute longer.

2. Transfer the onion mixture to the slow cooker. Stir in the barley, then add the bell pepper, mushrooms, beans, and broth. Season to taste with salt and black pepper. Cover and cook on High for 2½ hours. Taste and adjust the seasonings, if needed. If the barley is not quite tender, cook for another 30 minutes, with the lid off if the barley is too saucy. If it's too dry, stir in a small amount of hot water or broth. When the barley is tender, stir in the peas. Serve hot in shallow bowls.

THE IMPORTANCE OF CHECKING LABELS

If you're following a vegan diet, you already know how critical it is to scrutinize the labels of packaged goods for hidden animal products. Similarly, if you're living gluten- or soy-free, remain vigilant for hidden gluten or soy in products such as gluten in oats or hydrolyzed soy protein in vegan sauces.

Cheesy Chile Grits and Sweet Taters

SLOW COOKER SIZE: 4- TO 6-QUART (3.8 TO 5.7 L) | COOK TIME: 6 TO 8 HOURS ON LOW | GLUTEN-FREE | OIL-FREE | SOY-FREE OPTION

I love the contrasting flavor the sweet potatoes provide in this dish. If you're not a fan of sweet potatoes, substitute white potatoes, or try pinto or black beans for a different flavor experience. Your choice of mild or hot chiles will dictate whether this is a mild or spicy dish. Having been raised on polenta, I immediately took a liking to grits when I moved to the South. After all, they are both made from ground, dried corn kernels. Look for stone ground grits for the best flavor. Like polenta, grits can also be enjoyed fried. Simply transfer the cooked grits to a loaf pan or baking dish, smooth the top, cover, and refrigerate until chilled. Then cut the grits into ½-inch (1 cm)-thick slices and fry in olive oil or vegan butter until browned. For a more classic way to serve this dish, omit the chiles and sweet potatoes and serve with collard greens and black-eyed peas.

4½ cups (1 L) vegetable broth or water

1½ cups (210 g) stone ground grits

1 large or 2 medium-size sweet potatoes, peeled and cut into ½-inch (1 cm) dice (about 2 cups, or about 220 g)

4 scallions, minced

1 (4-ounce, or 115 g) can chopped mild or hot green chilies, drained

Salt and freshly ground black pepper

1 cup (240 ml) Cheesy Sauce (page 340)

1. Combine the broth and grits in the slow cooker, add the sweet potatoes, scallions, and chilies, and season to taste with salt and pepper. Cover and cook on Low until the sweet potatoes are tender, 6 to 8 hours.

2. Just before serving, stir in the cheesy sauce. Serve hot in shallow bowls.

1. Heat the water or oil in a medium-size skillet over medium-high heat. Add the onion and sauté until softened, about 5 minutes. Add the garlic, dried basil, rosemary, sage, and red pepper flakes, then stir in the tomato paste and cook for 1 minute longer. Stir in ½ cup (120 ml) of broth.

2. Transfer the onion mixture to the slow cooker. Add the carrots, celery, potato, tomatoes and their juices, beans, and remaining 2 cups (480 ml) of broth. Season to taste with salt and black pepper. Cover and cook on Low until the vegetables are tender, 4 to 6 hours.

3. Turn the heat to High, stir in the pasta, cover, and cook until the pasta is done, about 30 minutes. Alternatively, you can cook the pasta separately on the stovetop and add it to the slow cooker when ready to serve. Stir in the fresh basil and serve hot.

Ziti with Mushroom and Bell Pepper Ragu

SERVES 4

SLOW COOKER SIZE: 4- TO 6-QUART (3.8 TO 5.7 L) | COOK TIME: 2½ TO 3 HOURS ON HIGH | GLUTEN-FREE OPTION | OIL-FREE OPTION | SOY-FREE

Hard durum pasta (such as Barilla brand) works best in this recipe. If using a pasta other than a hard durum semolina, such as rice pasta, the pasta may become too soft when cooked directly in the slow cooker, so you may want to cook the pasta separately on the stovetop. In addition, this recipe needs to cook on High in order to properly cook the pasta. Alternatively, you may cook the sauce on Low for 6 to 8 hours, and then add stovetop-cooked pasta 20 minutes before serving. For gluten-free, use gluten-free pasta (and add it after the sauce has cooked).

¼ cup (60 ml) water, or 2 teaspoons olive oil

1 large yellow onion, minced

4 garlic cloves, minced

1 teaspoon dried basil, or 1 tablespoon (2.5 g) chopped fresh basil

2 teaspoons minced fresh oregano, or 1 teaspoon dried oregano

2 tablespoons (32 g) tomato paste

1 teaspoon granulated natural sugar

½ cup (120 ml) dry red wine

(continued)

1 large green or red bell pepper, seeded and minced

8 ounces (225 g) white mushrooms, coarsely chopped

8 ounces (225 g) dried ziti

1 (28-ounce, or 794 g) can plus 1 (14-ounce, or 395 g) can crushed tomatoes

1 cup (240 ml) hot water

Salt and freshly ground black pepper

2 tablespoons (8 g) chopped fresh flat-leaf parsley

Almond Parmesan (page 341), for garnish (optional)

1. Heat the water or oil in a large skillet over medium-high heat. Add the onion and cook for 5 minutes. Add the garlic, dried basil (if using), oregano, tomato paste, and sugar. Stir in the wine and cook for 1 minute longer. Add the bell pepper and mushrooms and cook for 3 minutes longer.

2. Transfer the onion mixture to the slow cooker. Add the ziti, tomatoes, hot water, and salt and black pepper to taste. Stir to combine, making sure all of the pasta is submerged. Cover and cook on High until the pasta is tender, 2½ to 3 hours.

3. Stir in the fresh basil (if using) and the parsley. Serve hot, sprinkled with the Almond Parmesan, (if using).

Lasagna Primavera

SERVES 6

SLOW COOKER SIZE: 4- TO 6-QUART (3.8 TO 5.7 L) | COOK TIME: 4 TO 5 HOURS ON LOW |
GLUTEN-FREE OPTION | OIL-FREE OPTION

Slow-cooked lasagna may sound unconventional, but it tastes great and is convenient to make. You will need to break the noodles to conform them to the shape of the slow cooker. For best results, use a large oval slow cooker. To make this gluten-free, use gluten-free lasagna noodles. I use regular dried lasagna noodles—no need to pre-boil. The added water is absorbed by the dried noodles and softens them as it cooks. You can also use no-boil lasagna noodles if you like (it may need a little less time to cook if you do) but be sure to check the label because some no-boil lasagna noodles contain eggs.

¼ cup (60 ml) water, or 2 teaspoons olive oil

1 small yellow onion, minced

3 garlic cloves, minced

1 cup (124 g) chopped zucchini

1 yellow bell pepper, seeded and chopped

8 ounces (225 g) white mushrooms, chopped

1 (10-ounce, or 280 g) package frozen chopped spinach, thawed and squeezed dry

Salt and freshly ground black pepper

1 pound (455 g) soft or medium tofu, drained

1 pound (455 g) firm tofu, drained

⅓ cup (20 g) nutritional yeast

¼ cup (16 g) minced fresh flat-leaf parsley

2 teaspoons dried basil

1 teaspoon dried oregano

4 cups (about 1 kg) Sunday Gravy (page 137) or your favorite marinara sauce

8 ounces (225 g) dried lasagna noodles (about 9 noodles)

¼ cup (33.5 g) Almond Parmesan (page 341)

1. Heat the water or oil in a large skillet over medium-high heat. Add the onion and sauté until softened, about 5 minutes. Add the garlic, zucchini, bell pepper, and mushrooms and cook for 2 minutes longer, adding a little more water if needed so the vegetables do not scorch. Stir in the spinach and season to taste with salt and pepper. Set aside.

2. Crumble all of the tofu into a large bowl. Add the nutritional yeast, parsley, basil, oregano, and salt and black pepper to taste. Mix well, then taste to make sure the mixture has enough salt and plenty of pepper.

3. Spread a layer of marinara sauce into the bottom of the slow cooker. Stir in ½ cup (120 ml) of water. Arrange a layer of the noodles over the sauce, breaking pieces to fit, as needed. Top the noodles with about one-third of the tofu mixture, followed by one-third of the vegetable mixture, and another layer of noodles. Spread a layer of marinara sauce over the noodles. Repeat the layering two more times, ending with a layer of marinara sauce. Sprinkle with Almond Parmesan. Cover and cook on Low for 4 hours or until the noodles are tender.

4. Remove the lid, turn off the cooker, and let the lasagna stand for about 15 minutes before serving.

Artichoke-Spinach Lasagna

SLOW COOKER SIZE: 4- TO 6-QUART (3.8 TO 5.7 L) | COOK TIME: 4 HOURS ON LOW | GLUTEN-FREE OPTION | OIL-FREE

If you're a fan of creamy artichoke-spinach dip, you'll love this lasagna. To make this gluten-free, use gluten-free noodles. I use regular dried lasagna noodles—no need to pre-boil. The added water is absorbed by the dried noodles and softens them as it cooks. You can also use no-boil lasagna noodles if you like (it may need a little less time to cook if you do), but be sure to check the label because some no-boil lasagna noodles contain eggs.

SAUCE

1 cup (140 g) raw cashews, soaked in hot water for 30 minutes, then drained
1 cup (240 ml) vegetable broth
1 (12-ounce, or 340 g) package soft or silken tofu, drained
⅓ cup (20 g) nutritional yeast
1 teaspoon garlic powder
1 teaspoon onion powder
1 teaspoon salt, or to taste

FILLING

1 pound (455 g) firm tofu, drained
1 (10-ounce, or 280 g) package frozen chopped spinach, thawed and squeezed dry
2 cups (600 g) chopped canned, jarred, or frozen artichoke hearts, thawed
⅓ cup (20 g) nutritional yeast
2 teaspoons dried basil
1 teaspoon dried oregano
1 teaspoon onion powder
1 teaspoon garlic powder
2 tablespoons (30 ml) fresh lemon juice
Salt and freshly ground black pepper

ASSEMBLY

8 ounces (225 g; 9 to 12 noodles) dried lasagna noodles
¼ cup (33.5 g) Almond Parmesan (page 341)
Marinara sauce, warmed, for serving

1. To make the sauce: Combine all the sauce ingredients in a high-powered blender and blend until smooth. Taste and adjust the seasonings, if needed. Set aside.

2. To make the filling: Crumble the tofu into a large bowl. Add the spinach, artichoke hearts, nutritional yeast, basil, oregano, onion powder, garlic powder, lemon juice, and salt and black pepper to taste. Mix well, then taste to make sure the mixture has enough salt and black pepper.

3. To assemble: Spread a thin layer of sauce into the bottom of the slow cooker. Mix ½ cup (120 ml) of water into the sauce. Arrange a layer of the dried noodles over the sauce, breaking pieces off the noodles as needed to make them fit. A bit of overlapping is fine. Top the noodles with about one-third of the filling, followed by another layer of noodles. Spread a thin layer of sauce over the noodles and repeat the layering until the ingredients are used up, ending with a layer of sauce. Pour another ½ cup (120 ml) of water around the perimeter of the sauce on top. Sprinkle the top with the Almond Parmesan.

4. Cover and cook on Low for 4 hours, or until the noodles are tender. Let the lasagna stand uncovered for about 15 minutes before serving. To serve, ladle some warm marinara sauce onto each plate and arrange a serving of the lasagna on top.

Mac and Cheesy

SERVES 4

SLOW COOKER SIZE: 4-QUART (3.8 L) | COOK TIME: 1½ HOURS ON HIGH | OIL-FREE

I like to add about 2 cups (260 g) of chopped cooked kale, chard, or spinach before serving this comforting mac-and-cheese casserole. The greens provide a lovely color contrast and added nutrients and flavor. Other good additions would be steamed broccoli florets or asparagus or frozen green peas, thawed, stirred in about 5 minutes before serving time. I recommend using a regular hard durum semolina pasta (such as Barilla brand). Other types of pasta may produce a too-soft pasta in the slow cooker. If you want to use one of those types, cook it separately on the stovetop and add it to the slow cooker shortly before serving time.

1 large russet potato, peeled and cut into ½-inch (1 cm) dice
1 medium-size yellow onion, chopped
1 large carrot, thinly sliced
1 cup (140 g) unsalted raw cashews, soaked overnight and drained

(continued)

3 cups (720 ml) vegetable broth

¼ cup (65 g) jarred pimientos or seeded and chopped jarred roasted red bell pepper, well drained

2 tablespoons (30 ml) fresh lemon juice

2 teaspoons white miso paste

1 teaspoon yellow mustard

½ cup (30 g) nutritional yeast

1 teaspoon onion powder

½ teaspoon garlic powder

½ teaspoon salt, or more to taste

½ teaspoon ground turmeric

8 ounces (225 g) dried elbow macaroni

Hot water or plain unsweetened plant milk, as needed

¼ cup (12.5 g) toasted panko crumbs (optional)

1. In a large saucepan, combine the potato, onion, carrot, cashews, and broth and bring to a boil. Lower the heat to medium, cover, and cook until the vegetables are tender, about 10 minutes.

2. Transfer the broth and vegetable mixture to a high-powered blender. Add the pimientos, lemon juice, miso, mustard, nutritional yeast, onion powder, garlic powder, salt, and turmeric. Blend until smooth. Taste and adjust the seasonings, if needed.

3. Place the macaroni in the slow cooker, then add the sauce mixture and stir to combine. Cover and cook on High for 1½ hours.

4. Uncover and stir, adding a little hot water if the mixture is too thick or if the pasta is not tender. Taste and adjust the seasonings. Cover and cook for an additional 10 to 15 minutes, if needed.

5. Just before serving, sprinkle on the toasted bread crumbs (if using).

Chili Mac

This shortcut recipe can have chili mac cooking in no time. Be sure to use regular hard durum semolina pasta (such as Barilla brand). Other types of pasta may produce a too-soft pasta in the slow cooker. If you want to use one of those types, cook it separately on the stovetop and add it to the slow cooker shortly before serving time.

1 (24-ounce, or 675 g) jar tomato salsa of your choice

2 tablespoons (15 g) chili powder

1 teaspoon ground cumin

4½ cups (774 g) cooked pinto or red kidney beans (page 114) or 3 (15-ounce, or 425 g) cans beans, rinsed and drained

1 (8-ounce, or 225 g) can tomato sauce

8 ounces (225 g) dried elbow macaroni

2 cups (480 ml) hot water

1 teaspoon salt

¼ teaspoon freshly ground black pepper

1 cup (240 ml) Cheesy Sauce (page 340), warmed

1. In the slow cooker, combine the salsa, chili powder, cumin, beans, tomato sauce, macaroni, hot water, salt, and pepper. Stir to combine. Cover and cook on High for 1½ hours.

2. Uncover and check to see whether the pasta is tender. If the mixture is too dry, stir in a little hot water. Taste and adjust the seasonings, if necessary. If the pasta is undercooked, cover and cook for 15 minutes longer or until tender; otherwise drizzle with the warm cheesy sauce and serve immediately.

Pasta and Vegetable Frittata

SERVES 4 OR 5

SLOW COOKER SIZE: 4- TO 6-QUART (3.8 TO 5.7 L) | COOK TIME: 3 HOURS ON LOW | GLUTEN-FREE OPTION | OIL-FREE

This frittata makes a satisfying one-dish meal and doesn't take too long to cook. It works best when made in a wide, shallow slow cooker. Depending on how shallow your slow cooker is, it can be a little tricky to remove the first wedge of the frittata, but after that, they should come out easily. Feel free to change up the type of vegetables used in this—cooked chopped asparagus, broccoli, and spinach are all good choices. Use gluten-free pasta for a gluten-free recipe.

1 pound (455 g) firm tofu, well drained

1¼ cups (300 ml) vegetable broth, divided

3 tablespoons (11.25 g) nutritional yeast

1 tablespoon (8 g) cornstarch

½ teaspoon onion powder

¼ teaspoon ground turmeric

Salt and freshly ground black pepper

1 jarred roasted red bell pepper, seeded and chopped

4 scallions, minced

1 cup (70 g) chopped white mushrooms

½ teaspoon dried basil

3 cups (420 g) cooked spaghetti or other pasta

¾ cup (97.5 g) frozen green peas, thawed

½ cup (120 ml) Cheesy Sauce (page 340), warmed (optional)

1. In a food processor or blender, combine the tofu, 1 cup (240 ml) of broth, nutritional yeast, cornstarch, onion powder, turmeric, and salt and black pepper to taste. Add 1 tablespoon (28 g) of the chopped roasted bell pepper and process until smooth and well blended. Set aside.

2. Heat the remaining ¼ cup (60 ml) of broth in a medium-size skillet over medium-high heat. Add the scallions, mushrooms, basil, and salt and black pepper to taste and cook for 3 to 4 minutes.

3. Coat the insert of the slow cooker with cooking spray. Spread the cooked vegetables evenly in the bottom of the cooker. Add the spaghetti, peas, and remaining chopped roasted bell pepper. Add the reserved tofu mixture, stirring to combine all of the ingredients, then spread the mixture evenly. Cover and cook on Low until the frittata is firm, about 3 hours.

4. Cut into wedges and serve hot topped with warm cheesy sauce (if using).

Hearty Main Dishes

Many of the recipes in this chapter are vegan versions of classic global dishes that lend themselves to slow cooking, such as a French pot-au-feu, a Moroccan tagine, and an Indian curry. There are some all-American classics as well, including one of my own favorites, Mom-Style Vegan Meatloaf. Many of these recipes traditionally call for meat, which the slow-cooking process helps to make tender. Since these meatless recipes don't require tenderizing, the slow cooker is used for the sheer convenience and enriched flavor that long, gentle cooking can bring to the ingredients.

This chapter also includes uniquely vegan recipes for braising tofu and making seitan from scratch. In addition, there are recipes for potpies and other casseroles—dishes usually associated with oven baking, all of which further illustrate the versatility of the slow cooker.

Vegetable Paella

SLOW COOKER SIZE: 4- TO 6-QUART (3.8 TO 5.7 L) | COOK TIME: 6 TO 8 HOURS ON LOW | GLUTEN-FREE |
SOY-FREE | OIL-FREE

The classic Spanish rice dish made with colorful vegetables is a terrific one-dish meal. Turmeric stands in for the traditional saffron to provide a more economical golden hue to the rice. Be sure to use short-grain brown rice for this recipe (long-grain rice cooks faster and will be too soft for this recipe). You can also substitute pearl barley for the rice. It holds up well to long slow cooking and retains its texture. (Note: If you use barley, the dish will no longer be gluten-free.)

1 yellow onion, chopped

3 garlic cloves, minced

1 red bell pepper, seeded and cut into thin strips

1 yellow bell pepper, seeded and cut into thin strips

1 cup (200 g) raw short-grain brown rice or pearl barley

1 teaspoon dried oregano

1 teaspoon smoked paprika

½ teaspoon ground turmeric

½ teaspoon red pepper flakes

1 (28-ounce, or 794 g) can diced fire-roasted tomatoes, undrained

3 cups (720 ml) vegetable broth

Salt and freshly ground black pepper

1½ cups (270 g) cooked cannellini beans (page 114)
    or 1 (15-ounce, or 425 g) can beans, drained and rinsed

1 (14-ounce, or 395 g) can artichoke hearts, drained, then halved or quartered

1 cup (130 g) frozen green peas, thawed

½ cup (50 g) sliced pimiento-stuffed green olives

2 tablespoons (18 g) capers, drained

2 teaspoons fresh lemon juice

2 tablespoons (8 g) chopped fresh parsley

Lemon wedges, for garnish

1. In a slow cooker, combine the onion, garlic, and bell peppers. Stir in the rice, oregano, paprika, turmeric, red pepper flakes, tomatoes and their juice, and the vegetable broth. Season with salt and pepper to taste.

2. Cover and cook on Low for 6 hours or until the rice is just tender. Stir in the cannellini beans, artichoke hearts, green peas, olives, capers, lemon juice, and parsley.

3. Cover and cook about 30 minutes longer to allow the flavors to blend. Taste and adjust the seasonings, if needed. Serve hot with lemon wedges.

Tempeh Cacciatore

SERVES 4

SLOW COOKER SIZE: 4- TO 6-QUART (3.8 TO 5.7 L) | COOK TIME: 6 TO 8 HOURS ON LOW | GLUTEN-FREE | OIL-FREE

Tempeh absorbs the savory goodness of the vegetables and seasonings as it cooks. Serve this tasty Italian stew over freshly cooked noodles.

8 ounces (225 g) tempeh, cut into 1-inch (2.5 cm) dice
1 yellow onion, cut into 1-inch (2.5 cm) dice
1 red or yellow bell pepper, seeded and cut into 1-inch (2.5 cm) dice
1 green bell pepper, seeded and cut into 1-inch (2.5 cm) dice
2 garlic cloves, minced
1½ cups (105 g) quartered cremini mushrooms
3 tablespoons (48 g) tomato paste
1 (14-ounce, or 395 g) can diced fire-roasted tomatoes, undrained
1 tablespoon (15 ml) tamari or coconut aminos
1 teaspoon dried oregano
1 teaspoon dried basil
1 teaspoon ground fennel seed
½ teaspoon red pepper flakes, or to taste
Salt and freshly ground black pepper
1½ cups (360 ml) vegetable broth
½ cup (120 ml) red wine (or more broth)
1 tablespoon (9 g) capers, drained

(continued)

1. In a large slow cooker, combine the tempeh, onion, bell peppers, garlic, and mushrooms. Stir in the tomato paste, tomatoes and their juice, and tamari; then add the oregano, basil, ground fennel seed, red pepper flakes, and salt and black pepper to taste. The amount of salt needed will depend on the saltiness of your broth.

2. Stir in the broth and wine. Cover, and cook on Low for 6 to 8 hours or until the vegetables are tender.

3. A few minutes before serving, stir in the capers and taste and adjust the seasonings, if needed. Serve hot.

Pulled Barbecue Jackfruit

SERVES 4 TO 6

SLOW COOKER SIZE: 4- TO 6-QUART (3.8 TO 5.7 L) | COOK TIME: 6 TO 8 HOURS ON LOW | GLUTEN-FREE | SOY-FREE OPTION | OIL-FREE

Jackfruit is a perfect ingredient to simmer slowly in barbecue sauce—and it even shreds beautifully to make wonderful sandwiches, served on your favorite rolls. I also like to serve it on a plate with corn bread and a side of cooked greens. To make this soy-free, use coconut aminos instead of tamari.

2 (20-ounce, or 560 g) cans young jackfruit in water or brine, drained and rinsed
½ cup (80 g) minced onion
3 garlic cloves, minced
⅓ cup (90 g) tomato paste
½ cup (120 ml) water
½ cup (120 g) ketchup
⅓ cup (80 g) brown sugar
2 tablespoons (30 ml) apple cider vinegar
1 tablespoon (15 ml) tamari or coconut aminos
1 tablespoon (15 ml) liquid smoke
½ teaspoon smoked paprika
¼ teaspoon garlic powder
¼ teaspoon onion powder
¼ teaspoon cayenne pepper
Salt and freshly ground black pepper

1. In a large slow cooker, combine the drained and rinsed jackfruit, onion, and garlic.

2. In a small bowl combine the tomato paste and water and blend until smooth. Add the tomato mixture to the slow cooker along with the remaining ingredients. Stir to combine.

3. Cover and cook on Low for 6 to 8 hours. About 30 minutes before serving, uncover and use two forks to shred the jackfruit pieces. Taste and adjust the seasonings, if needed.

4. Cover and cook another 30 minutes. Serve as desired.

Korean Bulgogi-Inspired Jackfruit   SERVES 6 TO 8

SLOW COOKER SIZE: 4- TO 6-QUART (3.8 TO 5.7 L) | COOK TIME: 6 TO 8 HOURS ON LOW | GLUTEN-FREE | SOY-FREE OPTION | OIL-FREE

Serve on buns or in tortillas with slaw or kimchi, or skip the bread and spoon into lettuce cups or serve over rice. Look for canned jackfruit (packed in water or brine—not syrup) and gochujang paste in Asian markets or online. The gochujang paste makes this dish fairly spicy, but if you want even more heat, add the optional sriracha sauce.

2 (20-ounce, or 560 g) cans young green jackfruit in water or brine, drained and rinsed
1 small yellow onion, finely chopped
1 ripe pear, cored and chopped
1 red bell pepper, seeded and finely chopped
3 garlic cloves, minced
2 tablespoons (16 g) grated peeled fresh ginger
⅓ cup (50 g) coconut sugar, (75 g) light brown sugar, or (106 g) agave nectar
¼ cup (80 g) gochujang paste
2 tablespoons (32 g) tomato paste
2 tablespoons (30 ml) rice vinegar
½ cup (120 ml) tamari or coconut aminos
½ cup (120 ml) water
1 teaspoon sesame oil (optional)
1 tablespoon (15 ml) sriracha sauce (optional)

(continued)

1. Combine the jackfruit, onion, pear, bell pepper, garlic, and ginger in a large slow cooker. In a bowl, combine the sugar, gochujang paste, tomato paste, vinegar, and tamari. Stir to blend well. Stir in the water and add the sesame oil and sriracha (if using). Pour the liquid over the jackfruit mixture and stir to combine.

2. Cover and cook on low for 6 to 8 hours. Remove the lid. Use two forks to pull apart and shred the jackfruit. Cook uncovered on High for 30 minutes to help absorb any remaining liquid. Taste and adjust the seasonings, if needed. Serve as desired.

Seitan in the Slow Cooker   MAKES ABOUT 1½ POUNDS (680 G)

SLOW COOKER SIZE: 4- TO 6-QUART (3.8 TO 5.7 L) | COOK TIME: 4 TO 6 HOURS ON LOW

It's easy to make your own homemade seitan (wheat meat). It tastes best when left to gently simmer for several hours—and, once again, the slow cooker comes to the rescue. For a firmer texture, add an additional ¼ cup (30 g) vital wheat gluten to the mix. The cooking liquid may be strained and used as a stock in sauces, soups, and other recipes.

1¾ cups (210 g) vital wheat gluten
¼ cup (30 g) chickpea flour
¼ cup (15 g) nutritional yeast
1 teaspoon onion powder
½ teaspoon garlic powder
½ teaspoon salt
¼ teaspoon freshly ground black pepper
6 tablespoons (90 ml) soy sauce
1 tablespoon (15 ml) olive oil
1¾ cups (420 ml) water or vegetable broth
1 medium-size yellow onion, quartered

1. In a large bowl, combine the vital wheat gluten, chickpea flour, nutritional yeast, onion and garlic powders, salt, and pepper. Stir in 3 tablespoons (45 ml) of soy sauce, the olive oil, and the water and continue stirring until well mixed. Knead for about 3 minutes.

2. Pour about 2 quarts (1.9 L) of water into the slow cooker. Depending on your preference, leave the seitan dough whole or divide into 4 to 6 pieces and add to the water along with the onion and remaining 3 tablespoons (45 ml) of soy sauce. Cover and cook on Low until firm, 4 to 6 hours.

3. Transfer the cooked seitan to a baking sheet to cool. If you are not using the seitan right away, it can be stored submerged in its cooking liquid in an airtight container for up to 5 days in the refrigerator, or for up to 3 weeks in the freezer.

Seitan Pot Roast

SERVES 4 TO 6

SLOW COOKER SIZE: 6-QUART (5.7 L) | COOK TIME: 6 TO 8 HOURS ON LOW | SOY-FREE OPTION

For this pot roast, the seitan cooks along with the vegetables for a delicious and satisfying meal that will fill your house with its wonderful aroma. To serve, you can simply spoon the cooking liquid over the seitan and vegetables or, if you prefer, you can thicken it into a sauce (see the note on page 24 for ways to thicken liquids). Or, instead, try serving it with the Mushroom Gravy (page 340). To make this soy-free, omit the soy sauce and use Soy-Free Sauce (page 344) or coconut aminos, or add some soy-free vegetable broth base or additional salt.

1½ cups (180 g) vital wheat gluten
½ cup (60 g) chickpea flour
¼ cup (15 g) nutritional yeast
1 teaspoon onion powder
1 teaspoon dried thyme, divided
½ teaspoon salt
¼ teaspoon freshly ground black pepper
2 tablespoons (30 ml) soy sauce
1 tablespoon (15 g) ketchup
3 teaspoons (15 ml) olive oil
1¼ cups (300 ml) water
¼ teaspoon paprika
1 large yellow onion, thinly sliced
3 carrots, cut into ½-inch (1 cm) slices
2 parsnips, cut into ½-inch (1 cm) slices

(continued)

1 pound (455 g) Yukon Gold potatoes, peeled and cut into
   1½-inch (3.5 cm) chunks
2 garlic cloves, crushed
Salt and freshly ground black pepper
1 cup (240 ml) vegetable broth
¼ cup (60 ml) dry white wine
1 tablespoon (15 ml) soy sauce
Mushroom Gravy (page 340), for serving (optional)

1. To make the seitan: In a large bowl, combine the vital wheat gluten, chickpea flour, nutritional yeast, onion powder, ½ teaspoon of thyme, salt, and pepper. Add the soy sauce, ketchup, 2 teaspoons of the oil, and the water. Mix well to form a stiff dough. Knead until smooth, about 3 minutes. Drizzle the remaining 1 teaspoon of oil onto the seitan and spread it with your fingers to coat. Sprinkle on the paprika and rub it in to coat the seitan. Leave the seitan dough in one piece or cut it into large chunks, depending on if you prefer to slice it from one large piece, or would rather have separate chunks to divide for different uses.

2. Add the onion, carrots, parsnips, potatoes, and garlic to the slow cooker. Sprinkle the vegetables with the remaining ½ teaspoon of thyme and season to taste with salt and black pepper. Pour in the broth, wine, and soy sauce. If the seitan is in chunks, arrange them among the vegetables. If the seitan is in one piece, place a small square of oiled parchment paper or aluminum foil (about the size of the seitan) on top of the vegetables and place the seitan on top. Cover and cook on Low until the seitan is cooked and the vegetables are tender, 6 to 8 hours.

3. Remove the seitan from the slow cooker and discard the parchment (if using). If the seitan is in one piece, cut it into thin slices. Arrange the seitan on a large serving platter. Surround with the cooked vegetables. Spoon the cooking liquid over the seitan and vegetables and serve hot with the gravy (if using).

Hoisin- and Miso-Braised Tofu

SERVES 4

SLOW COOKER SIZE: 4- TO 6-QUART (3.8 TO 5.7 L) | COOK TIME: 4 HOURS ON LOW | GLUTEN-FREE | OIL-FREE

The key to cooking tofu successfully in a slow cooker is braising. A wide, shallow slow cooker (such as a large oval) is needed for this recipe in order to arrange the tofu in a single layer. The beauty of this dish is in its simplicity. Serve with stir-fried Asian-style vegetables and rice.

4 scallions, finely minced

1 pound (455 g) extra-firm tofu, drained, pressed, and cut into ½-inch (1 cm)-thick slices

⅓ cup (80 g) hoisin sauce

2 tablespoons (34 g) miso paste

1 tablespoon (15 ml) rice vinegar

1 teaspoon agave nectar

1 teaspoon grated peeled fresh ginger

½ teaspoon Asian chili paste

⅓ cup (80 ml) water

1. Spread the scallions evenly in the bottom of the cooker. Arrange the tofu slices on top of the scallions, with as many slices in a single layer as possible and the rest arranged on top.

2. In a small bowl, whisk together the hoisin, miso, vinegar, agave, ginger, chili paste, and water. Spread the mixture evenly over the tofu. Cover and cook on Low for 4 hours, carefully turning over the tofu slices about halfway through the cooking time, if possible.

3. Carefully remove the tofu from the slow cooker and top with any remaining hoisin mixture.

Seitan Pot-au-Feu

This version of the rustic French "pot on fire" classic combines vegetables slow-simmered in broth with chunks of seitan cooked alongside for extra flavor. A large slow cooker is best for this recipe. To make it in a smaller cooker, cut the ingredient volume by half. Serve with French bread. To make this soy-free, omit the soy sauce and use Soy-Free Sauce (page 344), or coconut aminos, or add some soy-free vegetable broth base or additional salt.

1¼ cups (150 g) vital wheat gluten, plus more if needed

¼ cup (30 g) chickpea flour

3 tablespoons (11.25 g) nutritional yeast

½ teaspoon onion powder

¼ teaspoon salt

Freshly ground black pepper

1 teaspoon olive oil

2 tablespoons (30 ml) soy sauce

1¼ cups (300 ml) water, plus more if needed

2 medium-size carrots, peeled and cut into sticks about ¼ inch (0.6 cm) thick by 2 inches (5 cm) long

1 or 2 medium-size parsnips, peeled and cut into sticks about ¼ inch (0.6 cm) thick by 2 inches (5 m) long

3 or 4 small white potatoes, scrubbed and halved or quartered

2 leeks, white parts only, trimmed and cut into 2-inch (5 cm) pieces, or 1 medium-size yellow onion, diced

1 small (about 1 pound, or 455 g) savoy cabbage, cut into wedges

1 celery rib, halved lengthwise and cut into 2-inch (5 cm) pieces

4 garlic cloves, crushed

1 bouquet garni (see Note)

½ cup (120 ml) dry white wine

1 teaspoon dried thyme

2 tablespoons (8 g) chopped fresh flat-leaf parsley

1 teaspoon salt

4 cups (960 ml) vegetable broth

Coarse-ground brown mustard, horseradish, and cornichons, for serving

1. In a large bowl, combine the vital wheat gluten, chickpea flour, nutritional yeast, onion powder, salt, and a few grinds of pepper. Mix well, then stir in the oil, soy sauce, and water until well mixed. Use your hands to knead the mixture for about 5 minutes. If the mixture is dry, add a very small amount of extra water. If it is too wet, sprinkle on some additional vital wheat gluten. Divide the seitan into 4 to 6 smaller pieces and set aside.

2. Arrange the carrots, parsnips, potatoes, leeks, cabbage, celery, and garlic in the slow cooker. Add the bouquet garni and the seitan chunks. Add the wine, thyme, parsley, salt, and ¼ teaspoon of pepper, then pour in the broth. Cover and cook on Low until the seitan is cooked and the vegetables are tender, 6 to 8 hours.

3. Remove the bouquet garni and discard. Taste and adjust the seasonings, if needed. Transfer the seitan and vegetables to a large serving platter. Ladle the broth into small individual cups to serve with the pot-au-feu. Set out small serving bowls containing the mustard, horseradish, and cornichons.

NOTE: To make a bouquet garni, in a 5-inch (13 cm) square of cheesecloth (or in a coffee filter or tea ball, if you don't have cheesecloth), place 1 teaspoon peppercorns, 1 teaspoon whole cloves, 2 crumbled bay leaves, 1 teaspoon celery seeds, and 1 teaspoon dried thyme. Gather up the edges of the cheesecloth and tie with kitchen twine.

Vegetable Curry

SLOW COOKER SIZE: 4- TO 6-QUART (3.8 TO 5.7 L) | COOK TIME: 6 TO 8 HOURS ON LOW | GLUTEN-FREE |
OIL-FREE OPTION | SOY-FREE

Let the luscious fragrance of curry fill your house all day as it simmers in your slow cooker. Serve over hot cooked basmati rice with chutney on the side. For a creamier curry, stir in about ½ cup (120 ml) of unsweetened coconut milk or vegan yogurt just before serving.

¼ cup (60 ml) water, or 2 teaspoons avocado oil

1 large yellow onion, minced

3 garlic cloves, minced

2 tablespoons (32 g) tomato paste

2 tablespoons (12 g) curry powder

1 teaspoon ground coriander

¼ teaspoon cayenne pepper

1 bell pepper (any color), seeded and chopped

3 red-skinned potatoes, scrubbed and diced

3 cups (300 g) small cauliflower florets

1½ cups (150 g) green beans, cut into 1-inch (2.5 cm) pieces

1 (14.5-ounce, or 410 g) can diced tomatoes, drained

1½ cups (247.5 g) cooked chickpeas (page 114)
    or 1 (15-ounce, or 425 g) can chickpeas, rinsed and drained

2 bay leaves

½ cup (120 ml) vegetable broth

Salt and freshly ground black pepper

½ cup (65 g) frozen green peas, thawed

1. Heat the water or oil in a medium-size skillet over medium-high heat. Add the onion and sauté until softened, about 5 minutes. Add the garlic, tomato paste, curry powder, coriander, and cayenne and cook for 1 minute longer. Alternatively, place the onion in a microwave-safe bowl with 2 tablespoons (30 ml) of water, cover, and microwave for 2 minutes to soften, then stir in the garlic, tomato paste, and spices.

2. Transfer the onion mixture to the slow cooker. Add the bell pepper, potatoes, cauliflower, green beans, tomatoes, chickpeas, bay leaves, and broth. Season to taste with salt and black pepper. Cover and cook on Low until the vegetables are tender, 6 to 8 hours.

3. A few minutes before serving, stir in the green peas. Taste and adjust the seasonings, if needed. Remove the bay leaves. For a thicker curry, use an immersion blender to puree a portion of the mixture or scoop out about 2 cups (weight varies) of the mixture and puree it in a blender or food processor, then stir the puree back into the slow cooker. Serve hot.

Jackfruit Ropa Vieja

SERVES 4

SLOW COOKER SIZE: 4- TO 6-QUART (3.8 TO 5.7 L) | COOK TIME: 4 TO 6 HOURS ON LOW | GLUTEN-FREE |
OIL-FREE OPTION | SOY-FREE

There are many variations of this flavorful Latin American dish. This vegan version, made with a combination of jackfruit, black beans, and mushrooms, is my favorite. Served over rice, it makes a delicious dinner when accompanied by a green vegetable. It's also terrific spooned into warm tortillas and topped with diced avocado or Cashew Sour Cream (page 338).

¼ cup (60 ml) water, or 2 teaspoons olive oil

1 small yellow onion, sliced paper-thin

3 garlic cloves, minced

1 green bell pepper, seeded and sliced paper-thin

⅓ cup (85 g) tomato paste

1 teaspoon ground cumin

1 cup (242 g) crushed tomatoes

½ teaspoon dried oregano

½ teaspoon granulated natural sugar

2 portobello mushrooms caps, gills scraped and discarded, shredded or thinly sliced

1½ cups (258 g) cooked black beans (page 114) or 1 (15-ounce, or 425 g) can beans, rinsed and drained

1 (20-ounce, or 560 g) can young jackfruit in water or brine, drained and rinsed

1 cup (240 ml) vegetable broth

1 teaspoon chopped fresh cilantro

Salt and freshly ground black pepper

1 tablespoon (15 ml) fresh lime juice

Hot cooked rice or tortillas, for serving

(continued)

1. Heat the water or oil in a medium-size skillet over medium-high heat. Add the onion and sauté until softened, about 5 minutes. Add the garlic and bell pepper and continue cooking for 2 minutes. Stir in the tomato paste and cumin and cook for 1 minute longer. Alternatively, combine the onion, garlic, and bell pepper in a microwave-safe bowl with 2 tablespoons (30 ml) of water, cover, and microwave for 2 minutes to soften, then stir in the tomato paste and cumin.

2. Transfer the onion mixture to the slow cooker. Add the crushed tomatoes, oregano, sugar, mushrooms, beans, jackfruit, broth, cilantro, and salt and black pepper to taste. Stir until well combined. Cover and cook on Low until the vegetables are tender, 4 to 6 hours. About 30 minutes before serving, uncover and use two forks to shred the jackfruit pieces. Taste and adjust the seasonings, if needed.

3. Just before serving, add the lime juice. Serve hot, spooned over rice or into tortillas.

Rustic Potpie Topped with Chive Biscuits

SERVES 4

SLOW COOKER SIZE: 4- TO 6-QUART (3.8 TO 5.7 L) | COOK TIME: 4 TO 6 HOURS ON LOW, PLUS 1 HOUR ON HIGH | GLUTEN-FREE OPTION | SOY-FREE OPTION

This rustic potpie features a top crust of tender drop biscuits that cook right in the slow cooker. The steam heat produces a soft and tender biscuit topping. If you prefer a drier texture to the biscuits, let the cooked potpie sit uncovered for about 10 minutes before serving. To make this gluten-free, use diced tempeh or extra-firm tofu instead of seitan and use a gluten-free flour blend. For soy-free, omit the soy sauce and use Soy-Free Sauce (page 344), or coconut aminos, or add some soy-free vegetable broth base or additional salt, and a soy-free plant milk.

2 tablespoons (30 ml) plus 2 teaspoons olive oil
1 medium-size yellow onion, minced
2 large carrots, peeled and minced
2 tablespoons (32 g) tomato paste
1 teaspoon dried thyme
½ teaspoon dried marjoram
1 cup (124 g) plus 3 tablespoons (23.25 g) all-purpose flour
3 tablespoons (45 ml) dry red wine

1 tablespoon (15 ml) soy sauce

1 cup (240 ml) vegetable broth

2 medium-size Yukon Gold potatoes, peeled and cut into ½-inch (1 cm) dice

8 ounces (225 g) cremini mushrooms, coarsely chopped

8 ounces (225 g) seitan (page 154), cut into ½-inch (1 cm) dice

Salt and freshly ground black pepper

¾ cup (97.5 g) frozen green peas, thawed

1½ teaspoons baking powder

1 tablespoon (0.2 g) dried or (3 g) snipped fresh chives

½ cup (120 ml) plain unsweetened plant milk

1. Heat 2 teaspoons of oil in a large skillet over medium-high heat. Add the onion and carrots and sauté for 5 minutes. Stir in the tomato paste, thyme, and marjoram and cook for 1 minute longer. Sprinkle on 3 tablespoons (23.25 g) of flour and cook for 30 seconds. Add the wine, soy sauce, and broth, stirring after each addition.

2. Transfer the onion mixture to the slow cooker. Add the potatoes, mushrooms, seitan, ½ teaspoon of salt, and ¼ teaspoon of pepper. Cover and cook on Low until the vegetables are tender, 4 to 6 hours. Taste and adjust the seasonings, if needed, then stir in the green peas.

3. In a large bowl, combine the remaining 1 cup (124 g) of flour, the baking powder, chives, and ½ teaspoon salt. Quickly stir in the plant milk and the remaining 2 tablespoons (30 ml) of oil until just blended. Drop the biscuit mixture by large spoonfuls onto the surface of the simmering stew. Turn the heat setting to High, cover, and cook until the dough is cooked through, about 1 hour longer.

4. Serve within 15 minutes after the biscuit dough has finished cooking.

VARIATIONS

Instead of the seitan, use cooked chickpeas or chopped tempeh. You could also use sweet potatoes instead of the white potatoes, or add turnips in addition to the carrots, and so on. Different herbs could be used in the biscuits—instead of chives, try dill and a little dried savory, if you have some.

Chipotle-Polenta Bake

SERVES 4

SLOW COOKER SIZE: 4- TO 6-QUART (3.8 TO 5.7 L) | COOK TIME: 6 HOURS ON LOW | GLUTEN-FREE |
SOY-FREE

This yummy casserole couldn't be easier to make. Just combine all of the ingredients in the cooker, turn it on, and walk away—that is, until the wonderful fragrance draws you back to enjoy your meal. This soft and spicy polenta is spooned into bowls and topped with your garnishes of choice. If you prefer a milder flavor, cut back on the amount of chili powder and chipotle.

If you prefer fried polenta slices, transfer the cooked soft polenta to an oiled loaf pan and refrigerate to chill and firm up. Then cut the polenta into slices and pan-fry them in a small amount of olive oil. Serve topped with a little hot sauce or a dab of Cashew Sour Cream (page 338) and some salsa.

1¼ cups (175 g) medium-ground cornmeal
1¼ teaspoons salt
3 tablespoons (22.5 g) chili powder
2 teaspoons olive oil
5 cups (1.2 L) boiling vegetable broth
5 scallions, minced
1½ cups (258 g) cooked pinto beans (page 114)
  or 1 (15-ounce, or 425 g) can beans, rinsed and drained
1½ cups (232.5 g) fresh or (247.5 g) frozen corn kernels, thawed
2 tablespoons (34 g) minced chipotle chiles in adobo
Louisiana hot sauce, for seasoning
Your favorite salsa, for serving
2 tablespoons (2 g) minced fresh cilantro, for garnish
Sliced jalapeño chiles, sliced black olives, and/or Cashew Sour Cream (page 338),
  for garnish (optional)

1. Generously oil the insert of the slow cooker or spray it with nonstick cooking spray. Add the cornmeal, salt, chili powder, and oil. Stir in the boiling broth until well blended, then stir in the scallions, beans, corn, chipotle chiles, and hot sauce to taste. Cover and cook on Low for 6 hours.

2. Serve hot, topped with salsa and sprinkled with cilantro and any of the optional garnishes.

Wine-Braised Seitan and Cremini Mushrooms

SERVES 4

SLOW COOKER SIZE: 4- TO 6-QUART (3.8 TO 5.7 L) | COOK TIME: 6 TO 8 HOURS ON LOW | SOY-FREE OPTION

In this recipe, bite-size pieces of seitan and vegetables are braised in a fragrant red wine sauce redolent of thyme. The browning liquid deepens the color of the sauce to a rich brown. Serve this braise over freshly cooked noodles or rice or, if you prefer, add 1-inch (2.5 cm) chunks of potatoes to the cooker when you add the carrots and mushrooms. For soy-free, omit the soy sauce and use Soy-Free Sauce (page 344), or coconut aminos, or add some soy-free vegetable broth base or additional salt.

1¾ cups (210 g) vital wheat gluten

¼ cup (30 g) plus 3 tablespoons (22.5 g) tapioca starch, divided

1 tablespoon (3.75 g) nutritional yeast

½ teaspoon garlic powder

½ teaspoon onion powder

¼ teaspoon salt

¼ teaspoon freshly ground black pepper

1 tablespoon (15 ml) soy sauce

1 tablespoon (15 ml) olive oil

1 cup (240 ml) water

4 to 6 shallots, quartered

2 garlic cloves, minced

⅔ cup (160 ml) dry red wine

2 tablespoons (32 g) tomato paste

2 teaspoons minced fresh thyme, or 1 teaspoon dried thyme

2 carrots, peeled and thinly sliced

8 ounces (225 g) cremini mushrooms, quartered

1½ cups (360 ml) vegetable broth

Salt and freshly ground black pepper

1 teaspoon vegan gravy browner (such as Kitchen Bouquet)

(continued)

1. To make the seitan: In a large bowl, combine the vital wheat gluten, ¼ cup (30 g) of tapioca starch, nutritional yeast, garlic and onion powders, ¼ teaspoon salt, and ¼ teaspoon pepper. Stir in the soy sauce, 1 tablespoon (15 ml) of oil, and the water to make a stiff dough. Use your hands to knead for about 3 minutes, then pat the dough out flat on a work surface and cut it into ½-inch (1 cm) dice. Set aside.

2. In the slow cooker, combine the shallots, garlic, wine, tomato paste, and thyme, stirring to blend. Add the carrots and mushrooms and sprinkle with the remaining 3 tablespoons (22.5 g) of tapioca starch. Pour in the broth and season to taste with salt and black pepper.

3. Add the cubes of seitan dough, nestling them among the vegetables and submerging them as much as possible. Try not to let the seitan cubes touch each other, if possible. Cover and cook on Low for 6 to 8 hours, or until the vegetables are tender and the seitan is firm.

4. Gently stir in the browning liquid, then taste and adjust the seasonings, if needed. Serve hot.

NOTE: If a thicker sauce is desired, remove the solids from the cooker, turn the heat up to High, and stir in 1 tablespoon (8 g) of cornstarch blended with 2 tablespoons (30 ml) of water, stirring to thicken.

Topless Shepherd's Pie

SERVES 6

SLOW COOKER SIZE: 6-QUART (5.7 L) | COOK TIME: 6 TO 8 HOURS ON LOW | GLUTEN-FREE | OIL-FREE | SOY-FREE OPTION

Shepherd's pie is known for its topping of mashed potatoes, but try as I might I couldn't figure out how to both cook the shepherd's pie in the slow cooker and mash the potatoes in it. So this recipe keeps it "topless" and lets the bottom layer of sliced potatoes stand in for the mashers. If you're a stickler for tradition, then simply make the mashed on the stovetop and spread them on top of the shepherd's pie for the last 30 minutes of cooking. For soy-free, omit the soy sauce and use Soy-Free Sauce (page 344) or coconut aminos, or add some soy-free vegetable broth base or additional salt.

2 large russet potatoes, thinly sliced
Salt and freshly ground black pepper
2 carrots, finely chopped

8 ounces (225 g) mushrooms, coarsely chopped

½ cup (98.5 g) dried brown lentils, rinsed and picked over

⅔ cup (111 g) frozen baby lima beans

1 (14.5-ounce, or 410 g) can diced tomatoes, drained

1 cup (165 g) frozen corn kernels

1 cup (130 g) frozen green peas

1 cup (240 ml) vegetable broth

2 cups (480 ml) Mushroom Gravy (page 340)

1. Arrange the potato slices evenly in layers in the bottom of the slow cooker, seasoning each layer with salt and pepper. Top with the carrots, mushrooms, lentils, limas, tomatoes, corn, green peas, and broth.

2. Pour the gravy over the vegetable mixture, spreading evenly. Cover, and cook on Low for 6 to 8 hours or until the lentils and vegetables are tender.

Mom-Style Vegan Meatloaf   SERVES 4 TO 6

SLOW COOKER SIZE: 4- TO 6-QUART (3.8 TO 5.7 L) | COOK TIME: 4 HOURS ON LOW | OIL-FREE OPTION

An old-fashioned comfort food favorite made vegan—and in a slow cooker. This delicious loaf "bakes" in the slow cooker, right along with carrots and potatoes. Add a cooked green vegetable and dinner is served. The flavorful glaze makes a sauce unnecessary, but you can serve it with one if you like—or just pass the ketchup!

¼ cup (60 ml) water, or 2 teaspoons olive oil

1 small yellow onion, minced

2 garlic cloves, minced

1 tablespoon (3 g) dried thyme

1½ cups (258 g) cooked pinto beans (page 114)
    or 1 (15-ounce, or 425 g) can beans, rinsed and drained

12 ounces (340 g) extra-firm tofu, drained, squeezed, and crumbled

¾ cup (180 g) ketchup

2 tablespoons (30 ml) vegan Worcestershire sauce or soy sauce

1 tablespoon (15 g) Dijon mustard

½ cup (40 g) ground walnuts

(continued)

½ cup (78 g) old-fashioned rolled oats
¼ cup (28 g) dried bread crumbs
½ cup (60 g) vital wheat gluten
2 tablespoons (15 g) tapioca starch
2 tablespoons (8 g) minced fresh flat-leaf parsley
Salt and freshly ground black pepper
2 large carrots, cut into ¼-inch (0.6 cm) slices
2 or 3 Yukon Gold potatoes, cut into ½-inch (1 cm) slices
2 or 3 shallots, quartered lengthwise
2 tablespoons (22 g) yellow or brown mustard
2 teaspoons granulated natural sugar
1 tablespoon (15 ml) apple cider vinegar

1. Heat the water or oil in a small skillet over medium-high heat. Add the onion and sauté until softened, about 5 minutes. Add the garlic and thyme and cook 1 minute longer. Alternatively, place the onion in a microwave-safe bowl with 2 tablespoons (30 ml) of water, cover, and microwave for 2 minutes to soften, then stir in the garlic and thyme.

2. In a food processor, combine the beans, tofu, ½ cup (120 g) of ketchup, Worcestershire, mustard, and reserved onion mixture and process to mix well.

3. In a large bowl, combine the walnuts, oats, bread crumbs, vital wheat gluten, tapioca starch, and parsley. Season with 1 teaspoon of salt and ¼ teaspoon of pepper. Add the bean mixture and stir well to mix thoroughly.

4. Turn out the mixture onto a work surface and shape into a round or oval to fit inside your slow cooker, pressing to make sure the loaf holds together.

5. Arrange the carrot slices evenly in the bottom of the cooker. Season with a little salt and black pepper, then arrange the potato slices on top of the carrots. Set the reserved loaf on top of the potatoes and surround with the shallots.

6. In a small bowl, combine the remaining ¼ cup (60 g) of ketchup with the mustard, sugar, and vinegar and mix well. Spread the mixture on top of the loaf. Cover and cook on Low for 4 hours.

7. Remove the lid, turn off the cooker, and allow the loaf to rest for 10 minutes. Transfer the loaf carefully with a large spatula to a large serving platter and surround it with the carrots, potatoes, and shallots. Slice the loaf carefully with a serrated knife.

Chili-Potato Gratin

SERVES 4 TO 6

SLOW COOKER SIZE: 4- TO 6-QUART (3.8 TO 5.7 L) | COOK TIME: 4 TO 6 HOURS ON LOW |
GLUTEN-FREE OPTION | OIL-FREE OPTION | SOY-FREE

I first discovered how good chili and potatoes taste together years ago when I topped a baked potato with some chili. This gratin reunites those flavors by layering sliced potatoes and chili in a slow cooker for a tasty weeknight meal. The thinner you slice the potatoes, the more quickly they will become tender. To make the recipe gluten-free, omit the optional bread crumbs or use gluten-free crumbs. If you happen to have about 3 cups (about 600 g) of leftover chili on hand, you can use that in this recipe instead of making the chili from the first part of this recipe.

¼ cup (60 ml) water, or 2 teaspoons olive oil

1 small yellow onion, minced

3 garlic cloves, minced

3 tablespoons (48 g) tomato paste

¼ cup (60 ml) vegetable broth or water

1 to 2 tablespoons (7.5 to 15 g) chili powder

1 teaspoon dried oregano

½ teaspoon ground cumin

½ teaspoon smoked paprika

¼ teaspoon cayenne pepper

1 (14.5-ounce, or 410 g) can petite diced tomatoes, drained and juices reserved

1½ cups (258 g) cooked pinto beans (page 114)
    or 1 (15-ounce, or 425 g) can beans, rinsed and drained

2 or 3 large russet potatoes, peeled and sliced about ⅛-inch (0.3 cm) thick

Salt and freshly ground black pepper

1½ cups (360 ml) Cheesy Sauce (page 340)

¼ cup (12.5 g) toasted panko or other dried bread crumbs (optional)

1. Heat the water or oil in a medium-size skillet over medium-high heat. Add the onion and sauté until softened, about 5 minutes. Add the garlic and cook for 1 minute longer, then stir in the tomato paste, broth, chili powder, oregano, cumin, paprika, and cayenne. Stir in the juice from the tomatoes so the mixture doesn't burn. Stir in the tomatoes and beans and simmer for 5 minutes. Taste and adjust the seasonings of the chili mixture if needed.

2. Spoon a thin layer of the chili mixture in the bottom of the cooker. Arrange a layer of potato slices on top, overlapping slightly. Season to taste with salt and black pepper, then top with a thin layer of the chili mixture, followed by a drizzle of the cheesy sauce, another layer of potatoes, salt and black pepper, and so on, until all of the potatoes, chili, and sauce are used up, ending with a final drizzle of cheesy sauce on top. Cover and cook on Low until the potatoes are tender, 4 to 6 hours.

3. Remove the lid and let the gratin sit for 10 minutes before serving. Just before serving, sprinkle the panko on top (if using). Serve hot.

Jerk Tempeh with Sweet Potatoes   SERVES 4

SLOW COOKER SIZE: 4- TO 6-QUART (3.8 TO 5.7 L) | COOK TIME: 6 HOURS ON LOW | GLUTEN-FREE | OIL-FREE

Tempeh stands up well to jerk seasonings, as the flavorful sauce mingles nicely with the tempeh chunks as it all cooks. Sweet potatoes and dark red kidney beans provide color and complementary flavors. To save time, you can use a bottled jerk sauce instead of making your own.

1 small sweet yellow onion, coarsely chopped
2 scallions, coarsely chopped
1 hot green chile, seeded and coarsely chopped
1 garlic clove, crushed
1 tablespoon (8 g) grated peeled fresh ginger
2 tablespoons (40 g) lime or orange marmalade
1 tablespoon (15 ml) rice vinegar
2 teaspoons soy sauce
1 teaspoon granulated natural sugar
1 teaspoon dried thyme
½ teaspoon ground allspice
¼ teaspoon ground cinnamon
¼ teaspoon paprika
¼ teaspoon cayenne pepper
½ teaspoon salt
¼ teaspoon freshly ground black pepper
⅓ cup (80 ml) water

8 ounces (225 g) tempeh, cut into 1-inch (2.5 cm) dice

2 large sweet potatoes, peeled and cut into 1-inch (2.5 cm) dice

1½ cups (375 g) cooked dark red kidney beans (page 114) or 1 (15-ounce, or 425 g) can beans, rinsed and drained

1. To make the jerk sauce: In a food processor, combine the onion, scallions, chile, garlic, and ginger and process until finely minced. Add the marmalade, vinegar, soy sauce, sugar, thyme, allspice, cinnamon, paprika, cayenne, salt, and black pepper. Process to a paste. Add the water and process until well blended.

2. Combine the tempeh, sweet potatoes, and beans in the slow cooker. Add the jerk mixture and stir to coat. Cover and cook on Low until the potatoes and onions are tender, about 6 hours. Serve hot.

Layered Tortilla Pie

SERVES 6

SLOW COOKER SIZE: 4- TO 6-QUART (3.8 TO 5.7 L) | COOK TIME: 4 HOURS ON LOW | GLUTEN-FREE OPTION | OIL-FREE OPTION | SOY-FREE OPTION

This great weeknight meal is loaded with flavor and is also quick and easy to assemble ahead of time. For extra flavor, lightly toast the tortillas before using. Depending on your preference and the shape of your slow cooker, use 1 or 2 tortillas for each layer. For gluten-free, use tempeh or extra pinto beans instead of seitan; for soy-free, use seitan instead of tempeh.

¼ cup (60 ml) water, or 2 teaspoons olive oil

1 medium-size yellow onion, minced

4 garlic cloves, minced

2 canned chipotle chiles in adobo, minced

1 tablespoon (16 g) tomato paste

1 tablespoon (8 g) grated unsweetened dark chocolate

2 tablespoons (15 g) chili powder

1 teaspoon ground cumin

1 teaspoon smoked paprika

1 teaspoon dried oregano

1 teaspoon dark brown sugar

½ teaspoon salt

(continued)

¼ teaspoon freshly ground black pepper

1 (14.5-ounce, or 410 g) can crushed tomatoes

1½ cups (258 g) cooked pinto beans (page 114)
   or 1 (15-ounce, or 425 g) can beans, rinsed and drained

1 (15-ounce, or 425 g) can vegan refried beans, stirred

8 ounces (225 g) steamed diced tempeh, chopped seitan (page 154),
   or Tofu Chorizo (page 343)

1½ cups (232.5 g) fresh or (247.5 g) frozen corn kernels

6 to 12 soft corn tortillas

1½ cups (360 ml) Cheesy Sauce (page 340)

Cashew Sour Cream (page 338; optional), for serving

Your favorite tomato salsa (optional), for serving

1. Heat the water or oil in a large skillet over medium-high heat. Add the onion and sauté until softened, about 5 minutes. Add the garlic and cook for 1 minute longer, then stir in the chipotle chiles, tomato paste, chocolate, chili powder, cumin, paprika, oregano, sugar, salt, and pepper. Sprinkle with a little more water, if needed, so the mixture doesn't burn. Stir in the tomatoes and set aside.

2. In a bowl, combine the pinto beans, refried beans, tempeh, and corn. Season to taste with salt and black pepper. Add ½ cup (120 ml) of the sauce mixture and mix well.

3. Spoon a thin layer of the sauce in the bottom of the cooker, then place 1 or 2 tortillas on top. Top with a thin layer of the bean mixture, followed by another 1 or 2 tortillas, more sauce, and a drizzle of cheesy sauce. Repeat the layering until all of the ingredients are used, ending with the cheesy sauce. Cover and cook on Low for 4 hours. Serve hot, topped with sour cream and salsa (if using).

Sunday Supper Strata

SLOW COOKER SIZE: 4- TO 6-QUART (3.8 TO 5.7 L) | COOK TIME: 4 HOURS ON LOW | GLUTEN-FREE OPTION |
OIL-FREE OPTION

A strata is a casserole made with layers of bread and other ingredients, including a custard that is traditionally made with eggs and dairy. This version uses tofu and lots of flavorful vegetables. Stratas are especially popular for brunch, but I like to serve mine for Sunday supper. You can dry the bread cubes for this recipe by either leaving them spread on baking sheets all day or overnight or placing them in a very low oven (about 225°F, or 107°C) for about 30 minutes. To make this gluten-free, use a gluten-free bread.

2 cups (500 g) crumbled firm tofu

1 cup (240 ml) vegetable broth

2 tablespoons (7.5 g) nutritional yeast

½ teaspoon onion powder

½ teaspoon dried basil

¼ teaspoon ground turmeric

Salt and freshly ground black pepper

3 plum tomatoes, chopped, or 1 (14-ounce, or 395 g)
    can diced tomatoes, drained

½ cup (90 g) jarred roasted red bell pepper, seeded and chopped

½ cup (20 g) chopped fresh basil

¼ cup (60 ml) water, or 2 teaspoons olive oil

1 large yellow onion, minced

3 garlic cloves, minced

8 ounces (225 g) cremini mushrooms, chopped

2 medium-size zucchini, thinly sliced

1 cup (240 ml) Cheesy Sauce (page 340)

8 ounces (225 g) Italian bread, cut into ½-inch (1 cm) dice and dried
    (see headnote), 8 to 10 cups

(continued)

1. In a food processor or blender, combine the tofu, broth, nutritional yeast, onion powder, dried basil, turmeric, and salt and pepper to taste and process until smooth and well blended. Set aside. In a bowl, combine the tomatoes, roasted bell pepper, and fresh basil, stirring to mix. Set aside.

2. Heat the water or oil in a large skillet over medium-high heat. Add the onion and sauté until softened, about 5 minutes. Add the garlic, mushrooms, and zucchini and cook for 2 minutes longer.

3. Spread half of the dried bread in the bottom of the slow cooker. Top with half of the tomato mixture, followed by half of the mushroom-zucchini mixture, then drizzle on half of the cheesy sauce, the remaining bread, the remaining tomato mixture, and the remaining mushroom-zucchini mixture. Scrape the tofu mixture evenly over the top of the strata, pressing down on the bread with the back of a large spoon to moisten all the bread. Sprinkle on the remaining cheesy sauce. Cover and cook on Low until the strata is firm, about 4 hours. Serve hot.

Plant-Based Sausage Links

MAKES 6 LINKS

SLOW COOKER SIZE: 4- TO 6-QUART (3.8 TO 5.7 L) | COOK TIME: 4 HOURS ON LOW

Homemade plant-based sausage links are delicious, economical, and a cinch to make at home in the slow cooker. For spicier sausage, add up to 1 teaspoon red pepper flakes. Use these sausage links in any of the recipes calling for plant-based sausage, such as the Red Bean Gumbo (page 59) or the Crockery Cassoulet (page 121). They're also great sautéed with sliced onion and bell pepper and served in a roll, or sliced and added to your favorite pasta dish.

1 cup (120 g) vital wheat gluten
¼ cup (15 g) nutritional yeast
¼ cup (30 g) tapioca flour or chickpea flour
2 teaspoons paprika
1 teaspoon ground fennel seeds
½ teaspoon garlic powder
½ teaspoon onion powder
¼ teaspoon cayenne pepper
½ teaspoon salt
¼ teaspoon freshly ground black pepper

⅔ cup (171 g) cooked (page 114) or canned kidney beans, well drained
2 tablespoons (30 ml) soy sauce
1 tablespoon (15 ml) olive oil
1 tablespoon (15 g) ketchup
½ teaspoon liquid smoke
½ cup (120 ml) water, as needed

1. In a food processor, combine the vital wheat gluten, nutritional yeast, tapioca flour, paprika, fennel, garlic and onion powders, cayenne, salt, and black pepper. Pulse to mix. Add the kidney beans, soy sauce, oil, ketchup, liquid smoke, and ¼ cup (60 ml) of water and process until well mixed. If the mixture is too dry, add more water, a little at a time, until you have a medium-soft (but not wet) dough.

2. Turn out the dough onto a work surface and knead for 3 minutes, then divide the dough into 6 equal pieces. Roll and shape each piece into a link. Wrap each link separately in aluminum foil, twisting the ends to seal.

3. Place a rack, trivet, or a ring of crumpled aluminum foil in the bottom of the slow cooker insert and set a small heatproof plate on top for the links to rest on. Place the foil-wrapped links on the plate and pour in enough hot water to come up to the bottom of the plate. Cover and cook on Low for 4 hours.

4. Remove the links from the cooker, unwrap, and set aside to cool, then refrigerate them, loosely covered, for 1 to 2 hours to allow them to firm up before using. The sausage links may then be sautéed in a little oil until browned.

Spicy-Sweet Seitan Ribs

SERVES 4

SLOW COOKER SIZE: 4- TO 6-QUART (3.8 TO 5.7 L) | COOK TIME: 4 HOURS ON LOW | SOY-FREE OPTION

You can make a batch of these ribs up to 3 days in advance of when you want to serve them and refrigerate until needed. Then place them on the grill to reheat and give them some nice grill marks, brushing them with the barbecue sauce as they cook. I like to serve these with coleslaw and corn on the cob for a delicious (if messy) meal, or for the epitome of comfort food, serve them with the Scalloped Potatoes on page 236 and sautéed greens. For soy-free, omit the soy sauce and Worcestershire sauce and use Soy-Free Sauce (page 344), or coconut aminos, or add some soy-free vegetable broth base or additional salt.

1 chipotle chile in adobo
1 tablespoon (15 ml) soy sauce
1 tablespoon (15 ml) vegan Worcestershire sauce
1 tablespoon (15 ml) olive oil
1 teaspoon liquid smoke
2 cups (500 g) Better Barbecue Sauce (page 260)
1 cup (240 ml) water
2 tablespoons (7.5 g) nutritional yeast
2 teaspoons onion powder
1½ teaspoons garlic powder
1 teaspoon smoked paprika
½ teaspoon salt
2 cups (240 g) vital wheat gluten
½ cup (60 g) chickpea flour

1. In a food processor, combine the chipotle chile, soy sauce, Worcestershire sauce, olive oil, liquid smoke, ¼ cup (62.5 g) of barbecue sauce, and the water and process until smooth. Add the nutritional yeast, onion and garlic powders, paprika, and salt and process to blend. Add the vital wheat gluten and chickpea flour and process until a well-mixed dough forms.

2. Lightly oil a 7 × 9-inch (18 × 23 cm) shallow baking dish. Turn out the dough onto a work surface and use your hands to flatten it into a 6 × 9-inch (15 × 23 cm) rectangle. Cut the seitan crosswise into 1-inch (2.5 cm)-thick slices. Spread ½ cup (125 g) of barbecue sauce in the bottom of the baking dish and arrange the seitan strips in a single row on top of the sauce (they will fit snugly next to each other and the sides will touch). Pour 1 cup (250 g) of barbecue sauce over the seitan. Cover the baking dish tightly with aluminum foil and place inside a large slow cooker. Carefully pour about ½ inch (1 cm) of hot water into the slow cooker. Cover and cook on Low for 4 to 6 hours, or until firm.

3. Remove the baking dish from the slow cooker, then transfer the seitan to a work surface and re-cut the ribs. Brush with the remaining ¼ cup (62.5 g) of barbecue sauce and serve hot.

Moroccan Tempeh and Chickpeas with Prunes and Apricots

SERVES 4

SLOW COOKER SIZE: 4- TO 6-QUART (3.8 TO 5.7 L) | COOK TIME: 6 HOURS ON LOW | GLUTEN-FREE | OIL-FREE OPTION | SOY-FREE OPTION

The flavors of Morocco are a good match for the assertiveness of tempeh. I like to serve this with freshly cooked couscous or rice and steamed broccoli. The optional almond butter adds richness and depth to this dish, but it's also delicious without it. To make this soy-free, omit the tempeh entirely or substitute seitan (but remember that then it won't be gluten-free).

¼ cup (60 ml) water, or 2 teaspoons olive oil
1 large yellow onion, minced
3 garlic cloves, minced
1 tablespoon (16 g) tomato paste
1 tablespoon (16 g) almond butter (optional)
1½ teaspoons ground coriander
½ teaspoon ground cumin
¼ teaspoon paprika
¼ teaspoon ground cinnamon
¼ teaspoon cayenne pepper
1½ cups (360 ml) vegetable broth

(continued)

3 cups (495 g) cooked chickpeas (page 114)
   or 2 (15-ounce, or 425 g) cans chickpeas, rinsed and drained
8 ounces (225 g) tempeh, steamed (if desired) and cut into 1-inch (2.5 cm) dice
1 (14.5-ounce, or 410 g) can diced tomatoes, drained
⅓ cup (43 g) dried apricots, chopped
Salt and freshly ground black pepper
⅓ cup (58 g) prunes, halved and pitted
1 cup (130 g) frozen green peas, thawed
2 tablespoons (2 g) chopped fresh cilantro
1 tablespoon (15 ml) fresh lemon juice

1. Heat the water or oil in a large skillet over medium-high heat. Add the onion and sauté for 5 minutes. Stir in the garlic, tomato paste, and almond butter (if using). Add the coriander, cumin, paprika, cinnamon, and cayenne and cook, stirring, for 1 minute.

2. Stir in ½ cup (120 ml) of broth, then transfer the mixture to the slow cooker. Add the chickpeas, tempeh, tomatoes, apricots, and the remaining 1 cup (240 ml) of broth. Season to taste with salt and black pepper. Cover and cook on Low for 6 hours.

3. Stir in the prunes, green peas, cilantro, and lemon juice. Taste and adjust the seasonings, if needed. Serve hot.

Ethiopian-Style Tempeh and Lentils SERVES 4 TO 6

SLOW COOKER SIZE: 4- TO 6-QUART (3.8 TO 5.7 L) | COOK TIME: 6 TO 8 HOURS ON LOW | GLUTEN-FREE | OIL-FREE OPTION | SOY-FREE OPTION

Although it would be traditionally served with injera, a spongy crepe-like flatbread made with teff, this stew is also delicious served over couscous or rice. If you have berbere spice blend on hand, use 1 to 2 tablespoons (7.5 to 15 g) in place of the spices listed in the recipe. To make this soy-free, substitute seitan for the tempeh (but remember that then it won't be gluten-free).

¼ cup (60 ml) water, or 2 teaspoons olive oil
1 medium-size yellow onion, minced
2 garlic cloves, minced
2 tablespoons (32 g) tomato paste
1 teaspoon ground cumin
1 teaspoon ground coriander
1 teaspoon ground fenugreek
1 teaspoon sweet paprika
½ teaspoon cayenne pepper
¼ teaspoon ground cardamom or allspice
¼ teaspoon ground ginger or nutmeg
1 (28-ounce, or 794 g) can crushed tomatoes
8 ounces (225 g) tempeh, cut into ½-inch (1 cm) dice
1 cup (200 g) dried red lentils
3 cups (720 ml) vegetable broth
Salt and freshly ground black pepper

1. Heat the water or oil in a medium-size skillet over medium-high heat. Add the onion and sauté until softened, about 5 minutes. Alternatively, place the onion in a microwave-safe bowl with 2 tablespoons (30 ml) of water, cover, and microwave for 2 minutes to soften. Stir in the garlic, tomato paste, and all of the spices.

2. Transfer the onion mixture to the slow cooker. Stir in the tomatoes, then add the tempeh and lentils. Add the broth and season to taste with salt and black pepper. Cook on Low until the lentils and vegetables are soft, 6 to 8 hours.

3. Taste and adjust the seasonings, if needed. Serve hot.

Puttanesca Pizza

SLOW COOKER SIZE: 4- TO 6-QUART (3.8 TO 5.7 L) | COOK TIME: 1 HOUR 45 MINUTES ON HIGH |
SOY-FREE OPTION

This will make a thick and chewy pizza similar to a deep-dish personal pan pizza you'd get in a restaurant. It will serve 2 as a main dish or 4 as a side dish. Why make pizza in a slow cooker? you might ask. See page 182 for 10 great reasons provided by my blog readers when I posed the question to them. For soy-free, omit the optional cheese or use a soy-free vegan cheese.

DOUGH

1½ cups (186 g) unbleached all-purpose flour

1½ teaspoons instant yeast

½ teaspoon salt

½ teaspoon Italian seasoning

1 tablespoon (15 ml) olive oil

½ cup (120 ml) warm water, or as needed

SAUCE

½ cup (121 g) crushed tomatoes

¼ cup (38.75 g) pitted kalamata olives, sliced

¼ cup (25 g) pitted green olives, sliced

1 tablespoon (9 g) capers, drained

1 tablespoon (4 g) chopped fresh flat-leaf parsley

¼ teaspoon dried basil

¼ teaspoon dried oregano

¼ teaspoon garlic powder

¼ teaspoon granulated natural sugar

¼ teaspoon red pepper flakes

Salt and freshly ground black pepper

½ cup (57.5 g) shredded vegan mozzarella cheese (optional)

1. To make the dough: Lightly oil the inside of a large bowl. In a food processor, combine the flour, yeast, salt, and Italian seasoning. With the machine running, add the oil through the feed tube, then slowly add as much water as needed to form a slightly sticky dough ball. Transfer the dough to a floured surface and knead for 1 to 2 minutes, until it is smooth and elastic. Shape the dough into a ball and transfer to the prepared bowl, turning the dough to coat it with oil. Cover the bowl with plastic wrap and set aside to rise at warm room temperature until doubled in size, about 1 hour.

2. While the dough is rising, make the sauce. In a bowl, combine the tomatoes, both kinds of olives, capers, parsley, basil, oregano, garlic powder, sugar, red pepper flakes, and salt and black pepper to taste.

3. Generously oil the insert of a large slow cooker or spray it with nonstick cooking spray. Punch down the dough and transfer it to a lightly floured surface. Flatten the dough, then shape it to just fit inside your slow cooker. Place the dough in the cooker and spread the sauce over the dough. To prevent condensation from dripping onto the pizza, drape a clean kitchen towel over the cooker, then put on the lid. Cook on High for 1 hour, 45 minutes. If using the vegan mozzarella, sprinkle it on the pizza after 1 hour and 15 minutes, then cook for 30 minutes longer to allow it to melt.

10 GREAT REASONS TO MAKE PIZZA IN A SLOW COOKER

Once I excitedly discovered that I could make pizza in a slow cooker, I realized that "because I can" might not be enough reason to include the recipe in this cookbook, so I put the question out to my blog readers. The overwhelming majority encouraged me to include the pizza recipe. Here is just a sampling of the many responses I received:

1. "I like that you can put the pizza in the slow cooker, then go shopping, or go outside and do gardening, or shovel snow . . . and then when you come back home, it's ready!"

2. "You don't have to worry if it's going to burn in the oven."

3. "I live in Phoenix, where it is often over 100°F (38°C) during the day. I try not to use the oven and am using my slow cookers as much as possible."

4. "If you don't have an oven, like some students, it's good to know you can still 'bake.'"

5. "I think slow-cooker pizza would be awesome. I could get it ready before I picked up my son, and we could rush around to activities and get homework done and then sit down to a leisurely dinner."

6. "I would make pizza in a slow cooker if I were taking it to a party and didn't know if the oven would be available, or if I were having a party and needed the oven for other dishes, if I were remodeling the kitchen, or if I just needed to start dinner early and then be able to leave it alone."

7. "This would be great for people whose ovens don't heat very evenly, like the small ovens they often have in apartments."

8. "We're always struggling to find things to eat quickly enough with our weird soccer practice time and getting the kids off to bed—I often resort to PB&J in the car and then some fruit when we get home. This would be a nice alternative!"

9. "It is much more green to use the slow cooker than to heat an oven—especially to a high heat and then only use about 12 minutes' worth."

10 "Some nights anything other than plonking leftovers in the microwave is too much, so a slow-cooker pizza could be just the thing for a nice unwind while streaming a movie after a hectic day. Everyone loves pizza."

Black Bean and Sweet Potato Casserole

SERVES 4 TO 6

SLOW COOKER SIZE: 4- TO 6-QUART (3.8 TO 5.7 L) | COOK TIME: 4 HOURS ON LOW | GLUTEN-FREE | OIL-FREE OPTION | SOY-FREE

The combination of black beans and sweet potatoes is a favorite that tastes great in this easy weeknight meal. Instead of black beans, you could substitute 1½ cups (288 g) of Tofu Chorizo (page 343) or (382.5 g) finely chopped seitan (but remember it won't be gluten-free).

¼ cup (60 ml) water, or 2 teaspoons olive oil

1 small yellow onion, minced

3 garlic cloves, minced

3 tablespoons (48 g) tomato paste

3 tablespoons (22.5 g) chili powder

1 teaspoon dried oregano

1 teaspoon ground cumin

½ teaspoon smoked paprika

1 (16-ounce, or 455 g) jar tomato salsa

3 cups (516 g) cooked black beans (page 114)
   or 2 (15-ounce, or 425 g) cans beans, rinsed and drained

1½ pounds (680 g) sweet potatoes, peeled and thinly sliced

Salt and freshly ground black pepper

1½ cups (360 ml) Cheesy Sauce (page 340)

2 tablespoons (12 g) minced scallions, for garnish

1. Heat the water or oil in a medium-size skillet over medium-high heat. Add the onion and sauté until softened, about 5 minutes. Add the garlic and cook for 1 minute longer, then stir in the tomato paste, chili powder, oregano, cumin, and paprika. Stir in a small amount of water, if needed, so the mixture doesn't burn. Stir in the salsa and black beans, then taste and adjust the seasonings of the bean mixture, if needed.

(continued)

2. Spoon a thin layer of the bean mixture on the bottom of the cooker. Arrange a layer of sweet potato slices on top, overlapping slightly. Season to taste with salt and black pepper, then top with a thin layer of the bean mixture, followed by a drizzle of the cheesy sauce, more sweet potatoes, beans, cheesy sauce, salt and black pepper, and so on, until all of the sweet potatoes and beans are used up, ending with the remaining cheesy sauce on top. Cover and cook on Low until the potatoes are tender, about 4 hours.

3. When ready to serve, sprinkle with the scallions. Serve hot.

Slow-Cooked Seitan Fajitas

SERVES 4 TO 6

SLOW COOKER SIZE: 4- TO 6-QUART (3.8 TO 5.7 L) | COOK TIME: 6 HOURS ON LOW | SOY-FREE OPTION

Once the flavorful fajita filling is cooked, you can simply spoon it into tortillas and enjoy. Or, instead of using it in fajitas, try serving the filling over rice or quinoa for a tasty main dish. This recipe can be made soy-free by omitting the soy sauce and using Soy-Free Sauce (page 344), or coconut aminos, or adding some soy-free vegetable broth base or additional salt.

1½ cups (180 g) vital wheat gluten
¼ cup (30 g) chickpea flour
2 tablespoons (7.5 g) nutritional yeast
½ teaspoon garlic powder
½ teaspoon onion powder
¼ teaspoon salt, plus more for seasoning
¼ teaspoon freshly ground black pepper, plus more for seasoning
2 tablespoons (30 ml) soy sauce
2 teaspoons olive oil
1 cup (240 ml) water, plus more if needed
2 tablespoons (32 g) tomato paste
1½ cups (390 g) tomato salsa
1 tablespoon (7.5 g) chili powder
1 tablespoon (15 ml) soy sauce
2 large bell peppers (any color), seeded and cut into ¼-inch (0.6 cm)-thick strips
1 large yellow onion, thinly sliced
1 garlic clove, minced

2 tablespoons (30 ml) fresh lime juice
6 (7-inch, or 18 cm) flour tortillas, warmed
1 ripe Hass avocado, peeled, pitted, and diced, for garnish
1 large ripe tomato, diced, for garnish

1. To make the seitan: In a bowl, combine the vital wheat gluten, chickpea flour, nutritional yeast, garlic and onion powders, salt, and pepper. Stir in the soy sauce, oil, and as much water as needed to make a stiff dough. Use your hands to knead for about 3 minutes, then pat the dough out flat on a work surface and cut it into ¼ × 4-inch (0.3 × 10 cm) strips.

2. In a bowl, combine the tomato paste, salsa, chili powder, and soy sauce and stir to combine.

3. Combine the bell peppers, onion, and garlic in the slow cooker. Place the seitan strips on top of and in between the vegetables, arranging the seitan pieces so that they don't touch each other, if possible. Pour the salsa mixture on top of the seitan and vegetables. Season to taste with salt and black pepper. Cover and cook on Low for 6 hours.

4. Stir in the lime juice, then taste and adjust the seasonings, if needed. To serve, spoon the mixture into warm tortillas, topped with avocado and tomato.

CHAPTER

8

Simply Stuffed

Stuffed vegetables and slow cookers were made for each other. You can cook your stuffed summertime favorites like bell peppers, zucchini, and eggplant without heating up the kitchen with the oven. In the fall and winter, the slow cooker provides gentle heat to cook great stuffed winter squashes and stuffed cabbage rolls until tender and delicious, all without worrying about the burning or drying out that can happen in the oven.

A large oval slow cooker works best for the recipes in this chapter. If you have only a smaller cooker, then you may need to halve the recipe, or just make as much as will fit inside your cooker. In some cases, as with eggplant halves, you can even stack the stuffed vegetables on top of each other.

The slow cooker can also be used to cook just the stuffing, using the eponymous recipe in this chapter. There is also a recipe for a holiday-worthy stuffed and rolled seitan roast called Seitan Roulade.

Among the stuffed vegetables here are Stuffed Zucchini Puttanesca, Quinoa-Stuffed Bell Peppers, and Stuffed Collard Rolls. Best of all, you can mix and match the various stuffings with the vegetables of your choice. For example, you can use the red bean and bulgur stuffing to stuff bell peppers instead of eggplant.

TIPS FOR COOKING STUFFING IN A SLOW COOKER

When stuffing is cooked for too long or at too high a temperature in a slow cooker, it can sometimes harden at the edges. You can avoid this by taking the following precautions:

- Generously coat the bottom and sides of the crock with nonstick cooking spray.
- Pack the stuffing loosely in the slow cooker.
- Cook on Low for no longer than 4 hours.
- Stir around the edges occasionally while cooking.
- Line the sides of your slow cooker with a lightly oiled band of parchment paper.
- Place the stuffing in a covered casserole dish to cook inside the slow cooker.

Just the Stuffing

SERVES 6 TO 8

SLOW COOKER SIZE: 4- TO 6-QUART (3.8 TO 5.7 L) | COOK TIME: 3 TO 4 HOURS ON LOW |
GLUTEN-FREE OPTION | OIL-FREE OPTION | SOY-FREE

This is my go-to bread stuffing, based on my mom's recipe, but cooked in a slow cooker instead of a bird. In this recipe I use white Italian bread, just as my mother did, but you can use any type of bread you prefer, including gluten-free.

¼ cup (60 ml) water, or 2 teaspoons olive oil
1 large yellow onion, minced
2 celery ribs, minced
1½ teaspoons dried thyme
1 teaspoon dried marjoram
1 teaspoon ground sage
1 loaf Italian bread, cut into ½-inch (1 cm) dice (about 10 cups)
¼ cup (16 g) minced fresh flat-leaf parsley
1 teaspoon salt
½ teaspoon freshly ground black pepper
1½ cups (360 ml) vegetable broth, or as needed

1. Heat the water or oil in a large skillet over medium-high heat. Add the onion and celery and sauté until softened, about 5 minutes. Alternatively, combine the onion and celery in a microwave-safe bowl with 2 tablespoons (30 ml) of water, cover, and microwave for 2 minutes to soften, then stir in the thyme, marjoram, and sage.

2. Coat the slow cooker insert with nonstick cooking spray. Add the bread cubes, onion mixture, parsley, salt, and pepper. Stir in enough of the broth to just moisten. Taste and adjust the seasonings, adding more salt depending on the saltiness of your broth, and extra herbs, if desired. Cover and cook on Low until firm, 3 to 4 hours. Serve hot.

VARIATIONS

Mushroom Stuffing: Add up to 8 ounces (225 g) chopped mushrooms of your choice to the onion and celery mixture and cook for 1 minute before adding to the stuffing mixture.

Cranberry-Walnut Stuffing: Add up to 1 cup (120 g) toasted chopped walnuts and ⅓ cup (40 g) sweetened dried cranberries to the stuffing mixture.

Sausage Stuffing: Add up to 2 cups (220 g) cooked crumbled or chopped plant-based sausage to the stuffing mixture.

Chestnut Stuffing: Add 1½ cups (217.5 g) cooked chestnuts to the stuffing mixture.

Southwestern Stuffed Bell Peppers

SERVES 4

SLOW COOKER SIZE: 6-QUART (5.7 L) | COOK TIME: 4 HOURS ON LOW | GLUTEN-FREE | OIL-FREE | SOY-FREE

These zesty stuffed peppers are especially fun to make with "stoplight" peppers—a packaged combination of red, green, and yellow bell peppers. Make the stuffing as spicy as you like by increasing or decreasing the amount of chipotles.

3 garlic cloves, minced

4 scallions, chopped

1 tablespoon (7.5 g) chili powder

1 teaspoon ground cumin

1 teaspoon dried oregano

2 cups (400 g) cooked brown or white rice

1½ cups (258 g) cooked pinto beans or black beans (page 114) or 1 (15-ounce, or 425 g) can beans, rinsed and drained

1 cup (155 g) fresh or (165 g) frozen corn kernels, thawed

1 cup (180 g) diced fresh tomatoes or 1 (14-ounce, or 395 g) can diced tomatoes, drained

2 teaspoons minced chipotle chiles in adobo

Salt and freshly ground black pepper

4 large bell peppers (any color or a combination)

1 (14-ounce, or 395 g) can tomato sauce

½ teaspoon granulated natural sugar

1. In a large bowl, combine the garlic, scallions, chili powder, ½ teaspoon of cumin, and ½ teaspoon of oregano. Add the rice, beans, corn, tomatoes, and chipotles chiles and season to taste with salt and pepper. Mix well.

2. Slice off the tops off the bell peppers and remove and discard the seeds and membranes. Fill the peppers evenly with the rice mixture, packing lightly. Arrange the peppers upright in the slow cooker.

3. In a bowl, combine the tomato sauce, remaining ½ teaspoon of cumin, remaining ½ teaspoon of oregano, sugar, and salt and black pepper to taste. Pour the sauce over and around the peppers in the slow cooker. Cover and cook on Low until the peppers are fork-tender but still hold their shape, about 4 hours. Serve hot.

Tunisian-Inspired
Stuffed Bell Peppers

SLOW COOKER SIZE: 4- TO 6-QUART (3.8 TO 5.7 L) | COOK TIME: 4 HOURS ON LOW | OIL-FREE OPTION |
SOY-FREE

The flavors of North Africa infuse these peppers with an exotic flavor and aroma. Harissa, a North African chile paste, lends an authentic flavor, but another type of chile paste, such as sambal oelek, can be used in a pinch.

4 large bell peppers (assorted colors look great)
¼ cup (60 ml) water, or 2 teaspoons olive oil
1 medium-size yellow onion, minced
2 carrots, peeled and minced
1 large zucchini, minced
3 garlic cloves, minced
3 tablespoons (48 g) tomato paste
2 teaspoons harissa or hot chile paste
2 teaspoons ground coriander
1 teaspoon paprika
1 teaspoon ground cinnamon
1½ teaspoons ground cumin
1 teaspoon salt
¼ teaspoon freshly ground black pepper
2 cups (480 ml) boiling water or vegetable broth
2 cups (350 g) couscous
1 cup (165 g) cooked chickpeas (page 114)
    or 1 (15-ounce, or 425 g) can chickpeas
1 tablespoon (4 g) minced fresh flat-leaf parsley leaves, for garnish

(continued)

1. Slice off the tops of the peppers and remove and discard the seeds and membranes. Remove the stems and chop the pepper tops; set aside.

2. Heat the water or oil in a saucepan over medium-high heat. Add the onion and sauté for 4 minutes. Add the carrots, chopped pepper tops, zucchini, and garlic and cook, stirring, for 2 minutes. Stir in the tomato paste, harissa, coriander, paprika, cinnamon, cumin, salt, and pepper. Add the boiling water, stirring to blend, then stir in the couscous until well combined. Stir in the chickpeas and add a little more water if the stuffing is too dry. Taste and adjust the seasoning, if needed.

3. Lightly pack the stuffing into the peppers and arrange the peppers upright in the slow cooker. Pour hot water into the cooker to come about ½ inch (1 cm) up the sides of the peppers. Cover and cook on Low until the peppers are fork-tender but still hold their shape, about 4 hours. Serve hot, sprinkled with the parsley.

Quinoa-Stuffed Bell Peppers   SERVES 4

SLOW COOKER SIZE: 4- TO 6-QUART (3.8 TO 5.7 L) | COOK TIME: 4 HOURS ON LOW | GLUTEN-FREE | OIL-FREE OPTION | SOY-FREE

One recipe tester described these peppers as a "flavor explosion," and a quick look through the ingredient list tells you why. Nutty quinoa combines with tangy artichoke hearts and lemon juice, bold sun-dried tomatoes and red onion, sweet baby peas, and seasonings, all cooked slowly inside peppers to meld the flavors.

4 large bell peppers (any color or a combination)
¼ cup (60 ml) water, or 2 teaspoons olive oil
1 large red onion, minced
⅓ cup (38 g) minced oil-packed sun-dried tomatoes
½ teaspoon dried marjoram
1 (8-ounce, or 225 g) jar marinated artichoke hearts, drained and chopped
1 cup (130 g) frozen baby green peas, thawed
2 cups (370 g) cooked quinoa
½ cup (32 g) chopped fresh flat-leaf parsley leaves
2 teaspoons fresh lemon juice
Salt and freshly ground black pepper

1. Slice off the tops of the peppers and remove and discard the seeds and membranes. Remove the stems and chop the pepper tops; set aside.

2. Heat the water or oil in a large skillet over medium-high heat. Add the onion and sauté until softened, about 5 minutes. Add the chopped pepper tops and sauté for 3 minutes longer. Stir in the sun-dried tomatoes and marjoram.

3. Transfer the onion mixture to a bowl. Add the artichoke hearts, green peas, quinoa, parsley, lemon juice, and salt and black pepper to taste and mix well. Spoon the stuffing into the peppers, packing lightly. Arrange the peppers upright in the slow cooker. Pour hot water into the cooker to come about ½ inch (1 cm) up the sides of the peppers. Cover and cook on Low until the peppers are tender but still hold their shape, about 4 hours. Serve hot.

Chestnut- and Apple-Stuffed Squash

SERVES 4 TO 6

SLOW COOKER SIZE: 4- TO 6-QUART (3.8 TO 5.7 L) | COOK TIME: 5 TO 7 HOURS ON LOW |
GLUTEN-FREE OPTION | OIL-FREE OPTION | SOY-FREE

One of life's cold-weather pleasures is roasted chestnuts, usually available fresh in markets for only a short time each year. For preparation instructions, see page 194. For more convenient year-round choices, shelled chestnuts can be found at well-stocked supermarkets and gourmet shops, but they can be quite expensive. If you live near an Asian market, look for shelled roasted chestnuts in shelf-stable bags—that's where I get mine for about a dollar a bag.

For the best results, the bread cubes should be dried before using them in the stuffing. To do this, preheat the oven to 225°F (107°C). Spread the bread cubes in a single layer on baking pans and bake for about 30 minutes, then set aside to cool. Alternatively, set the bread cubes out at room temperature for a day or two to dry out. Use gluten-free bread to make this recipe gluten-free.

1 large kabocha or buttercup squash
¼ cup (60 ml) water, or 2 teaspoons olive oil
1 large yellow onion, minced
1 celery rib, minced
1 teaspoon ground sage

(continued)

½ teaspoon dried thyme

4 cups (140 g) cubed bread, dried (see headnote)

1 large Granny Smith apple, peeled, cored, and chopped

1 cup (145 g) coarsely chopped cooked chestnuts

3 tablespoons (12 g) minced fresh flat-leaf parsley

1 teaspoon salt

¼ teaspoon freshly ground black pepper

1 cup (240 ml) vegetable broth, or as needed

1. If you can fit two squash halves in your slow cooker, cut the squash in half and scoop out the seeds. Use a sharp knife to make a flat bottom on the two halves so they sit evenly. If you can fit only the whole squash in your slow cooker, slice off the top of the squash and scrape out the seeds. Set aside.

2. Heat the water or oil in a large skillet over medium-high heat. Add the onion and celery and sauté for 5 minutes. Stir in the sage and thyme.

3. Transfer the onion mixture to a large bowl. Add the dried bread, apple, chestnuts, parsley, salt, and pepper. Stir in just enough broth to moisten and mix well.

4. Lightly pack the stuffing mixture into the squash and place the squash inside the slow cooker. If cooking the squash whole, place the top back on the squash. Pour hot water into the slow cooker to come about ½ inch (1 cm) up the sides of the squash.

5. Cover and cook on Low until the squash is tender, 5 to 7 hours. Serve hot.

HOW TO PREPARE FRESH CHESTNUTS

Pierce the flat side of the chestnut shells with a sharp knife and make an "x." Boil the chestnuts or arrange them in a single layer in a baking dish and roast them at 350°F (180°C) until the shells curl back. For easier peeling, remove the outer shell and inner skin with a sharp paring knife while the chestnuts are still hot. The chestnuts are now ready to eat or use in recipes. (Alternatively, shelled roasted chestnuts are available in well-stocked supermarkets and Asian markets.)

Moroccan-Inspired Stuffed Winter Squash

SERVES 4

SLOW COOKER SIZE: 6-QUART (5.7 L) | COOK TIME: 6 TO 7 HOURS ON LOW | GLUTEN-FREE |
OIL-FREE OPTION | SOY-FREE

Combine your favorite cooked grain with vegetables, fruits, nuts, and spices to make a fragrant stuffing for squash. To making cutting the squash easier, place it in the microwave for a minute or so, then let it sit for another minute.

1 large kabocha or buttercup squash

¼ cup (60 ml) water, or 2 teaspoons olive oil

1 large yellow onion, minced

2 celery ribs, minced

1 carrot, peeled and minced

2 garlic cloves, minced

2 tablespoons (32 g) tomato paste

1½ teaspoons ground coriander

1 teaspoon dried thyme

1 teaspoon ground cinnamon

½ teaspoon ground allspice

½ teaspoon paprika

¼ teaspoon cayenne pepper

½ cup (120 ml) hot water

1 cup (130 g) chopped dried apricots or (145 g) golden raisins

½ cup (55 g) chopped toasted slivered almonds

2 cups (400 g) cooked rice, couscous, or quinoa

¼ cup (16 g) minced fresh flat-leaf parsley leaves

1 tablespoon (15 ml) fresh lemon juice

Salt and freshly ground black pepper

(continued)

1. If you can fit two squash halves in your slow cooker, cut the squash in half and scoop out the seeds. Use a sharp knife to make a flat bottom on the two halves so they sit evenly. If you can fit only the whole squash in your slow cooker, slice off the top of the squash and scrape out the seeds. Set aside.

2. Heat the water or oil in a large skillet over medium-high heat. Add the onion, celery, carrot, and garlic and sauté until softened, about 5 minutes. Stir in the tomato paste, coriander, thyme, cinnamon, allspice, paprika, and cayenne and cook, stirring, for 1 minute longer. Add the hot water, stirring to mix well.

3. Transfer the onion mixture to a large bowl. Add the apricots, almonds, rice, parsley, and lemon juice. Season to taste with salt and black pepper and mix well. Taste and adjust the seasonings, if needed.

4. Lightly pack the stuffing into the squash and place the squash inside the slow cooker. If cooking the squash whole, place the top back on the squash. Pour hot water into the slow cooker to come about ½ inch (1 cm) up the sides of the squash. Cover and cook on Low until the squash is tender, 6 to 7 hours. Serve hot.

Three Sisters Squash

SERVES 4 TO 6

SLOW COOKER SIZE: 6-QUART (5.7 L) | COOK TIME: 6 HOURS ON LOW | GLUTEN-FREE | OIL-FREE OPTION |
SOY-FREE

Large, orange-fleshed squash with dark green skin, such as kabocha or buttercup, are best for stuffing because they have a large cavity to hold more of the delicious ingredients. A 6-quart (5.7 L) oval slow cooker is the best size and shape to fit the squash halves inside. Otherwise, choose a squash that fits in your cooker whole and slice off the top few inches so you can scoop out the seeds and stuff it. If you like gravy on your stuffed squash, try the Mushroom Gravy on page 340.

1 large kabocha or buttercup squash
¼ cup (60 ml) water, or 2 teaspoons olive oil
1 medium-size yellow onion, minced
2 garlic cloves, minced
1 minced chipotle chile in adobo
1 teaspoon ground cumin
1 teaspoon ground coriander
1 teaspoon dried thyme
2 cups (400 g) cooked brown rice
1½ cups (258 g) cooked pinto beans (page 114)
  or 1 (15-ounce, or 425 g) can beans, rinsed and drained
1 cup (155 g) fresh or (165 g) frozen corn kernels, thawed
2 tablespoons (8 g) minced fresh flat-leaf parsley
Salt and freshly ground black pepper

1. If you can fit two squash halves in your slow cooker, cut the squash in half and scoop out the seeds. Use a sharp knife to make a flat bottom on the two halves so they sit evenly. If you can fit only the whole squash in your slow cooker, slice off the top of the squash and scrape out the seeds. Set aside.

2. Heat the water or oil in a medium-size skillet over medium-high heat. Add the onion and sauté until softened, about 5 minutes. Stir in the garlic, chipotle chile, cumin, coriander, and thyme and cook for 1 minute longer.

3. Transfer the onion mixture to a large bowl. Add the rice, beans, corn, parsley, and salt and black pepper to taste. Mix well, then taste and adjust the seasonings, if needed.

4. Lightly pack the stuffing into the squash and place the squash inside the slow cooker. If cooking the squash whole, place the top back on the squash. Pour hot water into the bottom of the slow cooker to come about ½ inch (1 cm) up the sides of the squash. Cover and cook on Low until the squash is tender, about 6 hours. Serve hot.

Great Scot Stuffed Squash

SLOW COOKER SIZE: 4- TO 6-QUART (3.8 TO 5.7 L) | COOK TIME: 4 HOURS ON LOW | GLUTEN-FREE |
OIL-FREE OPTION | SOY-FREE OPTION

In my previous slow cooker book, I included a groundbreaking recipe for vegan haggis wrapped in bean curd skin. I've since realized that there may be people disinclined to make a haggis recipe (vegan or not), so I wanted to use the delicious filling in a recipe that was more approachable. The result is a stuffed winter squash à la Robert Burns, so named because it was inspired by the traditional haggis that is served on January 25—Robert Burns's birthday. For gluten-free, be sure to use certified gluten-free oats; for soy-free, omit the soy sauce and use Soy-Free Sauce (page 344) or coconut aminos, or add some soy-free vegetable broth base or additional salt.

1 large kabocha or buttercup squash

¼ cup (60 ml) water, or 2 teaspoons olive oil

1 large yellow onion, minced

2 large carrots, peeled and finely shredded

4 ounces (115 g) white mushrooms, chopped

1¾ cups (420 ml) vegetable broth

¾ cup (117 g) old-fashioned rolled oats

1½ cups (384 g) cooked kidney beans (page 114)
   or 1 (15-ounce, or 425 g) can beans, rinsed and drained, coarsely mashed

⅔ cup (80 g) chopped walnuts

2 tablespoons (8 g) minced fresh flat-leaf parsley

2 tablespoons (30 ml) Scotch whisky

1½ tablespoons (23 ml) soy sauce

1½ teaspoons dried thyme

⅛ teaspoon ground nutmeg

⅛ teaspoon cayenne pepper

Salt and freshly ground black pepper

Mushroom Gravy (page 340), for serving

198   The Plant-Based Slow Cooker

1. If you can fit two squash halves in your slow cooker, cut the squash in half and scoop out the seeds. Use a sharp knife to make a flat bottom on the two halves so they sit evenly. If you can fit only the whole squash in your slow cooker, cut the top of the squash off and remove the seeds. Set aside.

2. Heat the water or oil in a large saucepan over medium-high heat. Add the onion and carrots and sauté for 5 minutes. Add the mushrooms and broth, then stir in the oats. Reduce the heat to a simmer and cook, stirring occasionally, for 10 minutes.

3. Stir the kidney beans into the oat mixture. Add the nuts, parsley, whisky, soy sauce, thyme, nutmeg, and cayenne and season to taste with salt and black pepper. Mix well to combine.

4. Lightly pack the stuffing mixture into the squash and place the squash inside the slow cooker. If cooking the squash whole, place the top back on the squash. Pour hot water into the bottom of the slow cooker to come about ½ inch (1 cm) up the sides of the squash. Cover and cook on Low until the squash is tender, about 4 hours.

5. A few minutes before serving time, heat the mushroom gravy. To serve, cut each squash half in half again (or cut the whole squash into quarters) and carefully serve each portion with the hot gravy.

NOTE: If your squash is on the smaller side, you may have some stuffing left over. It can be shaped into patties and sautéed in a skillet or spooned into an oiled baking dish, covered, and baked on its own.

Stuffed Zucchini Puttanesca

SERVES 4

SLOW COOKER SIZE: 6-QUART (5.7 L) | COOK TIME: 4 HOURS ON LOW | GLUTEN-FREE OPTION | OIL-FREE OPTION | SOY-FREE

As with most stuffed vegetable recipes, this one will need a large cooker (preferably oval) in order to accommodate the zucchini. It can be made heartier by adding 1½ cups (258 g) of your choice of cooked white beans or (165 g) cooked crumbled vegan sausage to the stuffing mixture, and using an additional zucchini to accommodate the extra stuffing. Use a gluten-free pasta to make this gluten-free.

2 large or 4 small zucchini
¼ cup (60 ml) water, or 2 teaspoons olive oil
6 garlic cloves, minced
3 ripe plum tomatoes, chopped
½ teaspoon red pepper flakes
Salt and freshly ground black pepper
⅓ cup (34 g) pitted green olives, chopped
⅓ cup (52 g) pitted kalamata olives, chopped
2 tablespoons (18 g) capers, drained
2 tablespoons (8 g) minced fresh flat-leaf parsley leaves
2 tablespoons (5 g) minced fresh basil leaves
1½ cups (210 g) cooked orzo or other tiny pasta
1 cup (250 g) marinara sauce

1. If using long zucchini, cut off the ends and cut the zucchini in half lengthwise. If using round zucchini, just cut off the top ½ inch (1 cm). Scoop out the zucchini flesh, leaving about ¼ inch (0.6 cm) of the flesh and the shells intact. Chop the scooped-out zucchini flesh. Slice off a tiny bit from the bottom of each zucchini if needed so they sit flat.

2. Heat the water or oil in a large skillet over medium heat. Add the garlic and chopped zucchini and sauté for 5 minutes, then remove from the heat. Stir in the tomatoes and red pepper flakes and season to taste with salt and black pepper. Stir in the green and black olives, capers, parsley, basil, and orzo. Mix well, then taste and adjust the seasonings, if needed.

3. Fill the zucchini shells with the stuffing mixture and place them in the slow cooker. Spoon the marinara sauce on top of the zucchini. Pour a little bit of hot water into the slow cooker just to cover the bottom of the insert and create steam. Cover and cook on Low until the zucchini is tender, about 4 hours.

Eggplant Stuffed with Red Beans and Bulgur

SERVES 4

SLOW COOKER SIZE: 6-QUART (5.7 L) | COOK TIME: 4 TO 5 HOURS ON LOW | OIL-FREE OPTION | SOY-FREE

A large oval slow cooker is best for this recipe to accommodate the eggplant. If your slow cooker is too small to accommodate both eggplant halves side by side, you can stack them crisscross. Bulgur, best known for its use in tabbouleh, is a quick-cooking grain made from wheat kernels that have been steamed, dried, and crushed.

1 large eggplant
¼ cup (60 ml) water, or 2 teaspoons olive oil
1 small onion, minced
½ small green bell pepper, seeded and minced
1 small celery rib, minced
4 garlic cloves, minced
1 jalapeño chile, seeded and minced
1 teaspoon dried thyme
Salt and freshly ground black pepper
1½ cups (384 g) cooked dark red kidney beans (page 114) or 1 (15-ounce, or 425 g) can beans, rinsed and drained
1 cup (182 g) cooked bulgur
1 chipotle chile in adobo, finely minced
1 (14.5-ounce, or 410 g) can crushed tomatoes
1 tablespoon (7.5 g) chili powder
1 teaspoon dried basil

1. Halve the eggplant lengthwise and scoop out the flesh, leaving ¼ to ⅓ inch (0.6 to 0.85 cm) of the flesh and the shells intact. Chop the scooped-out eggplant flesh.

(continued)

2. Heat the water or oil in a large skillet over medium-high heat. Add the onion, bell pepper, celery, garlic, jalapeño, thyme, and chopped eggplant. Season to taste with salt and black pepper and cook, stirring, for 5 minutes.

3. Transfer the onion mixture to a large bowl. Add the beans, bulgur, and chipotle chile, mix well, and season to taste with salt and black pepper. Fill the eggplant shells with the stuffing mixture and place them in the slow cooker, stacked crisscross if necessary.

4. In the same bowl, combine the tomatoes, chili powder, basil, and salt and black pepper to taste. Mix well, then pour the sauce on top of and around the eggplant. Cover and cook on Low until the eggplant shells are tender but still hold their shape, 4 to 5 hours. Serve hot.

Braciole-Inspired Stuffed Eggplant   SERVES 4 TO 6

SLOW COOKER SIZE: 4- TO 6-QUART (3.8 TO 5.7 L) | COOK TIME: 4 TO 6 HOURS ON LOW |
GLUTEN-FREE OPTION | OIL-FREE OPTION | SOY-FREE OPTION

Braciole is the name given to Italian beef roulades stuffed with a garlicky bread crumb mixture. In this recipe, that same flavorful crumb mixture is used to stuff eggplant. Be sure to choose an eggplant that will fit inside your slow cooker—a large oval slow cooker works best. If your slow cooker is too small to accommodate both eggplant halves side by side, just stack them crisscross. Use gluten-free bread crumbs to make this gluten-free and leave out the optional cheese to make it soy-free.

1 large eggplant
¼ cup (60 ml) water, or 2 teaspoons olive oil
5 garlic cloves, minced
6 ounces (170 g) white mushrooms, finely chopped
Salt and freshly ground black pepper
1 cup (115 g) dry bread crumbs
⅓ cup (20 g) nutritional yeast
⅓ cup (50 g) golden raisins
¼ cup (16 g) minced fresh flat-leaf parsley leaves
1 cup (250 g) marinara sauce
2 tablespoons (16.75 g) Almond Parmesan (page 341; optional)

4. Arrange the collard leaves on a flat surface. Cut off the thick part of the ribs near the base of the leaves so that the leaves will roll up easily. Place about ⅓ cup (weight varies) of the stuffing mixture near the stem end of each leaf. Beginning from the bottom of the leaf, roll it up around the stuffing, folding in the sides as you roll. Repeat the process until the stuffing and leaves are used up. Arrange the filled collard rolls in the slow cooker, seam-side down, stacking them if necessary. Pour the broth over the rolls. Cover and cook on Low until tender, 6 to 8 hours. If some of the rolls are not submerged in the broth, rotate them gently at some point during the cooking time, if possible. Serve hot, passing Cashew Sour Cream and Tabasco sauce at the table.

Corned Seitan and Cabbage Rolls   SERVES 4 TO 6

SLOW COOKER SIZE: 4- TO 6-QUART (3.8 TO 5.7 L) | COOK TIME: 6 TO 8 HOURS ON LOW | OIL-FREE OPTION | SOY-FREE

Liven up your next Saint Patrick's Day dinner with these cabbage rolls stuffed with a seitan mixture reminiscent of corned beef. They taste so good that you'll want to make them throughout the year.

1 large head green cabbage, cored
¼ cup (60 ml) water, or 2 teaspoons olive oil
1 medium-size yellow onion, minced
1 small carrot, peeled and grated
3 large Yukon Gold potatoes; 1 peeled and grated,
    2 peeled and cut into ½-inch (1 cm) dice
8 ounces (225 g) seitan (page 154), chopped
1 teaspoon ground coriander
¼ teaspoon ground allspice
Salt and freshly ground black pepper
3 tablespoons (33 g) brown mustard
¼ cup (60 ml) apple cider vinegar
2 tablespoons (25 g) granulated natural sugar
1½ teaspoons pickling spices
1 cup (240 ml) vegetable broth

(continued)

1. Steam the cabbage in a large covered pot with a steamer rack until the first few layers of leaves are softened, about 10 minutes. Remove from the pot and set aside to cool (keep the pot on the heat).

2. Heat the water or oil in a large skillet over medium-high heat. Add the onion and carrot and sauté for 5 minutes. Add the grated potato to the skillet and cook for 1 minute longer. Stir in the seitan and cook for 1 minute longer. Remove from the heat, and add the coriander, allspice, ½ teaspoon salt, and ¼ teaspoon black pepper. Stir in 1 teaspoon of the mustard and 1 teaspoon of the vinegar. Mix well to combine.

3. In a small bowl, combine the remaining mustard and vinegar with the sugar and pickling spices, stirring to blend. Slowly add the broth, stirring until smooth. Set aside.

4. Remove as many of the cabbage leaves as are soft and lay them out on a flat surface, rib-side down. Trim any thick ribs and the bottom end of the leaves. Place about ⅓ cup (weight varies) of the stuffing mixture in the center of each leaf. Roll up the leaf around the stuffing, folding in the sides as you roll. Repeat until the stuffing mixture is used up, steaming more cabbage leaves to soften if necessary.

5. Arrange the filled cabbage rolls in the slow cooker, seam-side down, stacking them if necessary. Arrange the diced potatoes around the rolls in the cooker. Pour the broth mixture over the rolls and potatoes and season to taste with salt and black pepper. Cover and cook on Low until tender, 6 to 8 hours.

Seitan Roulade

SLOW COOKER SIZE: 6-QUART (5.7 L) | COOK TIME: 6 TO 8 HOURS ON LOW | OIL-FREE OPTION

This delicious roast makes enough to serve a crowd and is especially good with mashed potatoes and roasted vegetables. It makes an ideal main dish for holiday dinners. Serve with the Mushroom Gravy (page 340) or your favorite brown gravy or sauce. If you prefer not to use wine in the seitan mixture, just use additional water or broth.

STUFFING

¼ cup (60 ml) water, or 2 teaspoons olive oil

3 shallots, minced

3 garlic cloves, minced

2 cups (140 g) finely minced cremini mushrooms

1 teaspoon fresh thyme, or ½ teaspoon dried thyme

1 teaspoon fresh minced sage, or ½ teaspoon dried crumbled sage

1 (10-ounce, or 280 g) package frozen chopped spinach, thawed and squeezed dry

1 jarred roasted red bell pepper, seeded and minced

Salt and freshly ground black pepper

2 Plant-Based Sausage Links (page 174), coarsely chopped (optional)

SEITAN

2 cups (240 g) vital wheat gluten

2 tablespoons (15 g) chickpea flour

2 tablespoons (15 g) tapioca flour

1 teaspoon onion powder

1 teaspoon dried thyme

½ teaspoon ground sage

½ teaspoon salt

¼ teaspoon freshly ground black pepper

3 tablespoons (45 ml) dry red wine or vegetable broth

2 tablespoons (30 ml) soy sauce

1¼ cups (300 ml) water or vegetable broth, plus more as needed

(continued)

1. To make the stuffing: Heat the water or oil in a large skillet over medium-high heat. Add the shallots and sauté for 3 minutes. Stir in the garlic, mushrooms, thyme, and sage and cook for 2 minutes longer. Add the spinach and bell pepper and season to taste with salt and pepper. Cook for 2 minutes longer. Remove from the heat. Stir in the sausage (if using) and mix well. Taste and the adjust seasonings, if needed. Set aside.

2. To make the seitan: In a bowl, combine the vital wheat gluten, chickpea flour, tapioca flour, onion powder, thyme, sage, salt, and pepper. Stir in the wine, soy sauce, and water and mix well to combine, adding up to ¼ cup (60 ml) more water if the mixture is too dry. You should end up with a soft dough. Knead the dough for a few minutes with your hands, then roll out the seitan on a work surface between two sheets of parchment paper, aluminum foil, or plastic wrap into a 9 x 12-inch (30 cm) rectangle.

3. Transfer the seitan to a large sheet of aluminum foil. Spread the reserved stuffing evenly on top of the seitan, leaving about a 1-inch (2.5 cm) border all the way around. Beginning at the shorter side, carefully roll up the seitan to enclose the filling. Place the rolled seitan, seam-side down, in the center of the foil and close up the foil around the roulade to enclose it.

4. Place the foil-wrapped roulade in the slow cooker, seam-side up. Pour hot water into the slow cooker to come about ½ inch (1 cm) up the sides of the roulade. Cover and cook on Low until firm, 6 to 8 hours.

5. Carefully remove the roulade from the slow cooker and open the foil. Let stand for 10 minutes before slicing. Use a serrated knife to cut the roulade into ½-inch (1 cm)-thick slices. Serve hot.

Vegetable Love

While a slow cooker may not be ideal for cooking delicate produce, it's a great way to prepare sturdier vegetables such as potatoes, carrots, parsnips, beets, and winter squash, as well as celery, tomatoes, cabbage, and onions. Slow cooking allows the flavor of the vegetables to intensify without drying out or dissipating their natural juices. This chapter includes a variety of slow-simmered vegetable dishes such as Classic Ratatouille, Citrus-Braised Beets, and Italian-Style Tomatoes and Zucchini.

The slow cooker can also be used to slow-steam or "bake" vegetables such as corn, artichokes, and potatoes—a boon during the hot summer months when you don't want to heat up the kitchen.

Some of these recipes, like Potatoes with Tomatoes and Butter Beans, can be enjoyed as main dishes, while others, like the Sweet and Sour Cabbage, make ideal side dishes.

Spice-Rubbed Whole Cauliflower

SERVES 4

SLOW COOKER SIZE: 4- TO 6-QUART (3.8 TO 5.7 L) | COOK TIME: 5 HOURS ON LOW | GLUTEN-FREE |
OIL-FREE OPTION | SOY-FREE

A whole cooked cauliflower tastes as good as it looks. You can change up the spice rub according to your whim (it's great with curry seasonings), or you can top it with a sauce such as a vegan cheese sauce or hollandaise. Be careful transferring it from slow cooker to platter—I like to use two wide metal spatulas to get the job done. To make this oil-free, use water instead of oil.

1 large whole cauliflower
2 tablespoons (7.5 g) nutritional yeast
½ teaspoon garlic powder
½ teaspoon onion powder
½ teaspoon dried basil
½ teaspoon salt
½ teaspoon ground turmeric
¼ teaspoon freshly ground black pepper
2 tablespoons (30 ml) olive oil or water
1 tablespoon (15 ml) fresh lemon juice
2 tablespoons (8 g) finely chopped fresh parsley

1. Remove the leaves and stem from the cauliflower. Place the whole cauliflower in a large slow cooker. Pour about ½ inch (1 cm) of water into the slow cooker around the cauliflower.

2. In a small bowl, combine the nutritional yeast, garlic powder, onion powder, basil, salt, turmeric, and pepper. Mix well.

3. In a separate small bowl, mix together the olive oil and lemon juice. Pour the oil mixture on top of the cauliflower and use your fingers to rub the liquid into the surface of the cauliflower. Sprinkle the cauliflower evenly with the spice mixture and rub the spices into the surface of the cauliflower.

4. Cover and cook on Low for 5 hours, or until the cauliflower is tender when pierced. Carefully remove the cauliflower from the slow cooker and place it on a platter. Sprinkle the cauliflower with the parsley. Slice the cauliflower to serve.

Cabbage Steaks with Barley and Tomatoes

SERVES 4

SLOW COOKER SIZE: 4- TO 6-QUART (3.8 TO 5.7 L) | COOK TIME: 6 TO 8 HOURS ON LOW | SOY-FREE | OIL-FREE

This rustic dish is like a deconstructed version of the Eastern European cabbage rolls known as *halupki*. If your cabbage is large, cut it in half (through the core) and place one half of the cabbage, cut-side down, onto a cutting board and cut your cabbage steaks from that half.

1 cup (200 g) raw pearl barley
3½ cups (840 ml) vegetable broth
¼ cup (64 g) tomato paste
1 cup (160 g) chopped onion
1 cup (100 g) sliced celery
1 cup (75 g) thinly sliced carrot
3 garlic cloves, minced
2 bay leaves
1 teaspoon dried thyme
1 teaspoon salt, plus more for seasoning
½ teaspoon freshly ground black pepper, plus more for seasoning
1 small head cabbage, stem end sliced off
1 (14-ounce, or 395 g) can fire-roasted diced tomatoes, undrained

1. Combine the barley and broth in a slow cooker. Stir in the tomato paste, onion, celery, carrot, garlic, bay leaves, thyme, salt, and pepper.

2. Place the cabbage on a cutting board, stem-end side down. Cut four ½-inch (1 cm) slices ("steaks") from the cabbage and arrange them on top of the barley mixture, reserving the remaining cabbage for another use.

3. Pour the tomatoes and their juices on top of the cabbage and season with salt and black pepper to taste.

4. Cover and cook on Low for 6 to 8 hours, or until the barley and cabbage are tender.

Portobello Pot Roast

SLOW COOKER SIZE: 4- TO 6-QUART (3.8 TO 5.7 L) | COOK TIME: 6 TO 8 HOURS ON LOW | GLUTEN-FREE | OIL-FREE | SOY-FREE OPTION

I like to cook the portobello caps whole and then slice them when ready to serve, but you can slice them before cooking, if you prefer. To make this soy-free, use coconut aminos instead of tamari.

1 red onion, diced
3 carrots, cut into ¼-inch (0.6 cm)-thick slices
1 celery rib, sliced
3 garlic cloves, minced
4 portobello mushroom caps
1½ pounds (680 g) baby red or yellow potatoes
1 teaspoon dried thyme
½ teaspoon dried marjoram or savory
½ teaspoon ground sage
3 tablespoons (48 g) tomato paste
2 tablespoons (30 ml) tamari or liquid aminos
⅓ cup (80 ml) dry red or white wine (optional)
2 cups (480 ml) vegetable broth
Salt and freshly ground black pepper

1. Spread the onion, carrots, celery, and garlic in the bottom of a slow cooker. Place the mushroom caps on top, cut-side down. Add the potatoes, thyme, marjoram, and sage.

2. In a small bowl, combine the tomato paste, tamari, and wine (if using), stirring to blend. Add the blended liquid to the slow cooker, then add the broth and season with salt and black pepper to taste.

3. Cover and cook on Low for 6 to 8 hours, or until the vegetables are tender. Serve hot.

Indian Eggplant Curry

SLOW COOKER SIZE: 4- TO 6-QUART (3.8 TO 5.7 L) | COOK TIME: 6 TO 8 HOURS ON LOW | GLUTEN-FREE | OIL-FREE | SOY-FREE

The slow cooker is ideal for making this flavorful eggplant dish because it allows the eggplant to soften and mingle with the other ingredients with no worries about scorching the pan.

1 medium-size yellow onion, chopped
3 garlic cloves, minced
1 jalapeño chile, seeded and minced
1 tablespoon (8 g) grated peeled fresh ginger
1 large or 2 medium-size eggplants, chopped
1 (14-ounce, or 395 g) can petite diced tomatoes, undrained
½ cup (120 ml) water
1 teaspoon garam masala
1 teaspoon ground coriander
½ teaspoon ground cumin
½ teaspoon ground turmeric
Salt
Cayenne pepper, to taste (optional)
½ cup (65 g) frozen green peas
Cooked brown basmati rice, for serving

1. Combine the onion, garlic, chile, and ginger in the slow cooker.

2. Add the eggplant, tomatoes, and water; then stir in the garam masala, coriander, cumin, turmeric, and salt to taste.

3. Cover and cook on Low for 6 to 8 hours.

4. About 30 minutes before serving, taste and adjust the seasoning, adding more salt, if needed, and adding cayenne (if using; if more heat is desired). Stir in the green peas. Serve hot over rice.

Slow-Steamed Artichokes

SLOW COOKER SIZE: 4- TO 6-QUART (3.8 TO 5.7 L) | COOK TIME: 6 TO 8 HOURS ON LOW | GLUTEN-FREE | OIL-FREE | SOY-FREE

Four small to medium-size artichokes (or six baby artichokes) will fit in a 4-quart (3.8 L) slow cooker. For larger artichokes (or more of them), you will need to use a larger cooker.

4 artichokes
3 cups (720 ml) hot water
Juice of 1 lemon

1. Slice off the stem end of each artichoke so that they sit upright. Use a serrated knife to cut off about 1 inch (2.5 cm) from the top of each artichoke and, with scissors, snip off the sharp tips from the leaves. Stand the artichokes upright in the slow cooker.

2. Pour the water into the bottom of the cooker, and drizzle the lemon juice over the tops of the artichokes. Cover and cook on Low until the artichokes are tender, 6 to 8 hours. Serve hot or at room temperature.

Citrus-Braised Beets

SLOW COOKER SIZE: 4- TO 6-QUART (3.8 TO 5.7 L) | COOK TIME: 6 TO 8 HOURS ON LOW | GLUTEN-FREE | OIL-FREE OPTION | SOY-FREE

Orange marmalade and lemon and lime juice combine to infuse the beets with citrus sweetness. For a shortcut, use purchased orange marmalade. Use the smallest beets you can find for the best flavor. The size of the beets will dictate the length of cooking time needed.

3 tablespoons (60 g) Orange Marmalade with a Twist of Lemon (page 258)
Juice of 1 lemon
Juice of 1 lime
2 teaspoons olive oil or water
8 to 10 small beets, trimmed and halved, or 4 large beets, trimmed and quartered
Salt and freshly ground black pepper

(continued)

1. In a small bowl, combine the marmalade, lemon juice, and lime juice. Add the oil or water, stirring to blend.

2. Place the beets in the slow cooker and add the citrus mixture, stirring to coat. Season to taste with salt and black pepper. Cover and cook on Low until the beets are tender, 6 to 8 hours, stirring once halfway through, if possible.

3. Before serving, remove the beet peels (they should slip off easily) and discard. Transfer the beets to a serving bowl. Pour the citrus mixture over the beets and serve.

Braised Brussels Sprouts and Chestnuts

SERVES 4

SLOW COOKER SIZE: 4-QUART (3.8 L) | COOK TIME: 4 HOURS ON LOW | GLUTEN-FREE | OIL-FREE | SOY-FREE

Brussels sprouts and chestnuts have a natural flavor affinity—and, conveniently, they're about the same shape and size, too. Seasoned with a sweet and sour braising liquid, the combination makes a flavorful autumn side dish. If you are using the optional vegan bacon, check to see that it's gluten-free or soy-free if necessary.

3 shallots, thinly sliced lengthwise
1½ pounds (680 g) Brussels sprouts, trimmed and halved lengthwise, if large
3 tablespoons (45 ml) vegetable broth
2 tablespoons (40 g) pure maple syrup
1 tablespoon (15 ml) apple cider vinegar
Salt and freshly ground black pepper
1 cup (145 g) roasted shelled chestnuts (page 194)
3 slices Tempeh Bacon (page 342), cooked and chopped (optional)

1. In the slow cooker, combine the shallots, Brussels sprouts, broth, maple syrup, vinegar, and salt and pepper to taste. Cover and cook on Low until the Brussels sprouts are tender, 3½ to 4 hours.

2. About 20 minutes before the end of the cooking time, stir in the chestnuts. Just before serving, stir in the bacon (if using). Serve hot.

Sweet and Sour Cabbage

SERVES 6

SLOW COOKER SIZE: 4- TO 6-QUART (3.8 TO 5.7 L) | COOK TIME: 4 TO 6 HOURS ON LOW |
GLUTEN-FREE OPTION | SOY-FREE

The slow-cooked flavor of this cabbage makes it an ideal side dish for a cold-weather supper. Turn it into an entrée by browning plant-based sausage links in a skillet and adding them to the cabbage when ready to serve. Use gluten-free flour to make this dish gluten-free.

2 teaspoons olive oil

1 yellow onion, minced

½ teaspoon caraway seeds

2 tablespoons (15.5 g) unbleached all-purpose flour

¼ cup (60 ml) water

3 tablespoons (45 ml) apple cider vinegar

3 tablespoons (37.5 g) granulated natural sugar

1 (2-pound, or 910 g) head green cabbage, cored and shredded

Salt and freshly ground black pepper

1. Heat the oil in a small skillet over medium-high heat. Add the onion and sauté for 5 minutes to soften. Add the caraway seeds and flour and cook, stirring, for 1 minute. Add the water, stirring until smooth.

2. Transfer the onion mixture to the slow cooker and stir in the vinegar and sugar. Add the cabbage and season to taste with salt and black pepper. Stir to combine. Cover and cook on Low until the cabbage is tender, 4 to 6 hours.

3. Taste to adjust the seasonings, if needed. Serve hot.

Sicilian-Style Cauliflower

SLOW COOKER SIZE: 4- TO 6-QUART (3.8 TO 5.7 L) | COOK TIME: 3 HOURS ON LOW | GLUTEN-FREE |
OIL-FREE OPTION | SOY-FREE

This flavorful side dish can also be enjoyed as a topping for pasta. To do so, either mash some of the cauliflower to make it "saucier" or stir in 1 tablespoon (16 g) of tomato paste to thicken the broth, then season to taste. A few shakes of red pepper flakes are a good addition as well.

¼ cup (60 ml) water, or 2 teaspoons olive oil
1 medium-size yellow onion, minced
3 garlic cloves, minced
1 large head cauliflower, trimmed, cored, and cut into small florets
1 (14.5-ounce, or 410 g) can diced tomatoes, drained
⅓ cup (50 g) golden raisins
1 tablespoon (9 g) capers, drained
⅓ cup (80 ml) white wine or vegetable broth
Salt and freshly ground black pepper
3 tablespoons (25.5 g) toasted pine nuts, for garnish
2 tablespoons (8 g) minced fresh flat-leaf parsley or basil, for garnish

1. Heat the water or oil in a medium-size skillet over medium-high heat. Add the onion and sauté until softened, about 5 minutes. Add the garlic and cook for 1 minute longer.

2. Transfer the onion mixture to the slow cooker. Add the cauliflower, tomatoes, raisins, capers, wine, and salt and black pepper to taste. Cover and cook on Low until the cauliflower is tender, about 3 hours.

3. Serve hot, sprinkled with the pine nuts and parsley.

Braised Collards with "Pot Likker"

SERVES 4

SLOW COOKER SIZE: 4-QUART (3.8 L) | COOK TIME: 4 TO 6 HOURS ON LOW | GLUTEN-FREE | OIL-FREE OPTION | SOY-FREE

I discovered the wonder of collard greens after moving down South in the early 1980s. Typically, collards are cooked for hours on top of the stove to make them tender and flavorful. A slow cooker does an even better job of cooking the greens, since you don't have to watch the pot, and there's no danger of cooking off all that delicious braising liquid known as "pot likker" (or "liquor"). Be sure to wash the collards well before using to remove any sand. A touch of liquid smoke, vinegar, and red pepper flakes add a nice depth of flavor to the collards. For a hearty meal, stir in cooked black-eyed peas and serve over rice, passing Tabasco sauce and Cashew Sour Cream (page 338) at the table.

1½ pounds (680 g) collard greens, trimmed of thick stems
¼ cup (60 ml) water, or 2 teaspoons olive oil
1 small yellow onion, chopped
3 large garlic cloves, minced
¼ teaspoon red pepper flakes
Salt and freshly ground black pepper
1 cup (240 ml) vegetable broth
1 tablespoon (15 ml) apple cider vinegar
1 teaspoon liquid smoke

1. Stack a few of the collard leaves at a time and roll them up tightly. Cut the rolls crosswise into thin strips. Repeat until all the collards are cut. You should end up with 8 to 10 cups (weight varies). Set aside.

2. Heat the water or oil in a small skillet over medium-high heat. Add the onion and sauté until softened, about 5 minutes. Stir in the garlic and cook for 1 minute longer.

3. Transfer the onion mixture to the slow cooker. Add the reserved collards, then sprinkle with the red pepper flakes and salt and black pepper to taste. Pour in the broth. Cover and cook on Low until the collards are tender, 4 to 6 hours.

4. Just before serving, stir in the vinegar and liquid smoke. Taste and adjust the seasonings, if needed.

Creamy Creamed Corn

SERVES 6 TO 8

SLOW COOKER SIZE: 4-QUART (3.8 L) | COOK TIME: 3 HOURS ON LOW | GLUTEN-FREE | OIL-FREE OPTION | SOY-FREE

Yes, canned "creamed" corn is vegan—there is no cream in it, despite the name. This rich, comforting side dish is great as is or, for extra zing, add some minced canned green chilies or chipotles in adobo. To make this recipe soy-free, use a soy-free plant milk.

¼ cup (60 ml) water, or 2 teaspoons avocado oil or vegan butter

1 medium-size yellow onion, minced

2 pounds (910 g) fresh or frozen corn kernels, thawed

1 (16-ounce, or 455 g) can creamed corn

Salt and freshly ground black pepper

½ cup (87.5 g) Cashew Cream Cheese (page 339), at room temperature

1 tablespoon (8 g) cornstarch or tapioca starch

1 cup (240 ml) plain unsweetened plant milk

1. Heat the water or oil in a small skillet over medium-high heat. Add the onion and sauté until softened, about 5 minutes. Alternatively, place the onion in a microwave-safe bowl with 2 tablespoons (30 ml) of water, cover, and microwave for 2 minutes to soften.

2. Transfer the onion to the cooker. Add the corn kernels and the creamed corn. Season to taste with salt and black pepper.

3. In a bowl, combine the cream cheese, cornstarch, and plant milk, stirring until smooth and well blended. Transfer the mixture to the slow cooker, stirring to combine. Cover and cook on Low for 3 hours.

4. Taste and adjust the seasonings, if needed. Use an immersion blender to blend a portion of the corn right in the slow cooker to thicken, or scoop out 2 to 3 cups (300 to 450 g) of corn and puree in a blender or food processer, then stir the puree back into the slow cooker. Serve hot.

Surprise Package Corn on the Cob

SERVES 4

SLOW COOKER SIZE: 6-QUART (5.7 L) | COOK TIME: 2 TO 4 HOURS ON LOW | GLUTEN-FREE |
OIL-FREE OPTION | SOY-FREE

Because corn on the cob is usually in season in the heat of summer, slow cooking can come in handy when you don't want to heat up the kitchen to cook your corn. You can either wrap the shucked corn in foil or leave the green husks on and place fresh herbs inside, allowing the flavor of the herbs to infuse the corn while it gently cooks. You can also omit the herbs if you prefer plain corn on the cob.

8 ears corn

8 to 16 sprigs thyme, rosemary, basil, or other fresh herbs or softened vegan
butter blended with your choice of minced chipotle chile, lime juice,
or your favorite spice blend

1 cup (240 ml) hot water

1. Set the ears of corn inside the slow cooker to make sure they fit. If using a shallow oval cooker, lay the corn on its side. If using a tall round cooker, stand the corn upright. Trim the ends or break the ears in half if necessary.

2. If using foil, shuck the corn. Tear off 8 sheets of aluminum foil (just large enough to fit an ear of corn inside) and place an ear of corn on each sheet. Divide the fresh herbs and/or other seasonings among the 8 ears of corn (you can use as many or as few different herbs and seasonings as you wish). Wrap each ear of corn tightly in its foil package to enclose the herbs or other seasonings with the corn. Alternatively, if cooking the corn in the husk, pull back the husk, remove the corn silk, place the herbs or seasonings on the corn, then pull the husk back up to enclose the herbs with the corn.

3. Place the corn in the slow cooker. Add the hot water, cover, and cook on Low until the corn is tender, 2 to 4 hours. Serve hot.

Lemony Edamame and Potatoes with Chard

SERVES 4

SLOW COOKER SIZE: 4- TO 6-QUART (3.8 TO 5.7 L) | COOK TIME: 6 HOURS ON LOW | GLUTEN-FREE |
OIL-FREE OPTION | SOY-FREE OPTION

I make it a point to use up whatever food is in the house before going to the supermarket. One time, these ingredients included some potatoes, frozen edamame, and a lone lemon, and the result was this light and lovely stew. This makes a hearty side dish as is. To transform it into a more substantial dish, add some sautéed seitan strips or baked diced tempeh. For a soy-free version, substitute lima beans for the edamame. Cooked cannellini beans also work well in this dish.

¼ cup (60 ml) water, or 2 teaspoons olive oil

1 large yellow onion, chopped

3 garlic cloves, minced

1 teaspoon dried oregano

½ cup (120 ml) dry white wine

2 bay leaves

1½ pounds (680 g) small white or red-skinned potatoes, scrubbed and halved or quartered if larger than 1 inch (2.5 cm)

3 cups (465 g) fresh or frozen shelled edamame, thawed

½ cup (120 ml) vegetable broth

1 teaspoon salt

¼ teaspoon freshly ground black pepper

2 tablespoons (30 ml) fresh lemon juice

8 ounces (225 g) fresh Swiss chard, stemmed and coarsely chopped

¼ teaspoon red pepper flakes (optional)

3 tablespoons (12 g) minced fresh flat-leaf parsley, for garnish

1 lemon, cut into wedges, for serving

1. Heat the water or oil in a medium-size skillet over medium-high heat. Add the onion and sauté until softened, about 5 minutes. Alternatively, place the onion in a microwave-safe bowl with 2 tablespoons (30 ml) of water, cover, and microwave for 2 minutes to soften. Stir in the garlic, oregano, and wine.

2. Transfer the onion mixture to the slow cooker. Add the bay leaves, potatoes, edamame, and broth. Add the salt and black pepper. Cover and cook on Low until the vegetables are tender, about 5 hours.

3. Stir in the lemon juice, then taste and adjust the seasonings, if needed.

4. Place the chard in a large bowl, cover with plastic wrap, and microwave for 2 to 3 minutes to wilt. Stir the chard and red pepper flakes (if using), into the slow cooker to combine. Sprinkle with the parsley and serve hot with the lemon wedges on the side.

Moroccan Eggplant and Artichokes   SERVES 6

SLOW COOKER SIZE: 4- TO 6-QUART (3.8 TO 5.7 L) | COOK TIME: 4 TO 5 HOURS ON LOW | GLUTEN-FREE |
OIL-FREE OPTION | SOY-FREE

This flavorful dish is ideal served over couscous. It will serve 6 as a side dish or 4 as a main dish. If using as a main dish, consider adding 1½ to 2 cups (247.5 to 330 g) cooked chickpeas to the mixture for added protein.

¼ cup (60 ml) water, or 2 teaspoons olive oil
1 medium-size yellow onion, minced
4 garlic cloves, minced
1½ teaspoons grated peeled fresh ginger
1 large eggplant, peeled and cut into ½-inch (1 cm) dice
Salt and freshly ground black pepper
1½ teaspoons ground coriander
1 teaspoon sweet paprika
½ teaspoon ground cumin
¼ teaspoon ground cinnamon
¼ teaspoon ground allspice or cardamom
¼ teaspoon cayenne pepper (optional)

(continued)

1½ cups (172.5 g) frozen artichoke hearts, thawed,
   or 1 (14-ounce, or 395 g) can artichoke hearts, drained and halved
1 large red bell pepper, seeded and cut into ½-inch (1 cm) dice
½ cup (77.5 g) pitted and halved kalamata olives
½ cup (75 g) golden raisins or chopped dried apricots
½ cup (120 ml) vegetable broth
1 tablespoon (15 ml) fresh lemon juice
¼ cup (16 g) chopped fresh flat-leaf parsley or (4 g) cilantro, for garnish
1 teaspoon grated lemon zest, for garnish

1. Heat the water or oil in a large skillet over medium-high heat. Add the onion and sauté until softened, about 5 minutes. Add the garlic and ginger and cook until fragrant, 1 minute longer. Add the eggplant and season to taste with salt and pepper. Cook, stirring, for 5 minutes, adding a little more water if needed to keep it from scorching. Sprinkle on the coriander, paprika, cumin, cinnamon, allspice, and cayenne (if using), and stir to combine.

2. Transfer the onion mixture to the slow cooker. Add the artichokes, bell pepper, olives, and raisins. Stir in the broth and season to taste with salt and black pepper. Cover and cook on Low until the vegetables are tender, 4 to 5 hours.

3. Taste and adjust the seasonings, if needed. Serve hot, sprinkled with the lemon juice, parsley, and lemon zest.

Classic Ratatouille

SERVES 6

SLOW COOKER SIZE: 4- TO 6-QUART (3.8 TO 5.7 L) | COOK TIME: 4 TO 5 HOURS ON LOW | GLUTEN-FREE | OIL-FREE OPTION | SOY-FREE

Slow cooking brings out the flavors of the vegetables in this consummate summer vegetable mélange inspired by the classic Provençal dish. If you have a lot of fresh tomatoes on hand, you can use them in this recipe; otherwise, canned tomatoes will do nicely. Ratatouille can be enjoyed as a main dish when you add cooked white beans and serve it over cooked grains, polenta, or pasta. It's also a wonderful side dish or can be enjoyed as a bruschetta topping— hot, warm, or cold.

¼ cup (60 ml) water, or 2 teaspoons olive oil
1 medium-size yellow onion, chopped
3 garlic cloves, minced
½ teaspoon dried marjoram
½ teaspoon dried basil
1 large eggplant, peeled and cut into ½-inch (1 cm) dice
4 small zucchini, cut into ½-inch (1 cm) dice
1 bell pepper (any color), seeded and cut into ½-inch (1 cm) dice
6 ripe red tomatoes, peeled and diced, or 1 (28-ounce, or 794 g)
    can diced tomatoes, drained
Salt and freshly ground black pepper
¼ cup (10 g) chopped fresh basil or (16 g) flat-leaf parsley

1. Heat the water or oil in a medium-size skillet over medium-high heat. Add the onion and sauté until softened, about 5 minutes. Alternatively, place the onion in a microwave-safe bowl with 2 tablespoons (30 ml) of water, cover, and microwave for 2 minutes to soften. Stir in the garlic, marjoram, and dried basil.

2. Transfer the onion mixture to the slow cooker. Add the eggplant, zucchini, bell pepper, and tomatoes. Season to taste with salt and black pepper. Cover and cook on Low until the vegetables are tender, 4 to 5 hours.

3. Just before serving, stir in the fresh basil. Taste and adjust the seasonings, if needed.

VARIATION

Golden Ratatouille: Use a yellow bell pepper, substitute yellow summer squash for the zucchini, and substitute fresh yellow tomatoes (peeled and diced) for the red tomatoes. For a vibrant garnish, sprinkle with sliced pitted kalamata olives.

Country French Green Beans and Tomatoes

SERVES 4

SLOW COOKER SIZE: 4- TO 6-QUART (3.8 TO 5.7 L) | COOK TIME: 4 TO 5 HOURS ON LOW | GLUTEN-FREE | OIL-FREE | SOY-FREE

These green beans simmered in a fragrant mixture of tomatoes, onions, and garlic are delicious as a side dish or as a topping for pasta, rice, or baked potatoes.

¼ cup (60 ml) water, or 2 teaspoons olive oil
4 garlic cloves, minced
1 pound (455 g) green beans, trimmed and cut into 1-inch (2.5 cm) pieces
4 or 5 ripe plum tomatoes, chopped, or 1 (14.5-ounce, or 410 g) can diced tomatoes, drained
Salt and freshly ground black pepper
2 tablespoons (5 g) minced fresh basil

1. In the slow cooker, combine the water, garlic, green beans, and tomatoes. Season to taste with salt and pepper, and stir to combine.

2. Cover and cook on Low until the beans are tender, 4 to 5 hours. Sprinkle with the basil when ready to serve.

Braised Manchurian-Style Cauliflower SERVES 6

SLOW COOKER SIZE: 4-QUART (3.8 L) | COOK TIME: 4 TO 5 HOURS ON LOW | GLUTEN-FREE | OIL-FREE OPTION | SOY-FREE OPTION

Now you can enjoy the amazing flavor of the popular Indian appetizer Gobi Manchurian in one easy step. Best of all, it's braised, not fried. If you miss that crunch from the fried version, sprinkle it with the optional crushed peanuts. To make this recipe soy-free, omit the soy sauce and use Soy-Free Sauce (page 344) or coconut aminos, or add some soy-free vegetable broth base or additional salt.

¼ cup (60 ml) water, or 2 teaspoons avocado oil
1 small yellow onion, chopped
4 garlic cloves, minced
1 teaspoon grated peeled fresh ginger
1 teaspoon ground coriander
½ teaspoon cayenne pepper
½ cup (120 g) ketchup
1 tablespoon (7.5 g) tapioca starch or cornstarch
½ cup (120 ml) vegetable broth
2 tablespoons (30 ml) soy sauce
2 teaspoons rice vinegar
¼ teaspoon red pepper flakes
Salt
1 head cauliflower, trimmed, cored, and cut into small florets
¼ cup (40 g) minced scallions, for garnish
¼ cup (4 g) minced fresh cilantro, for garnish
3 tablespoons (27 g) crushed dry-roasted peanuts (for garnish; optional)

1. Heat the water or oil in a small skillet over medium-high heat. Add the onion and sauté until softened, about 5 minutes. Add the garlic and ginger and cook for 1 minute longer. Add the coriander and ¼ teaspoon of cayenne, stirring to coat the vegetables. Alternatively, combine the onion and garlic in a microwave-safe bowl with 2 tablespoons (30 ml) of water, cover, and microwave for 2 minutes to soften, then stir in the ginger, coriander, and ¼ teaspoon of cayenne.

2. In a small bowl, combine the remaining ¼ teaspoon of cayenne, ketchup, tapioca, broth, soy sauce, 1 teaspoon of vinegar, and the red pepper flakes, stirring to blend, then stir it into the onion mixture. Season to taste with salt.

3. Place the cauliflower in the cooker and pour the sauce over and around the cauliflower. Cover and cook on Low until the cauliflower is tender, 4 to 5 hours. Gently stir in the remaining 1 teaspoon of vinegar about 1 hour before the cauliflower is done, if possible.

4. Taste and add more salt, if needed. Serve hot, garnished with a sprinkling of scallions and cilantro, and the peanuts (if using).

Green Bean Casserole Revisited

SERVES 4 TO 6

SLOW COOKER SIZE: 4- TO 6-QUART (3.8 TO 5.7 L) | COOK TIME: 4 TO 5 HOURS ON LOW | GLUTEN-FREE | OIL-FREE OPTION | SOY-FREE

The sauce, made with cashew cream cheese, is very rich and can be made with white beans or tofu if you prefer. I like to top the casserole with toasted ground almonds, but you can use canned fried onions as a nod to the traditional recipe, if you prefer.

¼ cup (60 ml) water, or 2 teaspoons olive oil

1 small yellow onion, chopped

2 garlic cloves, minced

1 cup (175 g) Cashew Cream Cheese (page 339)

¾ cup (180 ml) vegetable broth

½ teaspoon salt, plus more as needed

¼ teaspoon freshly ground black pepper

1½ pounds (680 g) green beans, trimmed and cut into 1-inch (2.5 cm) pieces

8 ounces (225 g) white mushrooms, sliced

½ cup (47.5 g) coarsely ground almonds, toasted

1. Heat the water or oil in a small skillet over medium-high heat. Add the onion and sauté until softened, about 5 minutes. Add the garlic and cook for 1 minute longer. Alternatively, combine the onion and garlic in a microwave-safe bowl with 2 tablespoons (30 ml) of water, cover, and microwave for 2 minutes to soften.

2. Transfer the onion mixture to a blender or food processor. Add the cream cheese, broth, salt, and pepper and process until smooth. Taste and adjust the seasonings—you may need to add more salt depending on the saltiness of your broth.

3. Combine the green beans and mushrooms in the cooker and pour the sauce over them, making sure the vegetables are covered with the sauce. Cover and cook on Low until the green beans are tender, 4 to 5 hours.

4. When ready to serve, sprinkle the almonds on top.

Colcannon

SLOW COOKER SIZE: 4- TO 6-QUART (3.8 TO 5.7 L) | COOK TIME: 4 TO 5 HOURS ON LOW | GLUTEN-FREE | SOY-FREE OPTION

Making colcannon in the slow cooker is especially convenient for a St. Patrick's Day party because you can make and serve it in the same (crock)pot. Of course, you don't need to wait until March 17 to enjoy this delicious combo of potatoes and kale. Instead of kale, you may substitute chard, spinach, or even cabbage. Use a soy-free vegan butter or olive oil to make this recipe soy-free.

2 pounds (910 g) Yukon Gold or russet potatoes,
    peeled and cut into 1-inch (2.5 cm) chunks (about 6 cups)
½ cup (120 ml) vegetable broth
Salt
8 ounces (225 g) kale, stemmed and finely chopped
2 tablespoons (28 g) vegan butter or (30 ml) olive oil
½ cup (120 ml) plain unsweetened plant milk, warmed
Freshly ground black pepper

1. Coat the insert of the slow cooker with nonstick cooking spray. Add the potatoes, broth, and ¾ to 1 teaspoon salt (depending on the saltiness of your broth). Cover and cook on Low until the potatoes are soft, 4 to 5 hours.

2. While the potatoes are cooking, steam the kale over boiling water on the stovetop until tender, 5 to 7 minutes. Set aside.

3. Use a potato masher to mash the potatoes right in the cooker. Use a wooden spoon to stir in the reserved kale, vegan butter, warm plant milk, and pepper to taste. Taste and adjust the seasonings, if needed. Serve hot.

Slow-Baked Taters and Sweets

SERVES 4

SLOW COOKER SIZE: 4- TO 6-QUART (3.8 TO 5.7 L) | COOK TIME: 4 TO 6 HOURS ON LOW | GLUTEN-FREE |
OIL-FREE | SOY-FREE

Foil-wrapped potatoes create their own steam as they cook gently in the slow cooker. The size and shape of the potatoes will determine the length of cooking time needed, and the size of your slow cooker will determine how many you can cook at one time. You can also cook all of one kind of potato instead of both kinds. Typically, russet potatoes take longer to cook than sweet potatoes. If cooking both kinds, or if some potatoes are smaller than others, check each one for doneness after 4 hours of cooking.

2 to 4 russet or other baking potatoes
2 to 4 medium-size sweet potatoes

1. Wash all the potatoes well, but do not dry them. Prick the russet potatoes with a fork and wrap each one in a sheet of aluminum foil. Wrap the sweet potatoes individually in foil as well.

2. Arrange the potatoes in a single layer in the slow cooker. Cover and cook on Low until tender, 4 to 6 hours.

Garlic Mashed Potatoes with Sour Cream and Chives

SERVES 4

SLOW COOKER SIZE: 4- TO 6-QUART (3.8 TO 5.7 L) | COOK TIME: 3 TO 4 HOURS ON HIGH | GLUTEN-FREE |
OIL-FREE OPTION | SOY-FREE OPTION

Mashed potatoes are easy to make in the slow cooker—and convenient, too, since you can cook and serve them in the same container. They also hold well on the Keep Warm setting if they finish cooking before the rest of the meal. The addition of sour cream and chives adds an extra flavor boost, but you can omit them (as well as the garlic) for more basic mashers. For soy-free, use soy-free vegan butter, Cashew Sour Cream (page 338), and plant milk.

3 garlic cloves, crushed

2 pounds (910 g) Yukon Gold or russet potatoes, peeled and cut into 1-inch (2.5 cm) chunks (about 6 cups)

2 cups (480 ml) water or vegetable broth

Salt and freshly ground black pepper

2 tablespoons (28 g) vegan butter, plus more if needed (optional)

½ cup (115 g) Cashew Sour Cream (page 338)

2 tablespoons (6 g) minced fresh chives, or 1 tablespoon dried chives

¼ cup (60 ml) plain unsweetened plant milk, heated (optional)

1. Combine the garlic and potatoes in the slow cooker. Add enough of the water to cover the potatoes. Season to taste with salt and pepper. (If using water, you'll need to add about 1 teaspoon salt.) Cover and cook on High until the potatoes are soft, 3 to 4 hours.

2. Carefully remove the insert of the slow cooker and drain the potatoes, then return the potatoes to the slow cooker. Add the vegan butter (if using) and the sour cream and mash the potatoes right in the slow cooker. Stir in the chives, then taste and adjust the seasonings, if needed. Add more vegan butter or a little warm plant milk, if needed for desired consistency. Serve hot.

Layered Tapenade Potatoes

SERVES 4 TO 6

SLOW COOKER SIZE: 4- TO 6-QUART (3.8 TO 5.7 L) | COOK TIME: 6 HOURS ON LOW | GLUTEN-FREE OPTION | OIL-FREE OPTION | SOY-FREE

A bold green olive, tomato, and artichoke tapenade combines with buttery Yukon Gold potatoes for a nice change from the usual potato dishes. Plan to make the tapenade the day before to save time when assembling this recipe. To make this recipe gluten-free, use gluten-free bread crumbs instead of panko.

1 (9-ounce, or 255 g) jar marinated artichoke hearts, drained

½ cup (77.5 g) pitted green olives

¼ cup (28.75 g) oil-packed or reconstituted sun-dried tomatoes, chopped

1½ tablespoons (13.5 g) capers, drained

¼ cup (60 ml) water, or 2 teaspoons olive oil

1 small yellow onion, chopped

(continued)

3 garlic cloves, minced

½ teaspoon dried basil

½ teaspoon dried thyme

2 pounds (910 g) Yukon Gold potatoes,
   peeled and cut into ⅛-inch (0.3 cm)-thick slices

Salt and freshly ground black pepper

3 tablespoons (9 g) toasted panko bread crumbs, for garnish

2 tablespoons (8 g) minced fresh flat-leaf parsley, for garnish

1. In a food processor, combine the artichoke hearts, olives, sun-dried tomatoes, and capers. Pulse to finely mince the tapenade ingredients. If making ahead, transfer to a container, cover, and refrigerate. Allow to come to room temperature before using.

2. Heat the water or oil in a small skillet over medium-high heat. Add the onion and sauté until softened, about 5 minutes. Stir in the garlic, basil, and thyme and cook for 1 minute longer. Alternatively, combine the onion and garlic in a microwave-safe bowl with 2 tablespoons (30 ml) of water, cover, and microwave for 2 minutes to soften. Stir in the basil and thyme.

3. Lightly coat the insert of the slow cooker with nonstick cooking spray. Arrange half of the potatoes in the bottom of the insert. Season with salt and black pepper and top with half of the onion mixture, followed by half of the tapenade. Top with a layer of the remaining potatoes and season to taste with salt and black pepper. Spread the remaining onion mixture on top, followed by the remaining tapenade. Cover and cook on Low until the potatoes are tender, about 6 hours.

4. Sprinkle the toasted bread crumbs and parsley over the top and serve.

Granny Apple Sweet Potatoes

SERVES 4

SLOW COOKER SIZE: 4- TO 6-QUART (3.8 TO 5.7 L) | COOK TIME: 5 TO 6 HOURS ON LOW | GLUTEN-FREE | OIL-FREE | SOY-FREE

Sweet potatoes and Granny Smith apples complement each other in this terrific side dish that's ideal for holiday meals. Not only is it a great change from the overly sweet marshmallow-topped sweet potato casserole, but it's also more practical because it's made in a slow cooker, so it frees up oven and stove space for the rest of your dinner. Use more or less sugar, according to your personal preference.

¼ to ⅓ cup (50 to 67 g) granulated natural sugar
¼ teaspoon ground cinnamon
¼ teaspoon salt
3 large sweet potatoes (about 2 pounds, or 910 g), peeled and thinly sliced
2 or 3 large Granny Smith apples, peeled, cored, and sliced
1 tablespoon (15 ml) fresh lemon juice

1. In a small bowl, combine the sugar, cinnamon, and salt.

2. Arrange a layer of sweet potato slices in the bottom of a slow cooker, followed by a layer of apple slices, sprinkling each layer with some of the sugar mixture. Continue layering until the ingredients are used up. Sprinkle the top layer with lemon juice.

3. Cover and cook on Low until the potatoes and apples are tender, 5 to 6 hours.

Scalloped Potatoes

SLOW COOKER SIZE: 4- TO 6-QUART (3.8 TO 5.7 L) | COOK TIME: 5 TO 6 HOURS ON LOW | GLUTEN-FREE |
OIL-FREE OPTION | SOY-FREE

As Melissa Chapman said after testing these potatoes, they're obviously not a diet food. What they are is delicious, rich, and creamy—so good, in fact, that Melissa's family couldn't stop raving about them.

¼ cup (60 ml) water, or 2 teaspoons olive oil
1 small onion, minced
3 garlic cloves, minced
½ teaspoon dried thyme
1 cup (175 g) Cashew Cream Cheese (page 339)
2 tablespoons (18 g) cornstarch
2 tablespoons (7.5 g) nutritional yeast
1 cup (240 ml) plain unsweetened plant milk
1 teaspoon Dijon mustard
Salt and freshly ground black pepper
1 cup (240 ml) vegetable broth, or as needed
2 pounds (910 g) russet potatoes, peeled and cut into ⅛-inch (0.3 cm)-thick slices

1. Heat the water or oil in a small skillet over medium-high heat. Add the onion and sauté until softened, about 5 minutes. Add the garlic and thyme and cook for 1 minute longer. Alternatively, combine the onion and garlic in a microwave-safe bowl with 2 tablespoons (30 ml) of water, cover, and microwave for 2 minutes to soften. Stir in the thyme.

2. In a blender or food processor, combine the onion mixture with the cream cheese, cornstarch, nutritional yeast, plant milk, mustard, and salt and black pepper to taste. Add as much of the broth as needed to make a smooth sauce.

3. Spread a thin layer of the sauce in the bottom of the cooker. Arrange a layer of potatoes over the sauce, and sprinkle with salt and black pepper. Top with a layer of sauce, and continue layering until all of the potatoes and sauce are used, ending with a layer of sauce. Cover and cook on Low until the potatoes are tender, 5 to 6 hours.

Potatoes with Tomatoes and Butter Beans

SERVES 4

SLOW COOKER SIZE: 4- TO 6-QUART (3.8 TO 5.7 L) | COOK TIME: 5 HOURS ON LOW | GLUTEN-FREE | OIL-FREE | SOY-FREE OPTION

This side dish can be made with either fresh or canned tomatoes. Or, serve it with a salad as a delicious main dish. To make this recipe soy-free, omit the soy sauce and use Soy-Free Sauce (page 344) or coconut aminos, or add some soy-free vegetable broth base or additional salt.

4 garlic cloves, minced

1 tablespoon (16 g) tomato paste

1 tablespoon (15 ml) soy sauce

½ teaspoon dried basil

½ teaspoon dried marjoram

¼ teaspoon red pepper flakes (optional)

¼ cup (60 ml) hot water

1½ pounds (680 g) Yukon Gold potatoes, peeled and thinly sliced

Salt and freshly ground black pepper

2 cups (344 g) cooked butter beans (page 114)
   or 1 (15-ounce, or 425 g) can beans, rinsed and drained (see Note)

1½ pounds (680 g) ripe tomatoes, diced, or 1 (14.5-ounce, or 410 g)
   can diced tomatoes, drained

2 tablespoons (5 g) chopped fresh basil or (8 g) flat-leaf parsley, for garnish

1. In a small bowl, combine the garlic, tomato paste, soy sauce, dried basil, marjoram, and red pepper flakes (if using). Add the hot water and stir to combine. Set aside.

2. Arrange half of the potatoes evenly in the bottom of the insert, seasoning with salt and black pepper. Top the potatoes with half each of the beans, the tomatoes, and the garlic mixture. Top with the remaining potatoes, seasoning with salt and black pepper. Add the remaining garlic mixture and beans, and end with a layer of tomatoes. Cover and cook on Low until the vegetables are tender, about 5 hours. Serve hot, sprinkled with the fresh basil.

NOTE: If butter beans are unavailable, substitute dried gigante beans, large lima beans, or cann ellini beans. If using fresh butter beans, cook them in a saucepan of boiling water for 10 minutes before adding them to the slow cooker.

Maple-Dijon Glazed Root Vegetables SERVES 4

SLOW COOKER SIZE: 4-QUART (3.8 L) | COOK TIME: 6 TO 8 HOURS ON LOW | GLUTEN-FREE | SOY-FREE

This recipe is a good way to serve root vegetables to your family. I like to use more carrots because they're popular and colorful, with a lesser amount of turnips and parsnips, but you can change the ratio however you like. Slow cooking combined with maple syrup brings out the natural sweetness of root vegetables, while the mustard adds just a touch of piquancy.

4 large carrots, peeled and cut into 1-inch (2.5 cm) chunks
1 medium-size turnip, peeled and cut into 1-inch (2.5 cm) cubes
1 large parsnip, peeled and cut into 1-inch (2.5 cm) pieces
4 shallots, halved
2 teaspoons olive oil
3 tablespoons (60 g) maple syrup
2 tablespoons (30 ml) water
1 tablespoon (15 g) Dijon mustard
Salt and freshly ground black pepper

1. Combine the carrots, turnip, parsnip, and shallots in the slow cooker.

2. In a small bowl, combine the oil, maple syrup, water, and mustard, stirring to blend, then pour it over the vegetables. Season to taste with salt and black pepper and stir to combine.

3. Cover and cook on Low until the vegetables are soft, 6 to 8 hours. Stir once about halfway through the cooking time, if possible.

Chimichurri Spaghetti Squash

SERVES 4

SLOW COOKER SIZE: 4- TO 6-QUART (3.8 TO 5.7 L) | COOK TIME: 7 TO 9 HOURS ON LOW | GLUTEN-FREE | SOY-FREE

An abundance of garlic, parsley, and oregano creates a bold, fresh taste in the Argentine chimichurri sauce that enlivens the delicate squash strands. To transform this side dish into a main dish, add sautéed seitan strips or plant-based sausage, or cooked white beans. Not only is it easier to cook a spaghetti squash in a slow cooker, but it also tastes better—the long and slow cooking results in a better texture and deeper flavor. A large oval slow cooker works best for this recipe. Make sure to buy a squash that will fit, whole, inside your slow cooker.

- 1 spaghetti squash (any size that fits inside your slow cooker)
- 2 cups (480 ml) water
- 4 or 5 garlic cloves, crushed
- 1 small bunch fresh flat-leaf parsley, coarsely chopped (about 1½ cups, or about 96 g)
- 1 teaspoon fresh oregano, or ½ teaspoon dried oregano
- Pinch of sugar
- ¾ teaspoon salt
- ½ teaspoon freshly ground black pepper
- ¼ teaspoon red pepper flakes
- 2 tablespoons (30 ml) red wine vinegar
- ¼ cup (60 ml) olive oil

1. Pierce the squash several times with a large fork or metal skewer. Place the squash in the slow cooker and add the water. Cover and cook the squash on Low until soft when pierced, 7 to 9 hours.

2. In a food processor, combine the garlic, parsley, oregano, sugar, salt, black pepper, and red pepper flakes and process to a paste. Add the vinegar and oil and process until smooth. Taste and adjust the seasonings, if needed.

3. Once the squash is cooked, turn off the slow cooker, remove the lid, and let the squash cool for 15 minutes, then cut it in half and scoop out the seeds. Drag a fork through the squash flesh to separate it into strands and transfer to a serving bowl. Add as much of the sauce as desired (depending on how much squash you have) and toss gently to coat. Serve immediately.

Winter Squash with Garlic and Ginger

SERVES 4

SLOW COOKER SIZE: 4-QUART (3.8 L) | COOK TIME: 6 HOURS ON LOW | GLUTEN-FREE | OIL-FREE | SOY-FREE OPTION

I enjoy making this dish for the lovely aroma it shares with the house while it cooks. Butternut squash is used in this recipe because it peels more easily than other winter squashes. However, you can use an unpeeled kabocha or buttercup squash if you prefer—just scrub the outside well. To make this recipe soy-free, omit the soy sauce and use Soy-Free Sauce (page 344) or coconut aminos, or add some soy-free vegetable broth base or additional salt.

4 garlic cloves, thinly sliced
1½ teaspoons grated peeled fresh ginger
2 tablespoons (30 ml) water
1 tablespoon (15 ml) soy sauce
1 large butternut squash, peeled, seeded, and cut into 2-inch (5 cm) chunks
1 tablespoon (12.5 g) granulated natural sugar
Salt and freshly ground black pepper

1. Spread the garlic and ginger in the bottom of the slow cooker. Stir in the water and soy sauce.

2. Add the squash chunks to the slow cooker, sprinkle with the sugar, and season to taste with salt and black pepper. Stir to coat the squash with the other ingredients. Cover and cook on Low until the squash is tender, 5 to 6 hours.

3. Taste and adjust the seasonings, if needed. Serve hot.

Italian-Style Tomatoes and Zucchini   SERVES 6

SLOW COOKER SIZE: 4- TO 6-QUART (3.8 TO 5.7 L) | COOK TIME: 4 TO 6 HOURS ON LOW | GLUTEN-FREE | OIL-FREE OPTION | SOY-FREE

This is a great way to enjoy those two prolific summer crops, tomatoes and zucchini. Plum tomatoes will yield less watery results. To reduce the liquid in the cooker, remove the cooked vegetables with a slotted spoon, turn the cooker to High, and let the liquid reduce. At this point, you can also stir in 1 tablespoon (15 ml) of cornstarch slurry (see page 25) to thicken it further, if you wish. To make this a main dish, add 1½ cups (270 g) cooked or canned cannellini beans (or other favorite), then toss with cooked pasta.

¼ cup (60 ml) water, or 2 teaspoons olive oil
1 medium-size yellow onion, minced
3 garlic cloves, minced
2 pounds (910 g) zucchini, diced
2 pounds (910 g) ripe plum tomatoes, diced
1 teaspoon dried basil
¾ teaspoon salt
⅛ teaspoon freshly ground black pepper
2 tablespoons (8 g) minced fresh flat-leaf parsley or (5 g) basil, for garnish

1. Heat the water or oil in a small skillet over medium heat. Add the onion and garlic and sauté until softened, about 5 minutes. Alternatively, combine the onion and garlic in a microwave-safe bowl with 2 tablespoons (30 ml) of water, cover, and microwave for 2 minutes to soften.

2. Transfer the onion and garlic to the slow cooker and add the zucchini and tomatoes. Sprinkle with the dried basil, salt, and pepper, then stir gently to combine. Cover and cook on Low until the vegetables are tender, 4 to 6 hours.

3. Serve hot, garnished with the parsley.

Braised Vegetables with Beans and Barley

SERVES 4

SLOW COOKER SIZE: 4- TO 6-QUART (3.8 TO 5.7 L) | COOK TIME: 3 HOURS ON HIGH | OIL-FREE OPTION | SOY-FREE

Barley is added to this simple vegetable braise to unify the other ingredients and give it a more substantial and homey feel. It also helps absorb the natural juices (and flavor) exuded by the vegetables as they cook.

¼ cup (60 ml) water, or 2 teaspoons olive oil

1 medium-size onion, minced

2 garlic cloves, minced

1 large carrot, thinly sliced

1 celery rib, thinly sliced

1 small red bell pepper, seeded and chopped

1 medium-size zucchini, chopped

1 small fennel bulb, thinly sliced crosswise

½ cup (100 g) raw pearl barley

1 cup (240 ml) vegetable broth

1½ cups (270 g) cooked cannellini beans (page 114)
   or 1 (15-ounce, or 425 g) can beans, rinsed and drained

Salt and freshly ground black pepper

1 cup (150 g) cherry tomatoes, halved

½ cup (65 g) frozen green peas, thawed

¼ cup (10 g) chopped fresh sage, basil, or marjoram

1. Heat the water or oil in a medium-size skillet over medium-high heat. Add the onion and sauté until softened, about 5 minutes. Add the garlic and cook for 1 minute longer. Alternatively, combine the onion and garlic in a microwave-safe bowl with 2 tablespoons (30 ml) of water, cover, and microwave for 2 minutes to soften.

2. Transfer the onion mixture to the slow cooker. Add the carrot, celery, bell pepper, zucchini, fennel, barley, broth, and beans. Season to taste with salt and black pepper and stir to combine. Cover and cook on High for 2 hours.

3. Add the tomatoes and green peas and continue cooking until the vegetables and barley are tender, about 1 hour.

4. When ready to serve, taste and adjust the seasonings, if needed. Stir in the sage and serve hot.

Balsamic Vegetable Crock

SLOW COOKER SIZE: 4- TO 6-QUART (3.8 TO 5.7 L) | COOK TIME: 2 HOURS ON HIGH | GLUTEN-FREE | OIL-FREE | SOY-FREE

More often than not, I come home from the farmers' market with more produce than my refrigerator can hold. I sometimes solve the storage problem by combining some of everything in a slow cooker. I especially enjoy using the slow cooker in the summer to avoid heating up the kitchen. The trick to keeping the just-picked flavor in these vegetables is cooking them on High until just tender. Feel free to mix and match with other vegetables and herbs. When ready to serve, a light drizzle of balsamic reduction provides the finishing touch.

2 shallots, thinly sliced

3 garlic cloves, minced

6 ounces (170 g) green beans, trimmed and halved lengthwise

1 red or yellow bell pepper, seeded and cut into ¼-inch (0.6 cm) strips

8 ounces (225 g) mushrooms (any kind), halved, quartered, or sliced

3 small zucchini, halved lengthwise and cut into ¼-inch (0.6 cm) slices

2 small yellow summer squash, halved lengthwise and cut into ¼-inch (0.6 cm) slices

Salt and freshly ground black pepper

2 cups (300 g) cherry tomatoes, halved

3 tablespoons (7.5 g) chopped fresh basil

2 tablespoons (8 g) chopped fresh flat-leaf parsley

Balsamic Reduction (page 345), for drizzling

1. Spread the shallots and garlic evenly in the bottom of the slow cooker. Add the green beans, bell pepper, mushrooms, zucchini, and yellow squash. Season to taste with salt and pepper. Cover and cook on High until the vegetables are tender, about 2 hours.

2. Stir the vegetables gently. Taste and adjust the seasonings, if needed. Add the tomatoes, basil, and parsley. Cover and cook for 10 minutes longer. Serve hot, drizzled with some of the balsamic reduction according to taste.

Condiments
from the Crock

I f you've ever cooked a jam, chutney, or fruit butter on top of the stove, you know that it requires careful monitoring and lots of stirring to prevent it from scorching. When you use a slow cooker to make such condiments, those problems virtually disappear. Just load your slow cooker, turn it on, and walk away. Now that's convenience!

Made with a cornucopia of fresh produce, the flavorful condiments in this chapter include a luscious Butternut Butter that is great spread on toast or a bagel—or even on pancakes—and a variety of zesty chutneys guaranteed to make you swear off the expensive store-bought stuff. You'll also find slow-cooker favorites such as applesauce, apple butter, orange marmalade, and cranberry sauce on these pages, along with homemade ketchup, stone fruit jam, and a tangy barbecue sauce.

Butternut Butter

SLOW COOKER SIZE: 4-QUART (3.8 L) | COOK TIME: 6 TO 8 HOURS ON LOW, PLUS 30 MINUTES
ON HIGH IF NEEDED | GLUTEN-FREE | OIL-FREE | SOY-FREE

The savory yet slightly sweet flavor of this spread is great on toast, English muffins, or bagels. It's also great slathered on pancakes or waffles, followed by a drizzle of maple syrup. This butter benefits from a good stirring about halfway through the cooking process, if possible.

1 large butternut squash, peeled, seeded, and diced
   (about 6 cups, or about 840 g)
1 cup (240 ml) apple juice
1 cup (200 g) granulated natural sugar
¼ cup (80 g) maple syrup
½ teaspoon ground cinnamon
¼ teaspoon ground allspice
⅛ teaspoon ground nutmeg
⅛ teaspoon ground ginger
½ teaspoon salt

1. Combine all of the ingredients in the slow cooker, stirring to mix well. Cover and cook on Low until the squash is very soft, 6 to 8 hours.

2. Remove the lid and stir the mixture. If it is at all watery, turn the cooker to High and continue to cook, uncovered, for an additional 30 minutes or more.

3. Turn off the slow cooker and allow to cool completely. When cool, use an immersion blender to puree it until smooth, or transfer the mixture to a food processor or blender and process until smooth. The butternut butter will keep in an airtight container in the refrigerator for up to 6 weeks.

Slow-Cooked Apple Butter MAKES ABOUT 4 CUPS (ABOUT 1.3 KG)

SLOW COOKER SIZE: 4-QUART (3.8 L) | COOK TIME: 8 HOURS ON LOW, PLUS 2 TO 4 HOURS ON HIGH |
GLUTEN-FREE | OIL-FREE | SOY-FREE

Apple butter requires a long, slow cooking process, making it ideal for a slow cooker, especially since it can easily scorch if left unattended on the stovetop. Unpeeled apples are used because the pectin contained in the skin helps to thicken the apple butter, so buy organic apples, if possible. You might want to make this overnight since it takes so long to cook. When you wake up, your house will smell like apple pie. The cooking time will depend on how juicy your apples are, and the amount of sugar used depends on how sweet you like your apple butter. It's great spread on toast or waffles or spooned into hot oatmeal.

2½ to 3 pounds (1.1 to 1.3 kg) cooking apples (I prefer McIntosh
    or Stayman for this recipe), washed, cored, and thickly sliced
1¼ cups (250 g) granulated natural sugar, or more to taste
⅓ cup (80 ml) apple juice
Juice of 1 lemon
1 tablespoon (7 g) ground cinnamon
¼ teaspoon ground allspice
¼ teaspoon ground nutmeg
¼ teaspoon ground ginger
¼ teaspoon ground cloves

1. Combine all of the ingredients in the slow cooker. Cover and cook on Low until the apples are very soft, about 8 hours.

2. Remove the lid, turn the heat to High, and stir the mixture. Continue to cook, uncovered, until the mixture thickens, 2 to 4 hours. When the apple butter has reached the thickness you prefer, turn off the slow cooker, remove the lid, and allow to cool completely. When cool, transfer the mixture to a food processor or blender and process until smooth. Alternatively, you can process the apples through a food mill to remove the bits of peel.

3. The apple butter will keep in an airtight container in the refrigerator for up to 2 months.

Cinnamon Applesauce

SLOW COOKER SIZE: 4-QUART (3.8 L) | COOK TIME: 3 TO 4 HOURS ON LOW | GLUTEN-FREE | OIL-FREE | SOY-FREE

Living in "apple country" in the Shenandoah Valley of Virginia, we get our pick of great apples. This applesauce is delicious made with a single variety of apple, but I prefer the complexity of combining a few different varieties. My favorites for applesauce are listed below. We love our applesauce spiced with cinnamon (the house smells like apple pie when this is cooking), but if you're not a cinnamon fan, just leave it out.

2½ pounds (1.1 kg) apples, such as Rome Beauty, Pink Lady, or McIntosh, peeled, cored, and diced

⅓ cup (67 g) granulated natural sugar

1 to 1½ teaspoons ground cinnamon, to taste

Pinch of salt

½ cup (120 ml) apple juice

1 tablespoon (15 ml) fresh lemon juice

1. Combine all of the ingredients in the slow cooker. Cover and cook on Low until the apples are very soft, 3 to 4 hours.

2. Turn off the slow cooker, remove the lid, and use a potato masher to mash the apples if they are still too chunky. Taste and adjust the seasonings, if needed. Serve warm or at room temperature. If not serving right away, allow to cool completely. The applesauce will keep in an airtight container in the refrigerator for up to 1 week.

Ginger Cran-Apple Chutney MAKES ABOUT 4 CUPS (ABOUT 1 KG)

SLOW COOKER SIZE: 4-QUART (3.8 L) | COOK TIME: 4 TO 5 HOURS ON LOW | GLUTEN-FREE | OIL-FREE | SOY-FREE

This chutney combines tart cranberries and sweet apples with zesty ginger for a luscious condiment that can be enjoyed in place of cranberry sauce around the holidays. The combination of fresh and crystallized ginger adds depth of flavor. If crystallized ginger is unavailable, you may simply omit it.

1 (12-ounce, or 340 g) bag fresh cranberries, rinsed and picked over
½ cup (60 g) sweetened dried cranberries
2 large apples, cored and finely chopped
2 shallots, minced
1½ teaspoons grated peeled fresh ginger
1 teaspoon chopped crystallized ginger (optional)
1¼ cups (250 g) granulated natural sugar
¼ cup (60 ml) apple cider vinegar
Grated zest of 1 lemon or orange

1. Combine all of the ingredients in the slow cooker, stirring to combine. Cover and cook on Low until the chutney becomes jam-like, about 4 hours.

2. Remove the lid, then taste and adjust the seasonings, if needed. Continue to cook, uncovered, until any liquid is evaporated and the chutney thickens, about 30 minutes. Taste and adjust the seasonings, if needed. Turn off the slow cooker and allow to cool completely.

3. The chutney will keep in an airtight container in the refrigerator for up to 2 months. Serve chilled or at room temperature.

Mixed Fruit Chutney

MAKES ABOUT 4 CUPS (ABOUT 1 KG)

SLOW COOKER SIZE: 4-QUART (3.8 L) | COOK TIME: 4 HOURS ON HIGH | GLUTEN-FREE | OIL-FREE |
SOY-FREE

This spicy-sweet chutney combines fresh and dried fruit, making it easy to adapt to whatever fruit you prefer or have on hand. You can mix and match the types of dried fruit, using a single variety or two, such as dried apricots and pears, or a mix of several. For fresh fruit, use your choice of apples, pears, peaches, or pineapple. In addition to serving with Indian food, this chutney is great on veggie burgers and makes a delicious accompaniment to Mom-Style Vegan Meatloaf (page 167) or roasted vegetables.

5 large apples or just-ripe pears, peeled, cored, and coarsely chopped, or 5 or 6 large underripe peaches, peeled (see Note), pitted, and diced

2 cups (weight varies) dried fruit (any kind), chopped

⅓ cup (50 g) golden raisins

2 shallots, minced

1 cup (200 g) granulated natural sugar

½ cup (120 ml) apple cider vinegar

2 teaspoons grated peeled fresh ginger

¼ teaspoon salt

¼ teaspoon red pepper flakes

1. Combine all of the ingredients in the slow cooker, stirring to combine. Cover and cook on High until the chutney becomes jam-like, about 3½ hours.

2. Remove the lid, then taste and adjust the seasonings, if needed. Continue to cook, uncovered, until the liquid is evaporated and the chutney thickens, about 30 minutes. Taste and adjust the seasonings, if needed. Turn off the slow cooker and allow to cool completely.

3. The chutney will keep in an airtight container in the refrigerator for up to 3 months. Serve chilled or at room temperature.

NOTE: To peel peaches, simply plunge them into boiling water for about 15 seconds and then into ice water—the skins will slip off easily.

Granny Apple–Green Tomato Chutney

MAKES ABOUT 3½ CUPS (ABOUT 875 G)

SLOW COOKER SIZE: 4-QUART (3.8 L) | COOK TIME: 4½ HOURS ON HIGH | GLUTEN-FREE | OIL-FREE | SOY-FREE

Green tomatoes and Granny Smith apples combine for a luscious chutney that is as at home with Indian meals as it is with a veggie burger, vegan meatloaf, or roasted vegetables.

5 large green tomatoes, peeled (see Note), seeded, and chopped
2 large Granny Smith apples, peeled, cored, and chopped
2 shallots, chopped
1 cup (145 g) raisins
¾ cup (150 g) granulated natural sugar
¼ cup (60 ml) apple cider vinegar
2 teaspoons grated peeled fresh ginger
1 teaspoon salt
¼ teaspoon ground cloves or allspice
¼ teaspoon red pepper flakes

1. Combine all of the ingredients in the slow cooker. Cover and cook on High until the chutney becomes jam-like, about 4 hours.

2. Remove the lid, then taste and adjust the seasonings, if needed. Continue to cook, uncovered, until any liquid is evaporated and the chutney thickens, about 30 minutes. Taste and adjust the seasonings, if needed. Turn off the slow cooker and allow to cool completely.

3. The chutney will keep in an airtight container in the refrigerator for up to 2 months. Serve chilled or at room temperature.

NOTE: To peel tomatoes, simply plunge them into boiling water for about 15 seconds and then into ice water—the skins will slip off easily.

Peach and Dried Blueberry Chutney

MAKES ABOUT 3½ CUPS (ABOUT 875 G)

SLOW COOKER SIZE: 4-QUART (3.8 L) | COOK TIME: 4½ HOURS ON HIGH | GLUTEN-FREE | OIL-FREE | SOY-FREE

When you need a tasty accompaniment to your meal, chutney may be just the thing. This one, made with fresh peaches and dried blueberries, is a terrific accompaniment for many seitan or tempeh recipes, as well as grain and bean dishes.

5 or 6 large underripe peaches, peeled (see Note), pitted, and chopped
¾ cup (120 g) dried blueberries
3 tablespoons (30 g) minced onion
1 cup (200 g) granulated natural sugar
⅓ cup (80 ml) apple cider vinegar
1 teaspoon grated peeled fresh ginger
½ teaspoon salt
¼ teaspoon red pepper flakes (optional)

1. Combine all of the ingredients in the slow cooker. Cover and cook on High until the chutney becomes jam-like, about 4 hours.

2. Remove the lid, then taste and adjust the seasonings, if needed. Continue to cook, uncovered, until any liquid is evaporated and the chutney thickens, about 30 minutes. Taste and adjust the seasonings, if needed. Turn off the slow cooker and allow to cool completely.

3. The chutney will keep in an airtight container in the refrigerator for up to 3 weeks. Serve chilled or at room temperature.

NOTE: To peel peaches, simply plunge them into boiling water for about 15 seconds and then into ice water—the skins will slip off easily.

Mango Chutney
with Dates and Lime

MAKES ABOUT 3 CUPS (ABOUT 750 G)

SLOW COOKER SIZE: 4-QUART (3.8 L) | COOK TIME: 4½ HOURS ON HIGH | GLUTEN-FREE | OIL-FREE | SOY-FREE

Mangoes and dates have a natural affinity. The addition of lime (rind and all) makes this one delicious chutney. Since you are using the entire lime, including the peel, try to buy organic limes. Enjoy this chutney with your favorite Indian food, or use it to enliven even a simple meal of rice and beans.

3 large ripe mangoes, peeled, pitted, and chopped
8 ounces (225 g) pitted dates, chopped
2 large shallots, minced
2 limes, washed, quartered, and chopped
2 teaspoons grated peeled fresh ginger
1 cup (200 g) granulated natural sugar
½ cup (120 ml) apple cider vinegar
½ teaspoon ground coriander
½ teaspoon ground cinnamon
½ teaspoon red pepper flakes

1. Combine all of the ingredients in the slow cooker. Cover and cook on High until the chutney becomes jam-like, about 4 hours.

2. Remove the lid, then taste and adjust the seasonings, if needed. Continue to cook, uncovered, until any liquid is evaporated and the chutney thickens, about 30 minutes. Taste and adjust the seasonings, if needed. Turn off the slow cooker and allow to cool completely.

3. The chutney will keep in an airtight container in the refrigerator for up to 3 weeks. Serve chilled or at room temperature.

Pear Confit

SLOW COOKER SIZE: 4-QUART (3.8 L) | COOK TIME: 6 TO 8 HOURS ON LOW, PLUS 1 HOUR ON HIGH |
GLUTEN-FREE | OIL-FREE | SOY-FREE

This delicious condiment is equally good served with sweet or savory foods. Serve it on vegan ice cream or a slice of cake or tea bread for an easy dessert, or on toast or a bagel for breakfast. It can also be used instead of a chutney or other relish, or to accompany Seitan Pot Roast (page 155).

6 to 8 underripe pears, peeled, cored, and chopped (about 3 pounds, or 1.3 kg)
½ cup (75 g) golden raisins
1 cup (200 g) granulated natural sugar
1 teaspoon grated peeled fresh ginger
½ teaspoon ground cinnamon
Pinch of salt
1 cup (240 ml) apple juice
Juice of 2 lemons
Zest of 2 lemons

1. Combine the pears, raisins, sugar, ginger, cinnamon, salt, apple juice, and lemon zest in the slow cooker. Cover and cook on Low until the pears are soft and the texture is jam-like, 6 to 8 hours.

2. Remove the lid and turn the setting to High. Continue to cook, uncovered, until thick, about 1 hour, stirring occasionally.

3. Stir in the lemon juice, then taste and adjust the seasonings, if needed. Turn off the slow cooker and allow to cool completely. Serve chilled or at room temperature. The confit will keep in an airtight container in the refrigerator for up to 2 weeks.

Easiest Cranberry Sauce

MAKES ABOUT 2 CUPS (ABOUT 560 G)

SLOW COOKER SIZE: 4-QUART (3.8 L) | COOK TIME: 2 HOURS ON HIGH | GLUTEN-FREE | OIL-FREE | SOY-FREE

Just three ingredients and two hours in the slow cooker result in a great-tasting cranberry sauce that thickens as it cools. This makes a fairly tart cranberry sauce, so if you prefer it sweeter, use more sugar and/or less lemon juice.

1 (12-ounce, or 340 g) bag fresh cranberries, rinsed and picked over
1 cup (200 g) granulated natural sugar
1 tablespoon (15 ml) fresh lemon, lime, or orange juice
Finely grated zest of 1 lemon, lime, or orange

1. Combine the cranberries, sugar, and juice in the slow cooker, stirring to mix. Cover and cook on High until the cranberries have popped, about 2 hours.

2. Stir in the zest, then taste and adjust the seasonings, if needed. Turn off the slow cooker, remove the lid, and allow to cool completely. Serve chilled or at room temperature. The cranberry sauce will keep in an airtight container in the refrigerator for up to 2 weeks.

Stone Fruit Jam

MAKES ABOUT 4 CUPS (ABOUT 1.3 KG)

SLOW COOKER SIZE: 4-QUART (3.8 L) | COOK TIME: 5 HOURS ON HIGH (2 HOURS COVERED; 3 HOURS UNCOVERED) | GLUTEN-FREE | OIL-FREE | SOY-FREE

This luscious fruit jam combines two of my summertime favorites—peaches and apricots. But you may also use plums, pluots, or plucots—they're all welcome additions, so feel free to mix and match your favorites, or use just one kind of fruit. If you can use locally grown fruit at the peak of its season, it will make this jam even more special. The jam needs to cool and then chill in the refrigerator in order for it to thicken nicely.

2 pounds (910 g) fresh firm peaches, peeled (see Note), pitted, and chopped
1 pound (455 g) fresh firm apricots, peeled (see Note), pitted, and chopped
3 tablespoons (45 ml) fresh lemon juice
1 (1.75-ounce, or 49 g) package pectin
2½ cups (500 g) granulated natural sugar, or to taste

1. Combine the peaches, apricots, and lemon juice in the slow cooker, stirring to mix. For a less chunky jam, crush the fruit with a potato masher. Sprinkle on the pectin and let stand for 20 minutes, then stir in the sugar. Cover and cook on High for 2 hours, stirring once about halfway through.

2. Remove the lid and continue to cook until the jam reaches your preferred consistency, about 3 hours. Turn off the slow cooker and allow to cool completely. Ladle the jam into jars or other containers with tight-fitting lids and refrigerate until chilled and thickened, at least 4 hours. The jam will keep in an airtight container in the refrigerator for up to 8 weeks, or in the freezer for up to 3 months.

NOTE: To peel peaches and apricots, simply plunge them into boiling water for about 15 seconds and then into ice water—the skins will slip off easily.

Orange Marmalade with a Twist of Lemon

MAKES ABOUT 4 CUPS (ABOUT 1.3 KG)

SLOW COOKER SIZE: 4-QUART (3.8 L) | COOK TIME: 6 TO 7 HOURS ON HIGH | GLUTEN-FREE | OIL-FREE | SOY-FREE

The addition of lemon juice and zest adds a nice twist to this flavorful marmalade. Orange marmalade can be used in lots of recipes, including the Artisanal Sweet and Spicy Wiener Balls (page 45) and the Citrus-Braised Beets (page 217). It's best to use organic oranges since you'll be including the peel in this recipe—and be sure to wash the oranges well.

4 Valencia or navel oranges (about 2 pounds, or 910 g), washed
3½ cups (840 ml) water
3 cups (600 g) granulated natural sugar, or to taste
Zest of 1 lemon
Juice of 1 lemon

1. Using a vegetable peeler or sharp paring knife, remove just the colored part of the peel from the oranges. Cut the strips of peel crosswise into very fine shards. Quarter the oranges and remove and discard any seeds and as much white pith as you can.

2. Transfer the orange pieces to a food processor and pulse until chopped. Transfer the oranges and peel to the slow cooker. Add the water, sugar, and lemon zest. Stir to combine. Cover and cook on High, stirring occasionally, until the peel becomes translucent, about 4 hours.

3. Remove the lid, stir in the lemon juice, and continue to cook, uncovered, until the mixture reduces and becomes syrupy, 2 to 3 hours.

4. Turn off the slow cooker and allow to cool completely; the marmalade will thicken more as it cools. The marmalade will keep in an airtight container in the refrigerator for up to 2 months.

Handcrafted Ketchup

MAKES ABOUT 3 CUPS (ABOUT 720 G)

SLOW COOKER SIZE: 4-QUART (3.8 L) | COOK TIME: 3 HOURS ON HIGH (FOR TOMATO PUREE) OR 4½ HOURS ON HIGH (FOR FRESH TOMATOES) | GLUTEN-FREE | OIL-FREE | SOY-FREE

Making your own ketchup elevates this all-purpose condiment from average to awesome. In addition to having a bright, fresh flavor (even when made with canned puree), this ketchup contains far less sodium and none of the high-fructose sweeteners that can be found in many store-bought brands. Note that the higher water content of fresh tomatoes necessitates the longer cooking time for that version.

1 small yellow onion, quartered

⅓ cup (67 g) granulated natural sugar

⅓ cup (80 ml) apple cider vinegar

2 (28-ounce, or 794 g) cans tomato puree or 4 pounds (1.8 kg) ripe tomatoes, peeled, seeded, and diced

½ teaspoon dry mustard

¼ teaspoon ground cinnamon

¼ teaspoon ground ginger

¼ teaspoon ground allspice

¼ teaspoon ground cloves or mace

Salt and freshly ground black pepper

1. Process the onion in a food processor until finely minced. Add the sugar and vinegar and process until smooth. Transfer the mixture to the slow cooker. Add the remaining ingredients and stir to combine. Cover and cook on High, stirring occasionally, for 2½ hours.

2. Remove the lid and cook until the ketchup thickens, about 30 minutes longer if using puree or about 2 hours longer if using fresh tomatoes. Taste and adjust the seasonings, adding more salt or sugar, if needed.

3. Turn off the slow cooker and allow to cool completely. The ketchup will keep in an airtight container in the refrigerator for several weeks.

Better Barbecue Sauce

MAKES ABOUT 3 CUPS (ABOUT 750 G)

SLOW COOKER SIZE: 4-QUART (3.8 L) | COOK TIME: 4 HOURS ON LOW | GLUTEN-FREE | OIL-FREE OPTION | SOY-FREE OPTION

This recipe makes a lot, but the sauce keeps well in the refrigerator or freezer. Since the flavor of the seasonings may dissipate after long cooking, you may need to add more spices near the end of the cooking time. This recipe can be made soy-free by omitting the soy sauce and Worcestershire sauce and using Soy-Free Sauce (page 344) or coconut aminos, or adding some soy-free vegetable broth base or additional salt.

1 small yellow onion, finely minced
2 garlic cloves, finely minced
1 chipotle chile in adobo, finely minced
1 (8-ounce, or 225 g) can tomato sauce
1 cup (240 g) ketchup
2 tablespoons (25 g) granulated natural sugar
1 tablespoon (15 ml) vegan Worcestershire sauce
1 tablespoon (15 ml) soy sauce
1 teaspoon smoked paprika
½ teaspoon ground cumin
½ teaspoon chili powder
½ teaspoon ground coriander
¼ teaspoon dry mustard
¼ teaspoon cayenne pepper
Salt and freshly ground black pepper
¼ cup (60 ml) water
⅓ cup (80 ml) apple cider vinegar
1 teaspoon liquid smoke

1. Combine the onion and garlic in a slow cooker. Add the chipotle, tomato sauce, ketchup, sugar, Worcestershire sauce, soy sauce, paprika, cumin, chili powder, coriander, mustard, cayenne, and salt and black pepper to taste. Stir in the water. Cover and cook on Low for 4 hours.

2. Stir in the vinegar and liquid smoke. Taste and adjust the seasonings, if needed. If a thicker sauce is desired, remove the lid, turn the setting to High, and continue to cook, stirring occasionally, until it is reduced to the desired consistency, about 30 minutes. Taste and adjust the seasonings, if needed.

3. Use an immersion blender to puree the mixture until smooth, or allow it to cool in the slow cooker, then transfer to a blender or food processor and process until smooth. When completely cool, transfer to an airtight container and store in the refrigerator for up to 8 weeks or in the freezer for up to 3 months.

Don't Forget Dessert

While you may expect a slow cooker to be useful for making bread puddings or even baked apples, you may be surprised to learn that you can also make cobblers, cakes, and even cheesecakes—all without turning on the oven. I like to see people's expressions when I tell them that the cheesecake they're enjoying not only contains no dairy, but was also "baked" in a slow cooker.

There are several advantages to making desserts in a slow cooker. For one thing, it's more economical than heating your oven, which, in the summer, provides the added advantage of keeping the kitchen cool. "Baking" in a slow cooker produces moist cakes and other desserts without the worry of scorching or burning, as the steamy heat of the cooker gently transforms ingredients into tasty treats.

Because many people have only one slow cooker—and it's usually either a 4-quart (3.8 L) or a 6-quart (5.7 L)—I've done my best to provide options for making these desserts using either size. Some desserts, such as puddings, are best made directly in the slow cooker insert, while other desserts, such as cakes, are best "baked" in pans that are set inside the slow cooker. Even so, instructions are provided to prepare most of these recipes either way.

If you plan to make a dessert using a baking pan, be sure you have a pan that fits inside your slow cooker. For example, a 7-inch (18 cm) springform pan will fit inside a 6-quart (5.7 L) slow cooker. You should also be able to find small cake pans, glass or ceramic baking dishes, or aluminum pans that will work. (Some people even use coffee cans for breads.) Also available are baking pans that are made to fit inside slow cookers.

Some of these recipes call for a rack or trivet to suspend the pan above a small amount of water in the bottom of the cooker. For this purpose, you may use virtually any heatproof object, including a ring made of crumpled aluminum foil or a small heatproof bowl. Special racks designed to fit inside your slow cooker may also be available from the manufacturer.

Whether you "bake" your cakes and other desserts directly in the slow cooker or in a pan set inside the cooker, you may want to place a piece of parchment paper, cut to fit, in the bottom of your pan or slow cooker insert for easy removal of your dessert. When baking cakes inside a slow cooker, I recommend draping a clean kitchen towel over the cooker before putting on the lid in order to prevent water condensation droplets from dripping onto the cake as it bakes.

Applesauce-Walnut Cake

SERVES 6 TO 8

SLOW COOKER SIZE: 4-QUART OR 6-QUART (3.8 OR 5.7 L) | COOK TIME: 2 HOURS ON HIGH FOR 4-QUART (3.8 L); 3 HOURS ON HIGH FOR 6-QUART (5.7 L) | GLUTEN-FREE OPTION | SOY-FREE

This flavorful old-fashioned treat can be made either directly in the insert of a 4-quart (3.8 L) round cooker or in a small baking pan set inside a 6-quart (5.7 L) oval cooker. To make this gluten-free, use an all-purpose gluten-free flour.

1¾ cups (217 g) unbleached all-purpose flour
⅔ cup (134 g) granulated natural sugar
1 teaspoon baking powder
½ teaspoon baking soda
½ teaspoon salt
1½ teaspoons ground cinnamon
¼ teaspoon ground allspice
¼ teaspoon ground nutmeg
⅛ teaspoon ground cloves
1 cup (245 g) unsweetened applesauce
1 tablespoon (15 ml) fresh lemon juice
1 teaspoon pure vanilla extract
¼ cup (60 ml) avocado oil or other neutral-tasting oil
½ cup (60 g) chopped walnuts

1. If using a 4-quart (3.8 L) slow cooker, place a round of parchment paper, cut to fit, in the bottom of the slow cooker insert. Coat the parchment and sides of the insert with nonstick cooking spray. If using a 6-quart (5.7 L) slow cooker, place a rack, trivet, or a ring of crumpled aluminum foil in the bottom of the insert. Lightly oil a baking pan that will fit in the cooker and set aside. If using a springform pan, wrap the outside bottom and sides of the pan with foil to prevent leakage.

2. In a large bowl, combine the flour, sugar, baking powder, baking soda, salt, cinnamon, allspice, nutmeg, and cloves. Mix well.

3. In a separate bowl, combine the applesauce, lemon juice, vanilla, and oil. Mix well. Stir the wet mixture into the dry mixture, mixing until smooth and well blended. Fold in the walnuts.

(continued)

4. If using a 4-quart (3.8 L) slow cooker, transfer the batter directly into the slow cooker, spreading evenly. Drape a clean kitchen towel over the cooker, put on the lid, and cook on High until a tester inserted in the center of the cake comes out clean, about 2 hours. Remove the lid and towel, turn off the cooker, and allow the cake to cool completely before serving.

If using a 6-quart (5.7 L) slow cooker, transfer the batter to the prepared baking pan. Pour about 1 inch (2.5 cm) of hot water into the bottom of the insert and place the pan on the rack inside the slow cooker. Drape a clean kitchen towel over the cooker, put on the lid, and cook on High until a tester inserted in the center of the cake comes out clean, about 3 hours. Remove the pan from the cooker and set aside to cool completely before serving.

Fat-Free Apple Crock Cake

SERVES 6 TO 8

SLOW COOKER SIZE: 4-QUART OR 6-QUART (3.8 OR 5.7 L) | COOK TIME: 2 TO 2½ HOURS ON HIGH FOR 4-QUART (3.8 L); 3 HOURS ON HIGH FOR 6-QUART (5.7 L) | GLUTEN-FREE OPTION | OIL-FREE | SOY-FREE

Apple cakes are so delicious that I thought I'd include two versions. Whereas the previous recipe is made with applesauce, nuts, and oil, this one uses fresh apples and eliminates the oil and nuts. Many thanks to recipe tester Barbara Bryan for testing this cake several times to get the texture just right while making it deliciously fat-free. This can be made either directly in the insert of a 4-quart (3.8 L) round cooker or in a small baking pan set inside a 6-quart (5.7 L) oval cooker. To make this gluten-free, use an all-purpose gluten-free flour.

1¾ cups (217 g) unbleached all-purpose flour
1 teaspoon baking powder
1 teaspoon baking soda
½ teaspoon salt
1 teaspoon ground cinnamon
¼ teaspoon ground allspice
¼ teaspoon ground nutmeg
Pinch of ground cloves
1 cup (200 g) granulated natural sugar
1 tablespoon (15 ml) fresh lemon juice
1 teaspoon pure vanilla extract

½ cup (122.5 g) unsweetened applesauce

2 Granny Smith or Stayman apples, peeled, cored, and chopped (about 2 cups, or about 300 g)

Confectioners' sugar, for dusting

1. If using a 4-quart (3.8 L) slow cooker, place a round of parchment paper, cut to fit, in the bottom of the slow cooker insert. Coat the parchment and sides of the insert with nonstick cooking spray. If using a 6-quart (5.7 L) slow cooker, place a rack, trivet, or a ring of crumpled aluminum foil in the bottom of the insert. Lightly oil a baking pan that will fit in the cooker and set aside. If using a springform pan, wrap the outside bottom and sides of the pan with foil to prevent leakage.

2. In a large bowl, combine the flour, baking powder, baking soda, salt, cinnamon, allspice, nutmeg, and cloves.

3. In a separate bowl, combine the granulated sugar, lemon juice, vanilla, and applesauce and mix well. Add the apples and stir to coat. Stir the wet mixture into the dry mixture, mixing until well blended.

4. If using a 4-quart (3.8 L) slow cooker, transfer the batter directly into the slow cooker, spreading evenly. Drape a clean kitchen towel over the cooker, put on the lid, and cook on High until a tester inserted in the center of the cake comes out clean, 2 to 2½ hours. Remove the lid and towel, turn off the cooker, and allow to cool completely. Dust the top with confectioners' sugar just before serving.

5. If using a 6-quart (5.7 L) slow cooker, transfer the batter to the prepared baking pan. Pour about 1 inch (2.5 cm) of hot water into the bottom of the insert and place the pan on the rack inside the slow cooker. Drape a clean kitchen towel over the cooker, put on the lid, and cook on High until a tester inserted in the center of the cake comes out clean, about 3 hours. Remove the pan from the cooker and set aside to cool completely. Dust the top with confectioners' sugar just before serving.

Piña Colada Cake

SLOW COOKER SIZE: 4-QUART OR 6-QUART (3.8 OR 5.7 L) | COOK TIME: 2 HOURS ON HIGH FOR 4-QUART (3.8 L); 3 TO 4 HOURS ON HIGH FOR 6-QUART (5.7 L) | GLUTEN-FREE OPTION | SOY-FREE OPTION

If you like piña coladas—or the flavor of creamy coconut and sweet pineapple with a hint of rum—you'll love this cake. This recipe can be made either directly in the insert of a 4-quart (3.8 L) round cooker or in a small baking pan set inside a 6-quart (5.7 L) oval cooker. To make this recipe soy-free, use a soy-free vegan butter or avocado oil. To make this gluten-free, use an all-purpose gluten-free flour.

2 cups (248 g) unbleached all-purpose flour

⅓ cup (67 g) granulated natural sugar

¼ cup (21.25 g) unsweetened shredded coconut, plus more for garnish (optional)

1½ teaspoons baking powder

½ teaspoon baking soda

½ teaspoon salt

1 cup (288 g) cream of coconut

3 tablespoons (42 g) vegan butter, softened, or (45 ml) avocado oil

¾ cup (116.25 g) finely chopped fresh or canned pineapple, well drained, juice reserved

⅓ cup plus 2 tablespoons (110 ml) pineapple juice from the chopped pineapple, plus more if needed (add purchased pineapple juice if necessary to yield the required amount)

1 tablespoon (15 ml) dark rum, or 1 teaspoon rum extract

½ teaspoon coconut extract

1 teaspoon apple cider vinegar

1 cup (120 g) confectioners' sugar

1. If using a 4-quart (3.8 L) slow cooker, place a round of parchment paper, cut to fit, in the bottom of the slow cooker insert. Coat the parchment and sides of the insert with nonstick cooking spray. If using a 6-quart (5.7 L) slow cooker, place a rack, trivet, or a ring of crumpled aluminum foil in the bottom of the insert. Lightly oil a baking pan that will fit in the cooker and set aside. If using a springform pan, wrap the outside bottom and sides of the pan with foil to prevent leakage.

2. In a large bowl, combine the flour, sugar, coconut, baking powder, baking soda, and salt and stir to combine.

3. In a separate bowl, combine the cream of coconut, vegan butter, chopped pineapple, ⅓ cup (80 ml) of the reserved pineapple juice, rum, coconut extract, and vinegar. Add the wet mixture to the dry mixture about one-third at a time, mixing well after each addition.

4. If using a 4-quart (3.8 L) slow cooker, transfer the batter directly into the slow cooker, spreading evenly. Drape a clean kitchen towel over the cooker, put on the lid, and cook on High until a tester inserted in the center of the cake comes out clean, about 2 hours. (Check the cake at 1 hour and 45 minutes if your cooker runs hot.) Remove the lid and towel, turn off the cooker, and allow the cake to cool completely.

5. If using a 6-quart (5.7 L) slow cooker, transfer the batter to the prepared baking pan, spreading it evenly. Pour about 1 inch (2.5 cm) of hot water into the bottom of the insert and place the pan on the rack inside the slow cooker. Drape a clean kitchen towel over the cooker, put on the lid, and cook on High until a tester inserted in the center of the cake comes out clean, 3 to 4 hours. Remove the pan from the cooker and set aside to cool completely.

6. Once the cake is cool, place the confectioners' sugar in a small bowl. Stir in the remaining 2 tablespoons (30 ml) of pineapple juice and continue stirring until it is a well-blended glaze, adding additional pineapple juice a teaspoon at a time if the glaze is too thick. Pour the glaze onto the cake, spreading with a spatula, if needed, to cover the top. Sprinkle the top with additional coconut, if desired. Serve immediately or refrigerate for 20 minutes to set the glaze.

Spiced Pumpkin Cake

SLOW COOKER SIZE: 4-QUART OR 6-QUART (3.8 OR 5.7 L) | COOK TIME: 2½ HOURS ON HIGH FOR 4-QUART (3.8 L); 3½ HOURS ON HIGH FOR 6-QUART (5.7 L) | GLUTEN-FREE OPTION | SOY-FREE

The daughter of one of the recipe testers who made this cake said that if she could bake autumn, this is what it would taste like. This cake can be made either directly in the insert of a 4-quart (3.8 L) round cooker or in a small baking pan set inside a 6-quart (5.7 L) oval cooker. The chocolate frosting on page 272 is wonderful on this cake. To make this gluten-free, use an all-purpose gluten-free flour.

1¾ cups (217 g) unbleached all-purpose flour
¾ cup (150 g) granulated natural sugar
1½ teaspoons baking powder
½ teaspoon salt
1 teaspoon ground cinnamon
½ teaspoon ground allspice
½ teaspoon ground nutmeg
¼ teaspoon ground cloves
1 cup (245 g) canned solid-pack pumpkin
¼ cup (60 ml) plain unsweetened plant milk
¼ cup (60 ml) avocado oil
1 teaspoon pure vanilla extract or rum extract
½ cup (55 g) chopped pecans (optional)

1. If using a 4-quart (3.8 L) slow cooker, place a round of parchment paper, cut to fit, in the bottom of the slow cooker insert. Coat the parchment and sides of the insert with nonstick cooking spray. If using a 6-quart (5.7 L) slow cooker, place a rack, trivet, or a ring of crumpled aluminum foil in the bottom of the insert. Lightly oil a baking pan that will fit in the cooker. If using a springform pan, wrap the outside bottom and sides of the pan with foil to prevent leakage.

2. In a large bowl, combine the flour, sugar, baking powder, salt, cinnamon, allspice, nutmeg, and cloves. Mix well.

3. In a separate bowl, combine the pumpkin, plant milk, oil, and vanilla. Mix well. Stir the wet mixture into the dry mixture, mixing until smooth and well blended. Fold in the pecans (if using).

4. If using a 4-quart (3.8 L) slow cooker, transfer the batter directly into the slow cooker, spreading evenly. Drape a clean kitchen towel over the cooker, put on the lid, and cook on High until a tester inserted in the center of the cake comes out clean, about 2½ hours. (Check the cake at 2 hours if your cooker runs hot.) Remove the lid and towel, turn off the cooker, and allow the cake to cool completely before serving.

5. If using a 6-quart (5.7 L) slow cooker, transfer the batter to the prepared baking pan, spreading it evenly. Pour about 1 inch (2.5 cm) of hot water into the bottom of the insert and place the pan on the rack inside the slow cooker. Drape a clean kitchen towel over the cooker, put on the lid, and cook on High until a tester inserted in the center of the cake comes out clean, about 3½ hours. Remove the pan from the cooker and set aside to cool completely before serving.

Chocolate Truffle Cake

SERVES 6 TO 8

SLOW COOKER SIZE: 4-QUART OR 6-QUART (3.8 OR 5.7 L) | COOK TIME: 2 HOURS ON HIGH FOR 4-QUART (3.8 L); 3 TO 4 HOURS ON HIGH FOR 6-QUART (5.7 L) | GLUTEN-FREE OPTION | SOY-FREE OPTION

This dense chocolate cake is rich and fudgy, so even a small piece will satisfy. This recipe can be made either directly in the insert of a 4-quart (3.8 L) round cooker or in a small baking pan set inside a 6-quart (5.7 L) oval cooker. For soy-free, use a soy-free vegan butter and soy-free plant milk. To make this gluten-free, use an all-purpose gluten-free flour.

CAKE

1½ cups (186 g) unbleached all-purpose flour
¼ cup (21.5 g) unsweetened cocoa powder
1½ teaspoons baking powder
¼ teaspoon baking soda
¼ teaspoon salt
3 tablespoons (42 g) vegan butter, softened
½ cup (100 g) granulated natural sugar
1 cup (240 ml) plant milk
1 teaspoon pure vanilla extract
½ teaspoon apple cider vinegar

(continued)

¼ cup (21.5 g) unsweetened cocoa powder

2 tablespoons (28 g) vegan butter, melted

1 teaspoon pure vanilla extract

2 tablespoons (30 ml) plant milk, plus more if needed

1 cup (120 g) confectioners' sugar, plus more if needed

1. If using a 4-quart (3.8 L) slow cooker, place a round of parchment paper, cut to fit, in the bottom of the slow cooker insert. Coat the parchment and sides of the cooker with nonstick cooking spray. If using a 6-quart (5.7 L) slow cooker, place a rack, trivet, or a ring of crumpled aluminum foil inside the slow cooker. Lightly oil a baking pan that will fit in the cooker. If using a springform pan, wrap the outside bottom and sides of the pan with foil to prevent leakage.

2. To make the cake: In a medium-size bowl, combine the flour, cocoa powder, baking powder, baking soda, and salt. Set aside.

3. In the bowl of an electric mixer, cream together the vegan butter and granulated sugar on high speed until blended. Beat in the plant milk, vanilla, and vinegar until blended. Add the flour mixture and incorporate on low speed until evenly mixed. Do not overmix.

4. If using a 4-quart (3.8 L) slow cooker, transfer the batter directly into the slow cooker, spreading evenly. Drape a clean kitchen towel over the cooker, put on the lid, and cook on High until a tester inserted in the center of the cake comes out clean, about 2 hours. Remove the lid and towel, turn off the cooker, and allow to cool completely. If using a 6-quart (5.7 L) slow cooker, transfer the batter to the prepared baking pan, spreading it evenly. Pour about 1 inch (2.5 cm) of hot water into the bottom of the insert and place the pan on the rack inside the slow cooker. Drape a clean kitchen towel over the cooker, put on the lid, and cook on High until a tester inserted in the center of the cake comes out clean, 3 to 4 hours. Remove the pan from the cooker and set aside to cool completely.

5. While the cake is cooling, make the frosting. Stir the cocoa into the melted vegan butter until well combined. Stir in the vanilla and plant milk and mix until smooth. Slowly stir in the confectioners' sugar until well blended. If the frosting is too thin, add more confectioners' sugar. If it's too thick, add more plant milk, 1 teaspoon at a time, until it reaches the desired consistency. Refrigerate the frosting for at least 1 hour before using, then frost the cooled cake and serve or refrigerate until needed. Refrigerate leftovers.

Carrot Cake with Pineapple

SERVES 6

SLOW COOKER SIZE: 4-QUART OR 6-QUART (3.8 OR 5.7 L) | COOK TIME: 2 TO 2½ HOURS ON HIGH FOR 4-QUART (3.8 L); 3 HOURS ON HIGH FOR 6-QUART (5.7 L) | GLUTEN-FREE OPTION | SOY-FREE

Carrot cake is a personal favorite that I make year-round. In the summer, I like to use freshly dug carrots from my garden and make it in the slow cooker so that I don't heat up the kitchen.

This cake can be made either directly in the insert of a 4-quart (3.8 L) round cooker or in a small baking pan set inside a 6- to 7-quart (5.7 to 6.7 L) oval cooker. Enjoy it plain or with a light dusting of confectioners' sugar, or whip up a cashew cream cheese frosting (recipe follows). To make this gluten-free, use an all-purpose gluten-free flour.

1½ cups (186 g) unbleached all-purpose flour

¾ cup (150 g) granulated natural sugar

1½ teaspoons baking powder

½ teaspoon salt

1 teaspoon ground cinnamon

¼ teaspoon ground nutmeg

2 carrots, peeled and finely shredded (1 cup packed, or 110 g)

⅓ cup (52 g) finely chopped fresh or canned pineapple, well drained, juice reserved

½ cup (120 ml) pineapple juice from the chopped pineapple, plus more if needed (add water, unsweetened plant milk, or purchased pineapple juice if necessary to yield ½ cup, or 120 ml)

¼ cup (60 ml) avocado oil

½ cup (67.5 g) chopped macadamia nuts (optional)

1. If using a 4-quart (3.8 L) slow cooker, place a round of parchment paper, cut to fit, in the bottom of the slow cooker insert. Coat the parchment and sides of the insert with nonstick cooking spray. If using a 6-quart (5.7 L) slow cooker, place a rack, trivet, or a ring of crumpled aluminum foil inside the slow cooker. Lightly oil a baking pan that will fit in the cooker. If using a springform pan, wrap the outside bottom and sides of the pan with foil to prevent leakage.

2. In a large bowl, combine the flour, sugar, baking powder, salt, cinnamon, and nutmeg. Mix well.

(continued)

3. In a separate bowl, combine the carrots, chopped pineapple, ½ cup (120 ml) of reserved pineapple juice, and oil. Mix well. Stir the wet mixture into the dry mixture, mixing until well blended. If the batter is too dry, add a little more pineapple juice, 1 to 2 tablespoons (15 to 30 ml) at a time. Fold in the macadamias (if using).

4. If using a 4-quart (3.8 L) slow cooker, transfer the batter directly into the slow cooker, spreading evenly. Drape a clean kitchen towel over the slow cooker, put on the lid, and cook on High until a tester inserted in the center of the cake comes out clean, 2 to 2½ hours. Remove the lid and towel, turn the cooker off, and allow to cool completely before serving.

5. If using a 6-quart (5.7 L) slow cooker, transfer the batter to the prepared baking pan, spreading it evenly. Pour about 1 inch (2.5 cm) of hot water into the bottom of the insert and place the pan on the rack inside the slow cooker. Drape a clean kitchen towel over the slow cooker, put on the lid, and cook on High until a tester inserted in the center of the cake comes out clean, about 3 hours. Remove the pan from the cooker and set aside to cool before frosting or serving.

CASHEW CREAM CHEESE FROSTING

MAKES ABOUT 1¾ CUPS (ABOUT 280 G)

¾ cup (131.25 g) Cashew Cream Cheese (page 339), softened
2 tablespoons (28 g) vegan butter, softened
1 cup (120 g) confectioners' sugar
1 teaspoon pure vanilla extract

Combine all of the ingredients in a food processor and process until smooth and well blended.

Orange-Topped Italian Polenta Cake SERVES 6

SLOW COOKER SIZE: 4-QUART OR 6-QUART (3.8 OR 5.7 L) | COOK TIME: 2 TO 2½ HOURS ON HIGH FOR 4-QUART (3.8 L); 3 HOURS ON HIGH FOR 6-QUART (5.7 L) | GLUTEN-FREE OPTION | SOY-FREE OPTION

Polenta cake is popular throughout Italy. There are many variations, including those that are fragrant with orange and almonds. This recipe can be made either directly in the insert of a 4-quart (3.8 L) round cooker or in a small baking pan set inside a 6-quart (5.7 L) oval cooker. For a shortcut version, use purchased orange marmalade. For soy-free, use a soy-free vegan butter. To make this gluten-free, use an all-purpose gluten-free flour.

⅔ cup plus 1 tablespoon (146 g) granulated natural sugar

1 navel orange, peeled and sliced into ⅛-inch (0.3 cm)-thick rounds

1¼ cups (155 g) all-purpose flour

⅓ cup (47 g) fine-ground cornmeal

¼ cup (23.75) finely ground almonds

1½ teaspoons baking powder

¾ teaspoon salt

¼ cup (56 g) vegan butter, softened

⅓ cup plus 2 tablespoons (147 g) Orange Marmalade with a Twist of Lemon (page 258)

1 teaspoon pure vanilla extract

1 cup (240 ml) unsweetened plant milk

1. If using a 4-quart (3.8 L) slow cooker, arrange two 3-inch (7.5 cm)-wide strips of parchment paper in a crisscross pattern across the bottom and up the sides of the slow cooker insert. Place a round of parchment paper, cut to fit, on top of the crisscross. Coat the parchment and sides of the insert with cooking spray.

2. If using a 6-quart (5.7 L) slow cooker, place a rack, trivet, or a ring of crumpled aluminum foil inside the cooker. Generously grease and flour a 7-inch (18 cm) springform pan or round cake pan. If using a springform pan, place it on a sheet of aluminum foil and bring up the sides of the foil to prevent leakage.

3. Sprinkle 1 tablespoon (12.5 g) of sugar onto the parchment circle or the bottom of the prepared pan. Arrange the orange slices on top of the sugar in a circular pattern, overlapping slightly, if necessary.

(continued)

4. In a bowl, combine the flour, cornmeal, almonds, baking powder, and salt.

5. In a separate large bowl, combine the remaining ⅔ cup (134 g) of sugar, vegan butter, ⅓ cup (107 g) of marmalade, and vanilla and beat until well blended. Slowly beat in the plant milk, then gradually stir in the dry ingredients until smooth.

6. If using a 4-quart (3.8 L) slow cooker, transfer the batter directly into the slow cooker, spreading evenly and being careful not to dislodge the orange slices. Drape a clean kitchen towel over the slow cooker, put on the lid, and cook on High until a tester inserted in the center of the cake comes out clean, about 2 hours. Remove the lid and towel, turn off the cooker, and allow the cake to cool completely. Carefully lift the cake out of the cooker, using the four ends of the parchment strips to help dislodge the cake, and invert onto a plate.

   If using a 6-quart (5.7 L) slow cooker, transfer the batter to the prepared baking pan, spreading evenly and being careful not to dislodge the orange slices. Pour about 1 inch (2.5 cm) of hot water into the bottom of the insert and place the pan on the rack inside the slow cooker. Drape a clean kitchen towel over the slow cooker, put on the lid, and cook on High until a tester inserted in the center of the cake comes out clean, 2 to 3 hours. Remove the lid and the towel, turn off the cooker, and let cool for 10 minutes, then remove the pan from the cooker and set aside to cool completely. When cool, carefully remove the sides from the springform pan (if using), and invert the cake onto a plate.

7. Heat the remaining 2 tablespoons (40 g) of marmalade in a saucepan over low heat or in the microwave in a heatproof bowl until warm. Stir until smooth. Brush the top of the cake with the warm marmalade. Allow the marmalade to cool completely before serving.

4. If using a 4-quart (3.8 L) slow cooker, spread the mixture in the prepared crock. Drape a clean kitchen towel over the cooker, put on the lid, and cook on High until a tester inserted in the center comes out clean, about 2 hours. Remove the lid, turn off the cooker, and allow to cool completely before cutting into wedges. Enjoy as is or sprinkle with a little confectioners' sugar to serve.

5. If using a 6-quart (5.7 L) slow cooker, spread the pumpkin mixture evenly in the prepared baking pan. Pour about 1 inch (2.5 cm) of hot water into the bottom of the insert and place the pan on the rack inside the slow cooker. Drape a clean kitchen towel over the slow cooker, put on the lid, and cook on High until a tester inserted in the center comes out clean, about 3 hours. Remove the pan from the slow cooker and set aside to cool completely before cutting into bars. Enjoy as is or sprinkle with a little confectioners' sugar (if using) to serve.

Tutti-Frutti Cobbler

SERVES 4 TO 6

SLOW COOKER SIZE: 4-QUART (3.8 L) | COOK TIME: 3 HOURS ON HIGH | GLUTEN-FREE OPTION | SOY-FREE

In addition to being the title of an old rock-and-roll song, tutti-frutti also means "all fruit" in Italian, making it an apt name for this cobbler, which can include as many varieties of fruit as you like. It's great made with a variety of berries or stone fruits such as peaches and plums. One of my favorite combinations includes blueberries, blackberries, peaches, and apricots. You may also use harder fruit, such as apples or pears, but you'll need to cut the pieces smaller and possibly cook the cobbler longer in order for the fruit to soften. Use this recipe as a guide (you'll need 5 to 6 cups, weight varies, total berries and/or cut fruit) to include your own favorites. The slow cooker is a great way to make cobblers during the heat of summer, when fresh fruit is abundant but you don't want to turn on the oven. Instead of fresh fruit, frozen fruit, thawed, or canned fruit pie filling may be substituted. For a gluten-free cobbler, use a gluten-free all-purpose flour.

(continued)

2 large ripe peaches, peeled (see Note), pitted, and sliced
2 ripe apricots, peeled (see Note), pitted, and sliced
1 cup (145 g) fresh blueberries, rinsed and picked over
1 cup (145 g) fresh blackberries, rinsed and picked over
¾ cup (150 g) granulated natural sugar
1½ tablespoons (11.25 g) tapioca starch or cornstarch
1¼ cups (155 g) unbleached all-purpose flour
1 teaspoon baking powder
¼ teaspoon ground cinnamon
¼ teaspoon salt
½ cup (120 ml) plain unsweetened plant milk
1 tablespoon (15 ml) avocado oil
½ teaspoon pure vanilla extract

1. Lightly coat the insert of the slow cooker with nonstick cooking spray. Add all of the fruit and ½ cup (100 g) of sugar. Sprinkle with the tapioca and stir to combine. Set the slow cooker on High, cover, and cook for 2 hours.

2. In a bowl, combine the flour, the remaining ¼ cup (50 g) of sugar, baking powder, cinnamon, and salt. Stir in the plant milk, oil, and vanilla, stirring until just combined to form a soft dough.

3. Stir the fruit in the slow cooker, then spread the dough evenly over the fruit mixture. Cover and continue to cook on High until the topping is cooked and a tester inserted in the center comes out clean, about 1 hour.

4. Remove the lid, turn off the cooker, and let the cobbler sit for 15 minutes before serving.

NOTE: To peel peaches and apricots, simply plunge them into boiling water for about 15 seconds and then into ice water—the skins will slip off easily.

Pear-Mincemeat Crisp

. . . .

SLOW COOKER SIZE: 4-QUART (3.8 L) | COOK TIME: 5 HOURS ON HIGH | SOY-FREE | OIL-FREE |
GLUTEN-FREE OPTION

. . . .

No meat or suet in this mincemeat—just delicious pears and a whole lot of fragrant spices. This comforting, intensely flavored crisp, with its crumbly granola topping, is best served warm accompanied by vegan vanilla ice cream for a harmonious combination of texture, temperatures, and flavors. I prefer Bosc pears for this recipe, but you may use another variety if you prefer. Be sure to remove the pith from the orange when peeling it to avoid any bitter taste. If you prefer not to include the brandy, simply omit it. To make this gluten-free, use gluten-free granola.

1 large orange
4 firm ripe Bosc pears, peeled, cored, and chopped
1 cup (145 g) raisins (dark, golden, or a combination)
1 cup (120 g) chopped dried apples, pears, or apricots, or a combination
1½ cups (360 ml) apple juice
½ cup (100 g) granulated natural sugar
¼ cup (60 ml) brandy, or 1 teaspoon brandy extract
2 tablespoons (30 ml) apple cider vinegar
½ teaspoon ground cinnamon
½ teaspoon ground nutmeg
½ teaspoon ground allspice
¼ teaspoon ground cloves
Pinch of salt
1¼ cups (152.5 g) granola of your choice
2 tablespoons (40 g) pure maple syrup or agave nectar

1. Remove 2 tablespoons (12 g) of zest from the orange and place it in a food processor. Peel and seed the orange and cut it into quarters. Remove and discard any white pith. Add the peeled and seeded orange quarters to the food processor and pulse until chopped, then transfer to the slow cooker.

2. Add the pears, raisins, dried apples, juice, sugar, brandy, vinegar, cinnamon, nutmeg, allspice, cloves, and salt. Stir to combine, then cover and cook on High for 2 hours.

(continued)

3. Remove the lid, stir the mixture, then continue to cook, uncovered, until the mixture thickens, about 2 hours.

4. In a bowl, combine the granola and maple syrup, stirring to coat. Stir the fruit mixture, then sprinkle the granola mixture over the top. Cover and cook for 1 hour longer. Serve warm, spooned into dessert dishes.

Banana Brown Betty

SERVES 4

SLOW COOKER SIZE: 4-QUART (3.8 L) | COOK TIME: 1½ TO 2 HOURS ON HIGH | GLUTEN-FREE OPTION | OIL-FREE | SOY-FREE

Bananas stand in for apples in this unusual take on the classic apple brown Betty dessert. In the words of recipe tester Jonathan Shanes, "Move over, bananas Foster!" This really does taste like bananas Foster—maybe it should be called Banana Brown Betty Foster? Whatever you call it, it's positively divine when topped with vegan vanilla ice cream. For gluten-free, use a gluten-free bread.

⅓ cup (107 g) pure maple syrup
¼ cup (60 ml) unsweetened plant milk
½ teaspoon ground cinnamon
¼ teaspoon ground ginger
¼ teaspoon ground nutmeg
⅛ teaspoon salt
6 cups (210 g) cubed bread
4 ripe bananas, peeled and chopped
⅓ cup (37 g) chopped toasted pecans
⅓ cup (67 g) granulated natural sugar
2 tablespoons (30 ml) brandy or rum, or 1 teaspoon brandy or rum extract

1. In a large bowl, combine the maple syrup, plant milk, cinnamon, ginger, nutmeg, and salt and mix well. Add the bread cubes and stir to coat.

2. In a separate bowl, combine the bananas, pecans, sugar, and brandy, stirring to mix.

3. Lightly oil the slow cooker insert or spray it with nonstick cooking spray. Spread half of the bread mixture in the bottom of the cooker, followed by half of the banana mixture. Repeat the layering, then cover and cook on High until firm, 1½ to 2 hours. Serve hot.

Three-Way Pumpkin Bread Pudding

SERVES 6 TO 8

SLOW COOKER SIZE: 4-QUART (3.8 L) | COOK TIME: 3 HOURS ON LOW | GLUTEN-FREE OPTION |
OIL-FREE OPTION | SOY-FREE OPTION

I've been a fan of pumpkin bread pudding for as long as I can remember, but sometimes the pumpkin flavor can get lost amid all the fragrant spices and boozy sauces. This version puts the "pumpkin" in pumpkin bread pudding because it includes both cubes of pumpkin cake and pumpkin puree and is topped with a lightning-quick pumpkin sauce. Bread may be substituted for the pumpkin cake, if desired—it will still have a delicious pumpkin-y flavor. You may also add ½ cup (60 g) sweetened dried cranberries to the mixture. For a gluten-free version, use gluten-free cake or bread; for soy-free, use a soy-free plant milk; for oil-free, use oil-free pumpkin cake.

BREAD PUDDING

2 cups (about 75 g) cubed Spiced Pumpkin Cake (page 270)
    or other pumpkin cake or bread

2 cups (70 g) cubed whole-grain bread (such as oat bread)

1 (16-ounce, or 455 g) can solid-pack pumpkin

¾ cup (150 g) granulated natural sugar

3 tablespoons (45 ml) rum or bourbon, or 1 teaspoon rum extract (optional)

1 teaspoon pure vanilla extract

1½ teaspoons ground cinnamon

¼ teaspoon ground nutmeg

¼ teaspoon ground ginger

¼ teaspoon ground allspice

¼ teaspoon salt

3 cups (720 ml) plant milk, warmed

(continued)

½ cup (120 ml) vegan creamer or a thick plant milk, plus more if needed

¼ cup (61.25 g) reserved pumpkin puree (from can used to make bread pudding)

1 teaspoon granulated natural sugar

⅛ teaspoon ground cinnamon

⅛ teaspoon ground nutmeg

⅛ teaspoon ground ginger

1 tablespoon (15 ml) rum or bourbon, or 1 teaspoon rum extract (optional)

1. To make the bread pudding: Lightly coat the slow cooker insert with vegan butter or nonstick cooking spray. Press half each of the cake and bread cubes into the bottom of the cooker.

2. Remove ¼ cup (61 g) of the pumpkin puree from the can and set aside for the sauce. In a large bowl, combine the remaining pumpkin puree, sugar, rum (if using), vanilla, cinnamon, nutmeg, ginger, allspice, and salt. Blend well, then slowly add the warm plant milk, stirring constantly. Carefully pour half of the pumpkin mixture over the cake and bread cubes in the slow cooker, pressing them into the wet mixture to moisten. Repeat with the remaining cake and bread cubes and the rest of the pumpkin mixture. Cover and cook on Low until firm, about 3 hours.

3. Turn off the slow cooker and let the pudding sit, covered, for 20 minutes before serving. In the meantime, make the sauce.

4. To make the pumpkin sauce: In a small saucepan, combine all of the ingredients over medium heat and stir to blend well. Cook, stirring, for about 4 minutes to mellow the flavor of the pumpkin and spices. For a thinner sauce, stir in a little more creamer. The sauce can be used warm, or it can be made ahead and chilled before using.

5. To serve, spoon the warm bread pudding into dessert bowls and drizzle with the sauce.

Zabaglione-Inspired Bread Pudding

SERVES 6

SLOW COOKER SIZE: 4-QUART (3.8 L) | COOK TIME: 3 HOURS ON LOW | GLUTEN-FREE OPTION | SOY-FREE

Zabaglione is a light custard made with Marsala that is traditionally served on its own or as a sauce over cake or fruit. In France it's called sabayon. Among the new twists in this recipe, the sauce becomes part of a delicious bread pudding and is topped with berries, with white chocolate added for an extra layer of flavor. The main twist, of course, is that this version is 100 percent vegan. For gluten-free bread pudding, use gluten-free bread.

½ cup (88 g) vegan white chocolate chips
3 cups (720 ml) plain unsweetened plant milk
½ cup (100 g) granulated natural sugar
½ cup (120 ml) dry Marsala wine
Pinch of salt
6 cups (210 g) cubed bread
2 cups (250 g) fresh raspberries or (340 g) sliced strawberries, for serving

1. In a saucepan, combine the white chocolate chips with 1 cup (240 ml) of plant milk. Cook, stirring, over low heat until the chocolate is melted and the mixture is smooth. Stir in the sugar, Marsala, and salt, then slowly add the remaining plant milk, stirring until well blended.

2. Lightly coat the slow cooker insert with vegan butter or nonstick cooking spray. Press half of the bread cubes into the bottom of the cooker. Pour half of the Marsala mixture over the bread cubes in the slow cooker, pressing them into the Marsala mixture to moisten. Repeat with the remaining bread and Marsala mixture. Cover and cook on Low until firm, about 3 hours.

3. Turn off the slow cooker and let the pudding rest, covered, for 20 minutes. Serve warm, topped with fresh berries.

Warm and Fudgy Chocolate Bread Pudding

SERVES 6

SLOW COOKER SIZE: 4- TO 6-QUART (3.8 TO 5.7 L) | COOK TIME: 2½ TO 3 HOURS ON HIGH |
GLUTEN-FREE OPTION | SOY-FREE OPTION

This chocolaty dessert gives you that "warm and fudgy" feeling inside. I highly recommend serving this bread pudding warm with vegan vanilla ice cream. For gluten-free, use gluten-free bread; for soy-free, use a soy-free vegan butter.

2 cups (480 ml) unsweetened plant milk
2 cups (350 g) vegan semisweet chocolate chips
4 cups (140 g) white bread cubes
½ cup (55 g) chopped pecans or walnuts (optional)
¾ cup (150 g) granulated natural sugar
¼ cup (21.5 g) unsweetened cocoa powder
½ teaspoon salt
1 teaspoon pure vanilla extract
1 tablespoon (14 g) vegan butter

1. Lightly coat the insert of the slow cooker with vegan butter or nonstick cooking spray. Heat 1½ cups (360 ml) of plant milk in a saucepan until it is just ready to boil. Take the pan off the heat and stir in 1⅔ cups (292 g) of chocolate chips. Stir until the chips are melted, then set aside.

2. Spread the bread cubes in the prepared slow cooker. Sprinkle with the nuts (if uinsg), and the remaining ⅓ cup (58 g) chocolate chips.

3. Heat the remaining ½ cup (120 ml) of plant milk in another saucepan. Add the sugar, cocoa, salt, and vanilla, stirring to dissolve, about 2 minutes. Combine the cocoa mixture with the chocolate chip mixture, then pour it all over the bread in the slow cooker. Press the bread cubes down so that they are submerged in the chocolate mixture. Dot the top of the bread pudding with bits of the vegan butter. Cover and cook on High until a tester inserted in the center comes out clean, 2½ to 3 hours.

4. Remove the lid, turn off the cooker, and let stand for at least 15 minutes before serving. Serve warm or at room temperature.

Coconut Rice Pudding with Mango

SERVES 6

SLOW COOKER SIZE: 4-QUART (3.8 L) | COOK TIME: 1½ TO 2 HOURS ON HIGH | GLUTEN-FREE | OIL-FREE | SOY-FREE

A favorite dessert in Thai restaurants, rice pudding with fresh mango is easy to make at home in your slow cooker. If you prefer a sweeter pudding, add up to ¼ cup (50 g) extra sugar.

1½ cups (300 g) raw jasmine rice

½ cup (100 g) granulated natural sugar, or more to taste

¼ teaspoon salt

2 (14-ounce, or 395 g) cans unsweetened coconut milk

½ cup (120 ml) unsweetened plant milk, plus more if needed

1 teaspoon coconut extract

1 teaspoon pure vanilla extract

1 large ripe mango, peeled, pitted, and chopped

1. Lightly coat the slow cooker insert with vegan butter or nonstick cooking spray. Combine the rice, sugar, and salt in the cooker. In a saucepan or the microwave, heat the coconut milk and plant milk just to boiling. Slowly add the heated milks to the slow cooker, stirring to dissolve the sugar. Cover and cook on High until the rice is tender, about 1½ hours.

2. Turn off the slow cooker and stir in the coconut and vanilla extracts. Allow to cool, uncovered, for 10 minutes, then stir in the mango. To help thicken the pudding, stir it gently to let it absorb any remaining liquid; it will continue to thicken as it cools. If the pudding is too thick, stir in a little more plant milk until it's the consistency you like. The pudding can be served warm, at room temperature, or chilled. To serve chilled, spoon the pudding into dessert glasses, cover, and refrigerate until cold.

Apricot Tapioca Pudding

SLOW COOKER SIZE: 4-QUART (3.8 L) | COOK TIME: 2 HOURS AND 20 MINUTES ON LOW | GLUTEN-FREE |
OIL-FREE | SOY-FREE

To make this homey dessert extra special, garnish each serving with a dollop of vegan whipped cream (soy-free, if desired).

⅓ cup (42 g) small pearl tapioca
½ cup (65 g) chopped dried apricots
⅓ cup (67 g) granulated natural sugar
2½ cups (600 ml) unsweetened plant milk
¼ cup (80 g) apricot preserves
1 teaspoon pure vanilla extract

1. Lightly coat the slow cooker insert with nonstick cooking spray. Combine the tapioca, apricots, sugar, and plant milk in the cooker. Stir to combine. Cover and cook on Low until the pudding has thickened and the liquid is absorbed, about 2 hours.

2. In a small bowl, combine the preserves and the vanilla, stirring to blend. Add the mixture to the pudding, stirring to mix well. Cover and continue to cook on Low for 20 minutes longer.

3. Remove the lid, turn off the cooker, and allow to cool. Serve at room temperature or chilled. To serve chilled, spoon the pudding into dessert bowls, cover tightly, and refrigerate until needed.

Lemon-Ginger Poached Pears

SERVES 4 TO 6

SLOW COOKER SIZE: 4- TO 6-QUART (3.8 TO 5.7 L) | COOK TIME: 2 HOURS ON LOW, PLUS 30 MINUTES ON HIGH | GLUTEN-FREE | OIL-FREE | SOY-FREE

These pears may be enjoyed warm or chilled; I especially like them served at room temperature with a scoop of vegan vanilla ice cream and a slice of vegan pound cake. I prefer Bosc pears in this recipe, although you may use Bartletts instead. Use more or less ginger, depending on your personal preference.

2½ cups (600 ml) white grape juice
¼ cup (50 g) granulated natural sugar, plus more if needed
2 to 3 teaspoons (6 g) grated peeled fresh ginger
4 to 6 strips lemon zest
Pinch of salt
½ cinnamon stick
4 to 6 firm ripe Bosc or Bartlett pears, peeled, halved, and cored
Juice of 1 lemon
Mint sprigs, for garnish (optional)

1. Heat the grape juice, sugar, ginger, lemon zest, and salt in a saucepan on the stove or in a bowl in the microwave until hot, stirring to dissolve the sugar. Transfer to the slow cooker and add the cinnamon stick.

2. Add the pears to the slow cooker. Cover and cook on Low until the pears are just tender, about 2 hours. Do not overcook.

3. Use a slotted spoon to transfer the pears to a shallow bowl and drizzle with the lemon juice. Taste the poaching liquid, adding more sugar if needed. Turn the setting to High and cook, uncovered, to reduce the poaching liquid by half, about 30 minutes. Strain the reduced liquid into a bowl and set aside to cool completely.

4. To serve, arrange the pears in shallow dessert bowls. Drizzle with some of the poaching liquid and garnish with mint sprigs (if using). Serve warm, chilled, or at room temperature.

Baked Cran-Apples

SLOW COOKER SIZE: 4- TO 7-QUART (3.8 TO 6.7 L) | COOK TIME: 2½ TO 4 HOURS ON HIGH | GLUTEN-FREE |
OIL-FREE | SOY-FREE

Baked apples are a wonderful autumn treat that fills the house with the fragrance of apple pie as they cook. Healthful and easy to make, these apples, stuffed with sweet-tart cranberries and bits of walnuts or pecans, are best served warm and are especially good paired with a scoop of vegan vanilla ice cream. They can also be enjoyed for breakfast (without the ice cream!) or even as a side dish at dinner. Use as many apples as will fit side by side in your slow cooker; the cooking time will depend on the number and size of the apples used. Because the peels will stay on, try to get organic apples for this recipe.

4 to 6 large firm apples, such as Granny Smith or Rome Beauty, washed
Juice of 1 lemon
⅓ cup (67 g) granulated natural sugar
⅓ cup (40 g) sweetened dried cranberries
¼ cup (24 g) crushed, chopped, or coarsely ground almonds, walnuts, or pecans
½ teaspoon ground cinnamon
½ cup (120 ml) naturally sweetened cranberry juice

1. Core the apples about three-quarters of the way down, leaving enough on the bottom so the stuffing doesn't leak out. Peel a ½-inch (1 cm) band of the peel from the cored apples about one-quarter of the way down from the top. Rub the exposed part of the apples with the lemon juice to avoid discoloration. Lightly oil the slow cooker insert or spray it with nonstick cooking spray and place the apples upright in a single layer in the cooker.

2. In a small bowl, combine the sugar, cranberries, nuts, and cinnamon. Pack the mixture into the cored center of each apple (it's okay if it heaps on top). Pour the cranberry juice into the slow cooker to surround the apples. Cover and cook on High until the apples are soft but not collapsing, 2½ to 4 hours. (If your slow cooker runs hot, check the apples after 2 hours.)

3. Remove the lid and turn off the cooker to allow the apples to cool slightly. Serve warm or at room temperature, drizzled with the cooking liquid.

Maple-and-Rum-Glazed Slow-Baked Apples

SERVES 6

SLOW COOKER SIZE: 4- TO 7-QUART (3.8 TO 6.7 L) | COOK TIME: 2 TO 4 HOURS ON HIGH | GLUTEN-FREE | OIL-FREE | SOY-FREE

This recipe is courtesy of Melissa Chapman, who tested many of the recipes for this book. She developed this luscious glazed-apple recipe when she scored loads of locally grown apples at the farmers' market. Use as many apples as will fit side by side in your slow cooker; the cooking time will depend on the number and size of the apples used. Because the peels will stay on, try to get organic apples for this recipe. For gluten-free, use certified gluten-free oats.

4 to 6 tart apples, washed
Juice of 1 lemon

FILLING

¼ cup (39 g) old-fashioned rolled oats
⅓ cup (75 g) packed light brown sugar
¼ cup (35 g) golden raisins
¼ cup (34 g) macadamia nut pieces or your favorite nut
¼ teaspoon ground nutmeg
½ teaspoon ground cinnamon

GLAZE

½ cup (160 ml) pure maple syrup
½ cup (120 ml) apple juice
¼ cup (60 ml) dark rum or spiced rum
¼ teaspoon ground nutmeg
¼ teaspoon ground cinnamon

(continued)

1. Core the apples about three-quarters of the way down, leaving enough on the bottom so the stuffing doesn't leak out. Peel a ½-inch (1 cm) band of the peel from the cored apples about one-quarter of the way down from the top. Rub the exposed part of the apples with the lemon juice to prevent discoloration.

2. To make the filling: In a small bowl, combine all of the filling ingredients, stirring to mix well. Pack the mixture into the cored center of each apple (it's okay if it heaps on top).

3. To make the glaze: In a small bowl, combine all of the glaze ingredients, stirring to mix well.

4. Arrange the stuffed apples upright in a single layer in the slow cooker and pour the glaze over the apples. Cover and cook on Low until the apples are soft but not collapsing, 2 to 4 hours, basting the apples with the glaze a few times throughout the cooking process.

5. Remove the lid and turn off the cooker to allow the apples to cool slightly. Serve warm or at room temperature, drizzled with the cooking liquid.

Granola-Stuffed Baked Apples   SERVES 4 TO 6

SLOW COOKER SIZE: 4- TO 7-QUART (3.8 TO 6.7 L) | COOK TIME: 2 TO 4 HOURS ON HIGH |
GLUTEN-FREE OPTION | SOY-FREE OPTION

When baked apples are stuffed with granola, it gives them an added dimension of texture and flavor, reminiscent of an apple crisp. Like the previous recipe, these are as good for breakfast as they are for dessert. Use as many apples as will fit side by side in your slow cooker. The cooking time and amount of granola needed will depend on the number and size of the apples used. For gluten-free, use gluten-free granola; for soy-free, use a soy-free vegan butter.

4 to 6 large firm apples, such as Granny Smith or Rome Beauty, washed
Juice of 1 lemon
1 to 1½ cups (122 to 183 g) granola of your choice
2 tablespoons (25 g) granulated natural sugar
½ teaspoon ground cinnamon
1½ tablespoons (21 g) vegan butter, cut into 4 to 6 pieces
½ cup (120 ml) apple juice

1. Core the apples about three-quarters of the way down, leaving enough on the bottom so the stuffing doesn't leak out. Peel a ½-inch (1 cm) band of the peel from the cored apples about one-quarter of the way down from the top. Rub the exposed part of the apples with the lemon juice to prevent discoloration. Lightly coat the slow cooker insert with vegan butter or nonstick cooking spray, and place the apples upright in a single layer in the cooker.

2. In a small bowl, combine the granola, sugar, and cinnamon. Pack the mixture into the cored center of each apple (it's okay if it heaps on top). Dot the tops of the apples with the vegan butter. Pour the apple juice into the slow cooker to surround the apples. Cover and cook on High until the apples are soft but not collapsing, 2 to 4 hours. (If your slow cooker runs hot, check the apples after 1½ hours.)

3. Remove the lid and turn off the cooker to allow the apples to cool slightly. Serve warm or at room temperature, drizzled with the cooking liquid.

Breakfast and Breads

Breakfast—or bread, for that matter—probably isn't the first thing you think of when you consider using a slow cooker. But there are ways to make them in a slow cooker that are as convenient as they are delicious.

In this chapter, you'll find some breakfast recipes made with nutritious whole grains that can cook overnight so they're ready by morning. Other recipes take only a few hours to cook but can easily be made overnight with the help of an automatic timer. If your slow cooker doesn't have a timer, you can purchase an inexpensive kitchen appliance timer, available at hardware stores, that will allow you to set your slow cooker to begin cooking up to two hours after you go to bed. (Remember, raw food should not be left at room temperature for longer than two hours.) Many slow cookers are also equipped with a Keep Warm setting, which can be handy if your breakfast is ready before you are. Another option is simply to make a large batch of oatmeal, for example, ahead of time in the slow cooker, store it in the refrigerator, and then reheat a portion each morning in the microwave.

If cooked grains aren't your thing, this chapter also includes a variety of frittatas and bread puddings that can be enjoyed for breakfast, brunch, or a light supper.

The breads in this chapter can be enjoyed any time of day as well. I call them "slow quick breads," since they are, in fact, quick breads that can be made in a slow cooker.

Carrot Cake Oatmeal

SERVES 6

SLOW COOKER SIZE: 4-QUART (3.8 L) | COOK TIME: 7 TO 8 HOURS ON LOW OR 4 HOURS ON HIGH |
GLUTEN-FREE OPTION

Carrot cake for breakfast may not sound like the healthiest choice, but when it comes in the form of a delicious slow-cooked oatmeal, there's no reason to say no. I like to load mine up with shredded coconut, vegan yogurt, walnuts, and a drizzle of maple syrup. To make this gluten-free, use certified gluten-free oats.

1½ cups (264 g) steel-cut oats
2 tablespoons (14 g) ground flaxseed
1½ teaspoons ground cinnamon
¼ teaspoon ground ginger
⅛ teaspoon ground nutmeg
½ teaspoon salt
2 large carrots, grated
½ cup (60 g) chopped walnuts
½ cup (75 g) golden raisins
¼ cup (80 g) pure maple syrup
1½ teaspoons vanilla extract
2 cups (480 ml) almond milk or other plant milk
1½ cups (360 ml) water
Optional toppings: shredded unsweetened coconut, chopped toasted walnuts, vegan vanilla yogurt, maple syrup

1. In a slow cooker, combine the oats, ground flaxseed, cinnamon, ginger, nutmeg, and salt. Stir in the carrots, walnuts, raisins, maple syrup, and vanilla. Add the almond milk and water and stir until well combined.

2. Cover and cook on Low for 7 to 8 hours or until the oats and carrots are soft. Serve hot topped with your choice of toppings (if using).

Chocolate Oatmeal with Raspberries and Rose Petals

SERVES 4

SLOW COOKER SIZE: 4-QUART (3.8 L) | COOK TIME: 6 TO 8 HOURS ON LOW OR 4 HOURS ON HIGH |
GLUTEN-FREE OPTION | OIL-FREE | SOY-FREE

Who says oatmeal can't be special? This one is all dressed up for Valentine's Day, but can be enjoyed any time you want a treat for breakfast. Look for food-grade dried rose petals in specialty markets or online. To make this gluten-free, use certified gluten-free oats.

1 cup (176 g) steel-cut oats

3¼ cups (780 ml) almond milk or other plant milk

¼ teaspoon salt

3 tablespoons (15 g) cocoa powder

¼ cup (80 g) pure maple syrup

2 tablespoons (14 g) ground flaxseed

½ teaspoon vanilla extract

Optional toppings: maple syrup, fresh raspberries, chocolate chips or cacao nibs, dried rose petals

1. In a slow cooker, combine the oats, plant milk, and salt.

2. In a small bowl, blend the cocoa powder with ⅓ cup (80 ml) of water until smooth. Add the cocoa mixture to the slow cooker, along with the maple syrup, ground flaxseed, and vanilla. Stir until well combined.

3. Cover and cook on Low for 6 to 8 hours or until the oats are tender. Serve hot topped with your choice of maple syrup, raspberries, chocolate chips, cacao nibs, and/or rose petals.

Slow-Cooker Granola

MAKES ABOUT 8 CUPS (ABOUT 1 KG)

SLOW COOKER SIZE: 4- TO 6-QUART (3.8 TO 5.7 L) | COOK TIME: 1 HOUR ON HIGH, PLUS 2 HOURS ON LOW |
GLUTEN-FREE OPTION | SOY-FREE

Making your own granola at home is easy and economical. It tastes better, too, since you make it fresh and can add whatever ingredients you like, substituting different dried fruits or nuts according to taste. To make this granola gluten-free, use certified gluten-free oats.

⅔ cup (213 g) pure maple syrup
¼ cup (60 ml) avocado oil or other neutral-tasting oil
¼ cup (50 g) granulated natural sugar
3 tablespoons (45 ml) water
1 teaspoon pure vanilla extract
5 cups (780 g) old-fashioned rolled oats
1 cup (110 g) slivered blanched almonds
½ cup (72.5 g) sunflower seeds
½ cup (42.5 g) unsweetened shredded coconut
½ cup (89 g) chopped dates or (65 g) dried apricots
½ cup (75 g) golden raisins or (60 g) sweetened dried cranberries

1. Lightly coat the slow cooker insert with vegan butter or nonstick cooking spray and turn on the setting to High. Add the maple syrup, oil, sugar, water, and vanilla and stir to blend and dissolve the sugar.

2. In a bowl, combine the oats, almonds, sunflower seeds, coconut, and dates, mixing well. Transfer about half of the oat mixture to the slow cooker, stirring to coat with the wet mixture. Add the remaining half of the oat mixture and stir to combine and coat evenly. Cook, uncovered, on High, stirring occasionally, for 1 hour.

3. Reduce the heat to Low, cover, and cook, stirring occasionally, until the granola is crisp and dry, about 2 hours. (If your slow cooker runs hot, it may be done a bit sooner, and be sure to stir occasionally so it doesn't burn if you have a "hot spot.") Stir in the raisins. Remove the lid and allow the granola to cool in the slow cooker, or spread the granola on a baking sheet to cool completely. Store in a tightly covered container at room temperature. The granola will keep well for several weeks, longer if frozen.

BREAKFAST BOWL TOPPERS

Here are some delicious ways to top your bowl of hot oatmeal or other hot breakfast cereal:

- Agave nectar
- Chopped dried plums
- Chopped fresh apple, pear, and/or peach
- Cinnamon
- Dark unsulfured molasses
- Dried cranberries, blueberries, or raisins
- Dried goji berries
- Fresh berries
- Fruit jam or preserves
- Granola
- Ground flaxseed
- Hemp hearts
- Maple syrup
- Pitted sliced dates
- Sliced fresh banana
- Slow-Cooked Apple Butter (page 248)
- Toasted chopped nuts or sunflower seeds
- Toasted sesame seeds
- Vegan yogurt

Granola Oatmeal

SERVES 4

SLOW COOKER SIZE: 4-QUART (3.8 L) | COOK TIME: 6 TO 8 HOURS ON LOW | GLUTEN-FREE OPTION | SOY-FREE

Granola is an easy way to add some sweetness and crunchy texture to your oatmeal. Use the homemade granola on page 300 or your favorite brand from the store. For gluten-free oatmeal, use gluten-free granola and certified gluten-free oats. Rolled oats generally take less time to cook than steel-cut oats.

1¼ cups (195 g) old-fashioned rolled oats or steel-cut oats
4½ cups (1 L) water
½ teaspoon salt
1½ teaspoons ground cinnamon
1 cup (122 g) granola
Unsweetened plant milk, for serving

1. Lightly coat the slow cooker insert with vegan butter or nonstick cooking spray. Combine the oats, water, salt, and cinnamon in the cooker. Cover and cook on Low until the oats are soft and the oatmeal is thickened, 6 to 8 hours.

2. Stir in the granola, adding more water or plant milk if the oatmeal is too thick. Serve hot, spooned into bowls and drizzled with a little plant milk.

302 The Plant-Based Slow Cooker

Overnight Apple-Cinnamon Oatmeal   SERVES 4

SLOW COOKER SIZE: 4-QUART (3.8 L) | COOK TIME: 7 TO 8 HOURS ON LOW | GLUTEN-FREE | OIL-FREE | SOY-FREE

You'll love waking up to this fragrant oatmeal. Turn on your slow cooker just before you go to bed and it will be ready in the morning. Leftover oatmeal can be reheated in the microwave or a saucepan, with a little water or plant milk added to thin out the consistency. Dried chopped apples may be substituted for fresh in this recipe, if desired. For extra flavor, toast the oats in a dry skillet over medium heat, stirring until golden and fragrant, before adding to the slow cooker. For gluten-free oatmeal, be sure to use certified gluten-free oats.

1¼ cups (220 g) steel-cut oats
3 cups (720 ml) water
2 cups (480 ml) apple juice
2 apples (I like Fuji or Gala in this recipe), peeled, cored, and chopped
½ cup (75 g) golden raisins or (60 g) sweetened dried cranberries
¼ cup (50 g) granulated natural sugar, or more to taste
1 tablespoon (7 g) ground flaxseed (optional)
1 teaspoon ground cinnamon
½ teaspoon salt
Unsweetened plant milk, for serving

1. Combine all of the ingredients except the plant milk in the slow cooker and mix well. Cover and cook on Low until the oatmeal is thickened and the oats are soft, 7 to 8 hours.

2. Serve hot, drizzled with a little plant milk.

PB & J Oatmeal

SLOW COOKER SIZE: 4-QUART (3.8 L) | COOK TIME: 7 TO 8 HOURS ON LOW | GLUTEN-FREE | OIL-FREE | SOY-FREE

Have your peanut butter at room temperature so that it is soft enough to streak into the oatmeal. If the peanut butter is especially firm, it's okay to add it into the oatmeal by the spoonful at any time during the cooking time. For gluten-free oatmeal, be sure to use certified gluten-free oats. Turn on your slow cooker just before going to bed so the oatmeal is ready in the morning.

1½ cups (264 g) steel-cut oats
5½ cups (1.3 L) water
¾ teaspoon salt
1 teaspoon ground cinnamon
½ cup (130 g) creamy peanut butter, at room temperature
½ cup (160 g) strawberry jam or your favorite fruit jelly, jam, or preserves
Unsweetened plant milk, for serving

1. Combine the oats, water, salt, and cinnamon in the slow cooker. Cover and cook on Low until the oatmeal is thickened and the oats are soft, 7 to 8 hours.

2. Stir the peanut butter into the oatmeal, followed by the jam—do not incorporate it, just streak it in. Serve hot, with drizzles of plant milk to achieve the desired consistency. Alternatively, you can serve the peanut butter and jam separately at the table, to be added as desired.

Amish Oatmeal

SERVES 6

SLOW COOKER SIZE: 4- TO 6-QUART (3.8 TO 5.7 L) | COOK TIME: 2 HOURS ON HIGH | GLUTEN-FREE |
SOY-FREE OPTION

Amish oatmeal is usually baked in a casserole, but I like to make it in my slow cooker. It cooks up in 2 hours or less, so it's great for a Sunday brunch. This oatmeal is typically firm and sweet (some say it's like eating an oatmeal cookie for breakfast), but you can add more or less sugar according to taste. Instead of dried cranberries, feel free to substitute raisins or another dried fruit—I especially like this made with dried blueberries, although it does turn the oatmeal a purplish color. For gluten-free oatmeal, be sure to use certified gluten-free oats; for soy-free, use a soy-free plant milk and vegan butter.

3 cups (720 ml) unsweetened plant milk
½ cup (100 g) granulated natural sugar or (160 g) maple syrup
2 tablespoons (28 g) vegan butter, melted
2 teaspoons pure vanilla extract
1½ teaspoons baking powder
1½ teaspoons ground cinnamon
½ teaspoon salt
2½ cups (390 g) old-fashioned rolled oats
⅔ cup (80 g) sweetened dried cranberries
½ cup (55 g) toasted slivered almonds or chopped walnuts

1. In a large mixing bowl, combine the plant milk, sugar, melted butter, vanilla, baking powder, cinnamon, and salt. Mix well until smooth and well blended. Add the oats, cranberries, and almonds and stir until combined.

2. Generously coat the slow cooker insert with vegan butter or nonstick cooking spray. Spread the mixture evenly in the cooker. Cover and cook on High until set in the middle, about 2 hours. Serve hot.

Pumpkin Breakfast Quinoa

SLOW COOKER SIZE: 4-QUART (3.8 L) | COOK TIME: 6 TO 7 HOURS ON LOW | GLUTEN-FREE | OIL-FREE | SOY-FREE

Wake up to the fragrance of pumpkin pie with this nourishing breakfast featuring protein-rich quinoa. Be sure to rinse the quinoa well before using to remove the bitter outer coating.

1 cup (184 g) quinoa, rinsed and drained
4 cups (960 ml) unsweetened plant milk
½ cup (122.5 g) canned solid-pack pumpkin
¼ cup (80 g) pure maple syrup or agave
1 teaspoon pure vanilla extract
½ teaspoon salt
1 teaspoon ground cinnamon
¼ teaspoon ground ginger
¼ teaspoon ground nutmeg
¼ teaspoon ground allspice
Sweetened dried cranberries, for garnish
Chopped toasted pecans, for garnish

1. Generously coat the slow cooker insert with vegan butter or nonstick cooking spray. Combine the quinoa, plant milk, pumpkin, maple syrup, vanilla, salt, cinnamon, ginger, nutmeg, and allspice in the cooker. Cover and cook on Low until the quinoa is soft and thickened, 6 to 7 hours.

2. Serve hot, spooned into bowls and sprinkled with cranberries and pecans.

Breakfast Polenta

SLOW COOKER SIZE: 4-QUART (3.8 L) | COOK TIME: 7 TO 8 HOURS ON LOW | GLUTEN-FREE |
OIL-FREE OPTION | SOY-FREE OPTION

Long before polenta became a darling of the dinner table, it was known to many as a breakfast food called cornmeal porridge or mush. I think "breakfast polenta" has a nicer ring to it. Instead of the sweet toppings listed below, you could omit the maple syrup and add savory toppings such as vegan bacon bits, cooked crumbled plant-based sausage, chopped sun-dried tomatoes, and so on. For oil-free, omit the vegan butter; for soy-free, use a soy-free vegan butter.

1 cup (140 g) medium- or coarse-ground polenta or cornmeal

4 cups (960 ml) water

1 teaspoon salt

1 tablespoon (14 g) vegan butter (optional)

2 tablespoons (40 g) pure maple syrup, plus more for serving

Fresh berries, sliced bananas, dried cranberries, and/or toasted nuts, for topping (optional)

1. Combine the cornmeal, water, and salt in the slow cooker. Cover and cook on Low, stirring occasionally, if possible, until thickened, 7 to 8 hours. Taste and adjust the seasonings, adding more salt if needed.

2. Just before serving, stir in the vegan butter (if using), and the maple syrup. Serve hot, passing additional maple syrup at the table, along with any of the optional toppings.

Indian Pudding

SLOW COOKER SIZE: 4-QUART (3.8 L) | COOK TIME: 3 HOURS ON HIGH OR 6 TO 8 HOURS ON LOW |
GLUTEN-FREE | SOY-FREE OPTION

This Native American classic is known for its rich molasses flavor. I've included it in the breakfast chapter because it's an excellent and nutritious option, but really it's probably at its best served warm for dessert with a scoop of vegan vanilla ice cream. For soy-free pudding, use a soy-free vegan butter.

3½ cups (840 ml) unsweetened plant milk
½ cup (70 g) medium-ground cornmeal
½ teaspoon salt
¼ cup (50 g) granulated natural sugar
¼ cup (85 g) molasses
½ teaspoon ground cinnamon
½ teaspoon ground ginger
¼ teaspoon ground nutmeg
⅔ cup (118 g) chopped dates
1 teaspoon pure vanilla extract
½ teaspoon baking powder
2 tablespoons (28 g) vegan butter

1. Lightly coat the insert of the slow cooker with nonstick cooking spray.

2. In a large saucepan, combine 2 cups (480 ml) of plant milk, the cornmeal, and salt and bring to a boil, stirring constantly. Reduce the heat to medium and stir in the sugar, molasses, cinnamon, ginger, nutmeg, and dates. Remove from the heat and add 1 cup (240 ml) of plant milk, the vanilla, and baking powder, stirring until blended.

3. Transfer the mixture to the slow cooker. Pour the remaining ½ cup (120 ml) of plant milk on top and dot with the vegan butter. Cover and cook on High for 3 hours or on Low for 6 to 8 hours. Serve warm.

Congee in a Crock

SLOW COOKER SIZE: 4- TO 6-QUART (3.8 TO 5.7 L) | COOK TIME: 4 TO 6 HOURS ON LOW, PLUS 30 MINUTES ON HIGH IF NEEDED | GLUTEN-FREE | OIL-FREE | SOY-FREE OPTION

Congee is a bland rice porridge served with a variety of savory toppings. It is enjoyed as a breakfast food in China. Serve it hot in small bowls accompanied by a variety of condiments, to be added according to taste. I use Arborio rice for a creamy texture, but any medium-grain rice may be used instead. Different types of rice require different cooking times. For soy-free congee, omit the soy sauce and use a Soy-Free Sauce (page 344) or coconut aminos, or add some soy-free vegetable broth base or additional salt.

1 cup (192 g) raw Arborio rice
1 small yellow onion, minced
2 teaspoons grated peeled fresh ginger
6 cups (1.4 L) hot vegetable broth
1 teaspoon salt
1 tablespoon (15 ml) soy sauce
Chopped scallions, crushed roasted peanuts, soy sauce, sriracha sauce, and/or toasted sesame oil, for serving

1. Combine the rice, onion, and ginger in the slow cooker. Stir in the hot broth, salt, and soy sauce. Cover and cook on Low until the texture is thick and creamy, 4 to 6 hours. If it is not done after 6 hours, remove the lid, turn the setting to High, and cook, uncovered, until the liquid is absorbed and the rice is tender, about 30 minutes.

2. Ladle the congee into soup bowls and sprinkle with some scallions and peanuts, with additional to pass at the table, along with bottles of soy sauce, sriracha, and sesame oil for diners to add according to their tastes.

French Toast Bread Pudding

SLOW COOKER SIZE: 4- TO 6-QUART (3.8 TO 5.7 L) | COOK TIME: 1½ TO 2 HOURS ON HIGH |
GLUTEN-FREE OPTION

Consider making this luscious bread pudding for a special breakfast or brunch. When Lori Maffei tested this recipe, she remarked that it was so good that she had to force herself to stop eating it right out of the slow cooker to save some for her children. Here's what else she said: "I thought this was just perfect. Delicious and very appealing visually as well, especially with the nuts. I can see using dried fruit or fresh apples, or both, as variations. Did I say how much I love this recipe?!" For a gluten-free version, use a gluten-free bread.

8 cups (280 g) soft white Italian bread cubes
6 ounces (170 g) soft or silken tofu, drained
½ cup (120 g) packed light brown sugar
2 teaspoons pure vanilla extract
1 teaspoon ground cinnamon
¼ teaspoon ground nutmeg
⅛ teaspoon ground allspice
¼ teaspoon salt
2 cups (480 ml) plant milk
¼ cup (80 g) pure maple syrup, plus more for serving
1 tablespoon (14 g) vegan butter
¼ cup (27.5 g) coarsely chopped pecans or walnuts

1. Preheat the oven to 275°F (140°C). Spread the bread cubes on a baking sheet and bake for 30 minutes to dry the bread.

2. Generously coat the slow cooker insert with vegan butter or nonstick cooking spray. Transfer the dried bread to the cooker.

3. In a food processor, combine the tofu, sugar, vanilla, cinnamon, nutmeg, allspice, and salt and process until well blended. Stir in the plant milk and maple syrup.

4. Pour the tofu mixture over the bread cubes in the slow cooker, pressing them into the wet mixture to moisten. Dot with bits of the vegan butter and sprinkle the top with the pecans. Cover and cook on High until firm, about 1½ hours. Serve topped with additional maple syrup.

Bananas Foster Bread Pudding

SERVES 4

This yummy bread pudding makes a special brunch dish—kind of a combination of bananas Foster and French toast, all in one fragrant and easy-to-make bread pudding. When topped with ice cream, it also makes a great dessert. For a gluten-free version, use a gluten-free bread.

½ cup (160 g) pure maple syrup
½ cup (100 g) granulated natural sugar
2 tablespoons (28 g) vegan butter
3 tablespoons (45 ml) dark rum or brandy (optional)
3 ripe bananas
6 ounces (170 g) firm silken tofu
1 cup (240 ml) plant milk
2 tablespoons (16 g) cornstarch
1 teaspoon pure vanilla extract
½ teaspoon salt
8 cups (280 g) cubed bread
1 cup (110 g) pecan pieces
⅓ cup (59 g) dried banana chips

1. In a saucepan, combine the maple syrup, sugar, and butter and cook over medium heat, stirring to dissolve the sugar and melt the butter. Stir in the rum (if using), then remove from the heat.

2. In a food processor, combine the bananas, tofu, plant milk, cornstarch, vanilla, and salt and process until smooth, scraping down the sides as needed. Add the maple syrup mixture and process to combine.

3. Generously coat the insert of the slow cooker with vegan butter or nonstick cooking spray. Combine the bread, pecans, and banana chips in the crock, stirring to mix well. Scrape the wet mixture onto the bread mixture, pressing the bread into the wet mixture to moisten. Cover and cook on High for 2 hours. Serve warm.

Sausage 'n' Scramble Casserole

SERVES 4 TO 6

SLOW COOKER SIZE: 4- TO 6-QUART (3.8 TO 5.7 L) | COOK TIME: 2 HOURS ON HIGH | OIL-FREE OPTION

This hearty casserole is ideal for breakfast or brunch, but it also makes a great main dish for a light supper.

2 teaspoons olive oil, or ¼ cup (60 ml) water

1 medium-size yellow onion, minced

3 garlic cloves, minced

1 red or green bell pepper, seeded and chopped

2 cups (140 g) sliced white mushrooms

½ teaspoon dried basil

½ teaspoon ground fennel seed

¼ teaspoon red pepper flakes, or more to taste

2 cups (220 g) chopped cooked Plant-Based Sausage Links (page 174)

1 pound (455 g) firm tofu, drained and crumbled

1½ cups (360 ml) plain unsweetened plant milk

3 tablespoons (11.25 g) nutritional yeast

1 tablespoon (8 g) cornstarch

1 teaspoon yellow mustard

1 teaspoon smoked paprika

¼ teaspoon ground cayenne pepper (optional)

Salt and freshly ground black pepper

6 cups (210 g) cubed French or Italian bread

¾ cup (180 ml) Cheesy Sauce (page 340)

2 tablespoons (8 g) chopped fresh flat-leaf parsley or basil, for garnish

1. For the best flavor, heat the oil in a large skillet over medium-high heat. Add the onion and sauté until softened, about 5 minutes. Add the garlic, bell pepper, and mushrooms and cook for 2 minutes longer. Stir in the dried basil, fennel, and red pepper flakes. Alternatively, omit the oil and sauté these ingredients in a few tablespoons of water or combine them in a microwave-safe bowl with a little water, cover, and microwave for 2 minutes. Drain off any liquid. Stir in the crumbled sausage and set aside.

2. In a food processor or blender, combine the tofu, plant milk, nutritional yeast, cornstarch, mustard, paprika, and cayenne (if using). Season to taste with salt and black pepper and blend until smooth. Taste and adjust the seasonings, adding more salt if needed.

3. Generously coat the slow cooker insert with vegan butter or nonstick cooking spray. Spread the bread cubes in the bottom of the slow cooker. Add the reserved sausage mixture, then add the tofu mixture and stir to combine. Spread the mixture out evenly in the slow cooker, and drizzle the top with the cheesy sauce. Cover and cook on High for 2 hours. Serve hot, sprinkled with the parsley.

Cheesy Mushroom-Chorizo Frittata   SERVES 4

SLOW COOKER SIZE: 4- TO 6-QUART (3.8 TO 5.7 L) | COOK TIME: 2 TO 3 HOURS ON HIGH | GLUTEN-FREE

To save time in the morning, assemble this the night before and then turn on the cooker first thing in the morning for a leisurely brunch main dish. (It also makes a good light supper choice.) Vegan frittatas hold well in the slow cooker and are best prepared in a wide, shallow cooker. It can be a little difficult to remove the first piece of the frittata, but after that, the pieces are easier to get out.

1 pound (455 g) firm tofu, well drained and lightly pressed
½ cup (120 ml) vegetable broth
¼ cup (15 g) nutritional yeast
1 tablespoon (8 g) cornstarch or tapioca starch
½ teaspoon onion powder
½ teaspoon garlic powder
½ teaspoon dried basil
½ teaspoon smoked paprika
Salt and freshly ground black pepper
2 teaspoons olive oil, or ¼ cup (60 ml) water
5 scallions, minced
8 ounces (225 g) white mushrooms, chopped
1 cup (192 g) Tofu Chorizo (page 343)
1 cup (240 ml) Cheesy Sauce (page 340)

(continued)

1. In a food processor or blender, combine the tofu, broth, nutritional yeast, cornstarch, onion powder, garlic powder, basil, paprika, and salt and pepper to taste. Process until smooth and well blended. Set aside.

2. For the best flavor, heat the oil in a large skillet over medium-high heat. Add the scallions, mushrooms, chorizo, and salt and black pepper to taste and cook until the mushrooms release their liquid and it evaporates. Alternatively, omit the oil and sauté these ingredients in a few tablespoons of water or combine them in a microwave-safe bowl with a little water, cover, and microwave for 2 minutes. Drain off any liquid exuded by the mushrooms.

3. Generously coat the slow cooker insert with vegan butter or nonstick cooking spray. Combine the chorizo mixture and the tofu mixture in the slow cooker, mixing well and spreading evenly. Top with the cheesy sauce. Cover and cook on High until firm, 2 to 3 hours.

4. Cut into wedges and serve hot.

Artichoke and Mushroom Frittata   SERVES 4

SLOW COOKER SIZE: 4- TO 6-QUART (3.8 TO 5.7 L) | COOK TIME: 3 TO 4 HOURS ON LOW | GLUTEN-FREE | OIL-FREE OPTION

Studded with pieces of artichoke heart and mushrooms, this frittata is a good choice for a brunch or light supper served with crusty bread. It holds well in the slow cooker and is best prepared in a wide, shallow cooker. It can be a little difficult to remove the first piece of the frittata, but after that, the pieces are easier to get out. For oil-free, use the water-sauté method and reconstituted sun-dried tomatoes.

1 pound (455 g) firm tofu, well drained and lightly pressed

1 cup (240 ml) vegetable broth

3 tablespoons (11.25 g) nutritional yeast

1 tablespoon (8 g) cornstarch or tapioca starch

½ teaspoon onion powder

Salt and freshly ground black pepper

⅓ cup (38 g) chopped oil-packed or reconstituted sun-dried tomatoes

¼ cup (60 ml) water, or 2 teaspoons olive oil

5 scallions, minced

8 ounces (225 g) white mushrooms, thinly sliced or chopped

½ teaspoon dried thyme

½ teaspoon dried basil

2 cups (600 g) canned artichoke hearts or (230 g) frozen artichoke hearts, thawed, chopped

1 teaspoon capers, drained, chopped if large

½ cup (120 ml) Cheesy Sauce (page 340)

1. In a food processor or blender, combine the tofu, broth, nutritional yeast, cornstarch, onion powder, and salt and pepper to taste. Add 1 tablespoon (7 g) of sun-dried tomatoes and process until smooth and well blended. Set aside.

2. Heat the water or oil in a medium-size skillet over medium-high heat. Add the scallions, mushrooms, thyme, basil, and salt and black pepper to taste and cook for 3 to 4 minutes. Drain off any liquid exuded by the mushrooms. Stir in the artichokes, the remaining sun-dried tomatoes, and the capers.

3. Coat the insert of the slow cooker with vegan butter or nonstick cooking spray. Spread the cooked vegetables evenly in the bottom of the cooker. Add the reserved tofu mixture, stirring to combine all of the ingredients, then spread the mixture evenly. Drizzle on the cheesy sauce. Cover and cook on Low until firm, 3 to 4 hours.

4. Cut into wedges and serve hot.

Greek Frittata

SLOW COOKER SIZE: 4- TO 6-QUART (3.8 TO 5.7 L) | COOK TIME: 2 HOURS ON HIGH | GLUTEN-FREE |
OIL-FREE OPTION

Kalamata olives, spinach, and red bell pepper make a colorful topping for this flavorful frittata seasoned with lemon juice, garlic, and herbs.

¼ cup (60 ml) water, or 2 teaspoons olive oil
1 small yellow onion, chopped
3 large garlic cloves, crushed
1 teaspoon dried basil
1 teaspoon dried oregano
1 pound (455 g) firm tofu, well drained and lightly pressed
2 to 3 tablespoons (7.5 to 11.25 g) nutritional yeast
1 tablespoon (15 ml) fresh lemon juice
Salt and freshly ground black pepper
3 cups (90 g) lightly packed fresh baby spinach
1 jarred roasted red bell pepper, seeded and chopped
½ cup (77.5 g) pitted kalamata olives, coarsely chopped

1. Heat the water or oil in a small skillet over medium-high heat. Add the onion and sauté until softened, about 5 minutes. Add the garlic, basil, and oregano and cook until fragrant, 1 minute longer.

2. Transfer the onion mixture to a food processor or blender. Add the tofu, nutritional yeast, lemon juice, and salt and black pepper to taste and process until smooth and well blended.

3. Generously coat the slow cooker insert with vegan butter or nonstick cooking spray. Scrape the tofu mixture into the cooker. Cover and cook on High for 1½ hours.

4. Meanwhile, lightly steam the spinach or microwave it until just wilted. Chop the spinach and place it in a bowl. Add the roasted bell pepper and olives and mix to combine. Spread the spinach and olive mixture on top of the frittata, cover, and cook for an additional 30 minutes, until set. Serve hot.

Autumn Fruit Crock

SLOW COOKER SIZE: 4- TO 6-QUART (3.8 TO 5.7 L) | COOK TIME: 6 HOURS ON LOW OR 3 HOURS ON HIGH, PLUS 30 MINUTES ON HIGH IF NEEDED | GLUTEN-FREE | OIL-FREE | SOY-FREE

A satisfying cold-weather breakfast alone or as a topping for oatmeal or other hot cereal, this compote also makes a great dessert. If your pears are ripe, the cooking time may be shorter, so check for doneness about 30 minutes ahead of time to see if it's cooked. If you'd like a little color in your compote, substitute fresh cranberries for dried, although you may need to add a little extra sugar if doing so.

3 large apples, peeled, cored, and cut into 1-inch (2.5 cm) dice
2 just-ripe pears, peeled, cored, and cut into 1-inch (2.5 cm) dice
1 cup (130 g) dried apricots, quartered
½ cup (60 g) sweetened dried cranberries
½ cup (87.5 g) pitted prunes, halved
¼ cup (50 g) granulated natural sugar
Grated zest of 1 lemon or orange
Juice of 1 lemon or orange
1 cinnamon stick
¼ cup (60 ml) water

1. Combine all of the ingredients in the slow cooker. Cover and cook on Low until the fruit is soft and the liquid is syrupy, about 6 hours on Low or 3 hours on High. If the liquid needs more reducing, remove the lid and cook uncovered on High for 30 minutes longer.

2. Set aside to cool and thicken. Serve warm or at room temperature. If not using right away, transfer to a bowl, cover, and refrigerate until ready to serve.

SLOW QUICK BREADS

Traditional quick breads are so-called because they are not made with yeast and therefore do not need extra time to rise. They go directly from mixing to baking, making them quick. Because the following quick bread recipes are made in a slow cooler, I call them "slow quick breads"—but you may want to simply call them "delicious."

Irish Soda Bread
MAKES 1 LOAF

- -
SLOW COOKER SIZE: 5- TO 6-QUART (4.8 TO 5.7 L) | COOK TIME: 3 HOURS ON HIGH
- -

No need to wait for St. Patrick's Day to make a fresh loaf of soda bread in your slow cooker.

¾ cup (180 ml) plain unsweetened plant milk
1 tablespoon (15 ml) apple cider vinegar
2½ cups (310 g) all-purpose flour
2 tablespoons (25 g) granulated natural sugar
1 teaspoon baking powder
1 teaspoon baking soda
¾ teaspoon salt
½ cup (75 g) raisins (optional but recommended)
3 tablespoons (42 g) vegan butter, softened

1. In a small bowl, combine the plant milk and vinegar, and set aside.

2. Generously coat the inside of a slow cooker with vegan butter or nonstick cooking spray or line it with parchment paper.

3. In a large bowl, combine the flour, sugar, baking powder, baking soda, and salt, whisking until well mixed. Add the raisins (if using). Cut in the softened butter with a pastry blender until the dough is crumbly. Stir in the milk mixture, slowly ¼ cup (60 ml) at a time, just until the dough forms a ball. If the dough is too sticky, add a little more flour; if it is too dry, slowly add a little more milk mixture, just until dough moves toward center of your bowl.

4. Turn the dough onto a lightly floured surface and knead by hand for about 1 minute until smooth.

5. Shape the dough into a round loaf about 6 to 8 inches (15 to 20 cm) in diameter. Place the loaf into the bottom of the prepared slow cooker. Cut an X about ½ inch (1 cm) deep across the top of the loaf.

6. Place a clean dish towel over the top of the slow cooker, then put on the lid and cook on High for about 3 hours. The bread is ready when it's golden on top and golden brown on the sides and bottom.

Chai-Spiced Breakfast Bread

MAKES 1 LOAF

SLOW COOKER SIZE: 4- OR 6-QUART (3.8 OR 5.7 L) | COOK TIME: 1½ HOURS ON HIGH FOR 4-QUART (3.8 L); 3 HOURS ON HIGH FOR 6-QUART (5.7 L) | SOY-FREE OPTION

This fragrant loaf is delicious served warm with hot tea or coffee—or even chai, if you're so inclined. To make soy-free bread, use soy-free vegan butter and soy-free plant milk.

1¾ cups (217 g) unbleached all-purpose flour
2 teaspoons baking powder
½ teaspoon baking soda
½ teaspoon salt
½ teaspoon ground cardamom
¾ teaspoon ground cinnamon
¼ teaspoon ground nutmeg
⅛ teaspoon ground cloves
¾ cup (150 g) granulated natural sugar
¼ cup (56 g) vegan butter, melted and cooled
2 tablespoons (30 g) unsweetened applesauce
¾ cup (180 ml) plant milk mixed with ½ teaspoon apple cider vinegar
½ cup (120 ml) double-strength brewed black tea
2 teaspoons pure vanilla extract
2 tablespoons (18 g) sunflower seeds or (15 g) chopped walnuts (optional)

(continued)

1. If using a 4-quart (3.8 L) slow cooker, lightly oil the insert or spray it with nonstick cooking spray. If using a 6-quart (5.7 L) slow cooker, place a rack, trivet, or a ring of crumpled aluminum foil in the bottom of the slow cooker insert. Lightly coat a 7 × 9-inch (18 × 23 cm) baking pan or other pan that will fit inside the cooker with vegan butter or nonstick cooking spray.

2. In a large bowl, combine the flour, baking powder, baking soda, salt, cardamom, cinnamon, nutmeg, and cloves. Mix well.

3. In a separate bowl, combine the sugar and vegan butter and beat until well combined. Add the applesauce, plant milk and vinegar mixture, tea, and vanilla and stir until blended. Add the wet mixture to the dry mixture, stirring to combine with a few quick strokes. Stir in the sunflower seeds (if using).

4. If using a 4-quart (3.8 L) slow cooker, transfer the batter to the slow cooker, smoothing evenly. If using a 6-quart (5.7 L) slow cooker, transfer the batter to the prepared pan, pour about ½ inch (1 cm) of hot water into the bottom of the cooker, and place the baking pan on the rack inside the slow cooker.

5. Drape a clean kitchen towel over the cooker, put on the lid, and cook on High until the bread is firm and a tester inserted in the center comes out dry, about 1½ hours if cooking directly in the cooker insert or about 3 hours if cooking in a baking pan inside the cooker.

6. Allow the bread to cool, uncovered, before slicing. This bread tastes best served warm, soon after it is made.

Pumpkin–Chocolate Chip Bread   SERVES 6 TO 8

SLOW COOKER SIZE: 4-QUART TO 6-QUART (3.8 TO 5.7 L) | COOK TIME: 2 TO 3 HOURS ON HIGH | SOY-FREE |
OIL-FREE OPTION

Pumpkin and chocolate have a natural affinity for each other, a fact that is evident in this delicious loaf. It's a great snack to keep on hand during the autumn months, especially around Halloween or Thanksgiving. To make an oil-free bread, use the applesauce instead of the oil and omit the chocolate chips (they contain cocoa butter).

1 cup (245 g) canned solid-pack pumpkin

⅓ cup (67 g) granulated natural sugar

¼ cup (80 g) pure maple syrup

2 tablespoons (30 ml) avocado oil (or other neutral-tasting oil) or (30 g) applesauce

1 teaspoon pure vanilla extract

1¾ cups (217 g) unbleached all-purpose flour

2 teaspoons baking powder

½ teaspoon salt

½ teaspoon ground cinnamon

¼ teaspoon ground nutmeg

¼ teaspoon ground allspice

½ cup (87.5 g) semisweet vegan chocolate chips

1. If using a 4-quart (3.8 L) slow cooker, generously oil the insert or spray it with nonstick cooking spray. If using a 6-quart (5.7 L) slow cooker, lightly coat a 7 × 9-inch (18 × 23 cm) baking pan or other pan that will fit inside your cooker with vegan butter or nonstick cooking spray. Place a rack, trivet, or a ring of crumpled aluminum foil in the bottom of the cooker insert.

2. In a medium-size bowl, combine the pumpkin, sugar, maple syrup, oil, and vanilla and mix well.

3. In a separate large bowl, combine the flour, baking powder, salt, cinnamon, nutmeg, and allspice. Stir the wet ingredients into the dry ingredients, mixing with a few quick strokes. Add the chocolate chips and stir until just combined.

4. If using a 4-quart (3.8 L) slow cooker, scrape the batter into the insert, spreading evenly. If using a 6-quart (5.7 L) slow cooker, transfer the batter to the prepared pan, pour about ½ inch (1 cm) of hot water into the bottom of the cooker, and place the pan on the rack in the slow cooker.

5. Drape a clean kitchen towel over the cooker and put on the lid. Cook on High until the bread is firm and a tester inserted in the center comes out clean, about 2 hours if cooking directly in the cooker insert or about 3 hours if cooking in a baking pan inside the cooker.

6. Allow the bread to cool, uncovered, before slicing.

Three-Corn Corn Bread

SERVES 6 TO 8

SLOW COOKER SIZE: 4-QUART OR 6-QUART (3.8 OR 5.7 L) | COOK TIME: 2 HOURS ON HIGH FOR 4-QUART (3.8 L); 3 HOURS ON HIGH FOR 6-QUART (5.7 L) | GLUTEN-FREE OPTION | SOY-FREE

In addition to being a great chili accompaniment, corn bread makes a delicious breakfast bread when served warm and slathered with Slow-Cooked Apple Butter (page 248) or a little vegan butter. To make this gluten-free, use a gluten-free all-purpose flour.

1¼ cups (175 g) medium- or coarse-ground cornmeal
1 cup (124 g) unbleached all-purpose flour
2 teaspoons baking powder
½ teaspoon salt
1 (15-ounce, or 425 g) can creamed corn
½ cup (77.5 g) fresh or (82.5 g) frozen corn kernels, thawed
¼ cup (80 g) pure maple syrup
2 tablespoons (30 ml) avocado oil or other neutral-tasting oil

1. If using a 4-quart (3.8 L) slow cooker, generously coat the insert of the cooker with vegan butter or nonstick cooking spray. If using a 6-quart (5.7 L) slow cooker, lightly coat a 7 × 9-inch (18 × 23 cm) baking pan or other pan that will fit inside the cooker with vegan butter or nonstick cooking spray. Place a rack, trivet, or a ring of crumpled aluminum foil in the bottom of the slow cooker insert.

2. In a large bowl, combine the cornmeal, flour, baking powder, and salt.

3. In a separate large bowl, combine the creamed corn, corn kernels, maple syrup, and oil. Add the wet ingredients to the dry ingredients and mix well with a few quick strokes.

4. If using a 4-quart (3.8 L) slow cooker, scrape the batter into the insert, spreading evenly. If using a 6-quart (5.7 L) slow cooker, transfer the batter to the prepared pan, pour about ½ inch (1 cm) of hot water into the bottom of the cooker, and place the pan on the rack.

5. Drape a clean kitchen towel over the top and put on the lid. Cook on High until the bread is firm and a tester inserted in the center comes out clean, about 2 hours if cooking directly in the cooker insert or about 3 hours if cooking in a baking pan inside the cooker.

6. Allow the bread to cool, uncovered, before slicing.

Berry-Banana Breakfast Bread

MAKES 1 LOAF

SLOW COOKER SIZE: 4-QUART OR 6-QUART (3.8 OR 5.7 L) | COOK TIME: 2 HOURS ON HIGH FOR 4-QUART (3.8 L); 3 HOURS ON HIGH FOR 6-QUART (5.7 L) | OIL-FREE | SOY-FREE

I like to make this slow cooker bread in the summer when fresh blueberries are abundant, although it can also be made with frozen or dried blueberries. To vary this, leave out the blueberries, or add a different kind of berry or fruit, or add walnuts or chocolate chips.

⅓ cup (82 g) unsweetened applesauce
½ cup (120 g) packed light brown sugar
3 ripe bananas, mashed
1 teaspoon pure vanilla extract
1¾ cups (217 g) unbleached all-purpose flour
2 teaspoons baking powder
½ teaspoon salt
¾ cup (109 g) fresh, frozen, thawed, or dried blueberries

1. If using a 4-quart (3.8 L) slow cooker, generously coat the insert of the cooker with vegan butter or nonstick cooking spray. If using a 6-quart (5.7 L) slow cooker, place a rack, trivet, or a ring of crumpled aluminum foil in the bottom of the cooker insert. Lightly coat a 7 × 9-inch (18 × 23 cm) baking pan or other pan that will fit inside the cooker with vegan butter or nonstick cooking spray.

2. In a large bowl, combine the applesauce, brown sugar, bananas, and vanilla and mix well.

3. In a separate bowl, combine the flour, baking powder, and salt. Add the dry ingredients to the wet ingredients and mix well. Gently stir in the blueberries.

4. If using a 4-quart (3.8 L) slow cooker, pour the batter into the insert. If using a 6-quart (5.7 L) slow cooker, pour the batter into the prepared pan, pour about ½ inch (1 cm) of hot water into the bottom of the cooker, and place the pan on the rack. Drape a clean kitchen towel over the top of the cooker, put on the lid, and cook on High until the bread is firm and a tester inserted in the center comes out dry, 1½ to 2 hours if cooking directly in the cooker insert or about 3 hours if cooking in the baking pan inside the cooker.

5. Allow the bread to cool, uncovered, before slicing.

Hot Drinks

From a steaming crock of spiced cider at a Halloween party to a festive punch on New Year's Eve, hot drinks are a welcome addition to cold-weather gatherings of all kinds. A slow cooker is a great way to keep hot drinks at an ideal serving temperature. You can make and serve your beverage from the same crock and, when turning on the Keep Warm setting, it will do just that throughout the evening. You can set the slow cooker right on the table or countertop, leaving you free from monitoring a simmering pot on top of the stove.

Of course, you don't need a crowd to serve your favorite hot beverages. The Vanilla-Spice Chai or Mexican Hot Chocolate can be enjoyed as your own private indulgence, while the Hot Sangria is a good choice for a cozy evening for two. Whatever your choice, these drinks can be served piping hot directly from the slow cooker into waiting mugs or heatproof punch cups. Since the contents of a slow cooker will remain at a good serving temperature for several hours, it can also be convenient when you go out for an hour or two—to build a snowman, for example—and want to come home to a nice hot drink that's waiting for you. With this varied selection of hot drinks, there's something delicious to warm up everyone in the house.

Blushing Spiced Cider

MAKES ABOUT 2 QUARTS (1.9 L)

SLOW COOKER SIZE: 4-QUART (3.8 L) | COOK TIME: 1 TO 2 HOURS ON LOW | GLUTEN-FREE | OIL-FREE | SOY-FREE

The first cold nip of autumn is occasion enough to put on a pot of this warming cider. It's a great beverage for a gathering and can be made as a spiked punch by adding a generous splash of vodka or rum to the slow cooker when ready to serve, or to individual servings as desired.

2 cinnamon sticks, broken into pieces
1 teaspoon whole cloves
1 teaspoon allspice berries
2 quarts (1.9 L) apple cider
2 cups (480 ml) cranberry juice
½ cup (120 g) packed light brown sugar
2 tablespoons (30 ml) fresh lemon juice
1 medium-size orange, unpeeled, sliced

1. Place the cinnamon, cloves, and allspice in the center of a 6-inch (15 cm) square piece of cheesecloth. Gather the ends of the cloth together and tie with kitchen string to enclose the spices.

2. Combine the apple cider, cranberry juice, and brown sugar in the slow cooker and stir to dissolve the sugar. Stir in the lemon juice and add the spice bag. Cover and cook on Low until hot, 1 to 2 hours.

3. Just before serving, remove and discard the spice bag and float the orange slices on the top. Serve hot. If not serving right away, turn the slow cooker to the Keep Warm setting.

Hot Sangria

SLOW COOKER SIZE: 4- TO 6-QUART (3.8 TO 5.7 L) | COOK TIME: 1 HOUR ON HIGH | GLUTEN-FREE |
OIL-FREE | SOY-FREE

Prepare a fun and fruity alternative to mulled wine with the convenience of a slow cooker. Put it together, turn it on, and then forget it. Guests can help themselves, and the wine stays at the perfect serving temperature for hours.

2 (750 ml each) bottles dry red wine
½ cup (120 ml) brandy or orange-flavored liqueur
1 cup (200 g) granulated natural sugar
1 cup (240 ml) fresh orange juice
1 cup (240 ml) cranberry juice
1 cup (170 g) fresh or frozen sliced peaches or cherries
1 orange, unpeeled, halved lengthwise and sliced crosswise
1 lemon, unpeeled, halved lengthwise and sliced crosswise

1. Combine all of the ingredients in the slow cooker. Cover and cook on High for 1 hour.

2. Serve hot, in clear punch cups or heat-resistant glasses, including some of the fruit with each serving. If not serving right away, turn the slow cooker to the Keep Warm setting.

Celebration Punch

SLOW COOKER SIZE: 4-QUART (3.8 L) | COOK TIME: 2 HOURS ON LOW | GLUTEN-FREE | OIL-FREE | SOY-FREE

Fruit juice seasoned with spices makes for a refreshing alcohol-free punch. For a spiked version, add a splash or two of rum when ready to serve.

3 cinnamon sticks, broken into pieces
1 teaspoon whole cloves
1 cup (240 ml) water
½ cup (100 g) granulated natural sugar
1 (6-ounce, or 170 g) can frozen lemonade concentrate, thawed
2 cups (480 ml) cranberry juice
1½ quarts (1.4 L) apple cider or apple juice
1 navel orange, unpeeled, sliced

1. Place the cinnamon and cloves in the center of a 6-inch (15 cm) square piece of cheesecloth and tie it with kitchen string to enclose the spices.

2. Combine the water and sugar in the slow cooker and stir to dissolve the sugar. Stir in the lemonade concentrate, then add the cranberry juice, stirring to dissolve the lemonade. Add the spice bag and stir in the apple cider. Cover and cook on Low for 2 hours.

3. Just before serving, remove and discard the spice bag and float the orange slices in the punch. Serve hot. If not serving right away, turn the slow cooker to the Keep Warm setting.

Spiced Rum Punch

SLOW COOKER SIZE: 2- TO 4-QUART (1.9 TO 3.8 L) | COOK TIME: 45 MINUTES TO 1 HOUR ON LOW |
GLUTEN-FREE | SOY-FREE OPTION

Spiced rum provides depth and complexity to this bracing and delicious punch. It may well be the hit of your next get-together. Use a soy-free vegan butter for soy-free punch.

½ cup (120 g) packed dark brown sugar
¼ cup (56 g) vegan butter, at room temperature
¼ cup (80 g) agave nectar
½ teaspoon ground cinnamon
¼ teaspoon ground nutmeg
¼ teaspoon ground cloves
½ teaspoon pure vanilla extract
1 cup (240 ml) spiced rum
3 cups (720 ml) boiling water
Cinnamon sticks, for garnish

1. Combine the brown sugar, butter, agave, cinnamon, nutmeg, cloves, and vanilla in the slow cooker and stir until well blended. Add the rum and the boiling water. Stir to blend well. Cover and cook on Low until hot, 45 minutes to 1 hour.

2. Serve hot in mugs and garnish with cinnamon sticks. If not serving right away, turn the slow cooker to the Keep Warm setting.

Hot and Spicy
Virgin Mary Sipper

MAKES ABOUT 6 CUPS (1.4 L)

SLOW COOKER SIZE: 4-QUART (3.8 L) | COOK TIME: 2 HOURS ON HIGH | GLUTEN-FREE | OIL-FREE | SOY-FREE OPTION

You can spike this with vodka, if desired. With or without, it's a great way to warm up on a cold night! To make this soy-free, omit the Worcestershire sauce and use a Soy-Free Sauce (page 344) or coconut aminos, or add some soy-free vegetable broth base or additional salt.

1 (46-ounce, or 1.4 L) can blended vegetable juice, such as V8
1½ tablespoons (18.75 g) granulated natural sugar
1½ tablespoons (23 ml) fresh lemon juice
1 to 2 teaspoons horseradish
1 teaspoon vegan Worcestershire sauce
½ teaspoon celery salt
½ teaspoon Tabasco sauce
Celery sticks, for garnish

1. Combine the vegetable juice, brown sugar, lemon juice, horseradish, Worcestershire sauce, celery salt, and Tabasco in the slow cooker. Cover and cook on High until hot, about 2 hours.

2. Serve hot, ladled into cups or mugs. Garnish each serving with a celery stick. If not serving right away, turn the slow cooker to the Keep Warm setting.

Hot White Chocolate

SLOW COOKER SIZE: 4-QUART (3.8 L) | COOK TIME: 2 HOURS ON HIGH | GLUTEN-FREE | SOY-FREE

If you're a fan of white chocolate like I am, you enjoy it any way you can get it—and this white version of hot chocolate is no exception. Because white chocolate is so sweet, this recipe requires very little additional sweetener.

4 cups (960 ml) unsweetened plant milk
½ cup (87.5 g) vegan white chocolate chips
2 tablespoons (40 g) agave nectar
2 teaspoons pure vanilla extract
Ground nutmeg or unsweetened cocoa powder, for garnish (optional)

1. Combine the plant milk, white chocolate, agave, and vanilla in the slow cooker, stirring to mix well. Cover and cook on High, stirring occasionally, until the chocolate is melted and the mixture is hot, about 2 hours.

2. Stir well before serving in warm cups or mugs. Garnish with a sprinkling of nutmeg or cocoa (if using). If not serving right away, turn the slow cooker to the Keep Warm setting.

Mocha Affogato

SLOW COOKER SIZE: 4-QUART (3.8 L) | COOK TIME: 1 TO 2 HOURS ON LOW | GLUTEN-FREE |
SOY-FREE OPTION

Inspired by an Italian dessert where hot espresso is poured over a scoop of gelato, this decadent concoction is like having coffee and dessert rolled into one—especially if you add the optional scoop of vanilla ice cream to each serving. Add the Kahlúa or not at your own discretion—it's delicious either way. For soy-free, use soy-free vegan ice cream. This recipe is easily doubled for a crowd.

1 pint (425 g) vegan chocolate ice cream
4 cups (960 ml) hot brewed coffee
½ cup (120 ml) Kahlúa, or to taste (optional)
1 pint (425 g) vegan vanilla ice cream (optional)

1. Place the chocolate ice cream in the slow cooker. Pour the hot coffee over the ice cream, stirring to melt. Cover and cook on Low until hot, 1 to 2 hours. If not serving right away, turn the slow cooker to the Keep Warm setting.

2. Just before serving, stir in the Kahlúa (if using). Serve as is in coffee mugs, or place a small scoop of vanilla ice cream in the bottom of each coffee mug before ladling the mocha mixture on top, and serve with a spoon.

Mexican Hot Chocolate

SLOW COOKER SIZE: 4-QUART (3.8 L) | COOK TIME: 2 HOURS ON HIGH | GLUTEN-FREE | SOY-FREE

Nothing beats the flavor and aroma of homemade hot chocolate, and this Mexican version, with cinnamon sticks and an optional pinch of cayenne, really hits the spot on a cold day or evening. The addition of vegan whipped cream (soy-free, if desired) makes it extra special.

½ cup (87.5 g) semisweet vegan chocolate chips
¼ cup (80 g) agave nectar
3 cinnamon sticks
Pinch of cayenne pepper (optional)
4 cups (960 ml) unsweetened plant milk
Vegan whipped cream, for serving (optional)

1. Combine the chocolate, agave, cinnamon, and cayenne (if using) in the slow cooker. Add the plant milk, stirring to mix well. Cover and cook on High, stirring occasionally, until the chocolate is melted, about 2 hours. If not serving right away, turn the slow cooker to the Keep Warm setting.

2. Stir well and remove the cinnamon sticks before serving in warm cups or mugs. Top with a dollop of vegan whipped cream (if using).

Vanilla-Spice Chai

SLOW COOKER SIZE: 4-QUART (3.8 L) | COOK TIME: 4 HOURS AND 15 MINUTES ON HIGH, PLUS 30 MINUTES ON LOW | GLUTEN-FREE | OIL-FREE | SOY-FREE

Chai tea can be pricey in coffee shops, and even chai tea concentrate is expensive to buy for making at home. This recipe allows you to have it your way. You can increase or decrease the spices according to your own taste preference. If you don't have a whole vanilla bean, add a little vanilla extract just before serving. If you don't have whole cardamom pods, sprinkle a little ground cardamom into the spice mixture before closing up the cheesecloth.

6 (¼-inch, or 0.6 cm-thick) slices peeled fresh ginger
8 whole cloves
½ teaspoon fennel seeds
½ teaspoon cardamom seeds
½ teaspoon peppercorns
4 cinnamon sticks, whole or broken into pieces
1 vanilla bean, whole or cut into pieces
4 cups (960 ml) water
6 black or rooibos tea bags, regular or decaf
4 cups (960 ml) vanilla plant milk
Agave nectar, to taste (optional)

1. Place the ginger, cloves, fennel seeds, cardamom seeds, and peppercorns in the center of a small square of cheesecloth and tie it with kitchen string to enclose the spices. If using pieces of cinnamon sticks and vanilla bean, rather than whole ones, you may add them to the bag, although you may need to make two spice bags for all to fit.

2. Place the spice bag in the slow cooker along with the whole cinnamon sticks and whole vanilla bean (if using). Add the water, cover, and cook on High for 4 hours.

3. Add the tea bags, cover, and allow to steep for 15 minutes, then turn the setting to Low. Remove the tea bags and the spices. Stir in the plant milk and agave (if using). Cover and continue to cook for 30 minutes longer to heat the plant milk. Serve hot in mugs. If not serving right away, turn the slow cooker to the Keep Warm setting. (See Note for make-ahead instructions.)

NOTE: To make ahead, do not add the plant milk in step 3. Instead, transfer the chai to a container and refrigerate. When ready to serve, add the plant milk and heat on the stovetop or in the microwave until hot, or serve chilled. Alternatively, you can use the chai mixture as your homemade version of chai concentrate—simply store it in the refrigerator and combine any amount with an equal amount of plant milk. Heat it up or add a few ice cubes for refreshing iced chai.

Not from the Crock

I n this chapter you will find the supporting players: recipes that, while not made in a slow cooker, help make the slow cooker recipes even better. Here are the recipes for making homemade versions of cashew sour cream, cream cheese, and Parmesan. There are also recipes for Cheesy Sauce, Tempeh Bacon, Cashew Cream—all made with wholesome plant-based ingredients.

Cashew Cream

MAKES ABOUT 1 CUP (230 ML)

GLUTEN-FREE | OIL-FREE | SOY-FREE

When you blend soaked raw cashews with water, the result is cashew cream, a versatile ingredient that can be used in a number of savory and sweet recipes.

1 cup (125 g) raw cashew pieces, soaked in hot water for 30 minutes, then drained
½ cup (120 ml) water, plus more if needed

In a high-powered blender, combine the drained cashews and water. Blend until completely smooth and creamy. The cashew cream should be very thick. For a thinner cream, add a little more water, 1 tablespoon (15 ml) at a time. Transfer to an airtight container and refrigerate up to 4 or 5 days.

Cashew Sour Cream

MAKES ABOUT 1½ CUPS (ABOUT 345 G)

GLUTEN-FREE | OIL-FREE | SOY-FREE

Use this soy-free cashew sour cream in any recipe calling for cashew sour cream, or when you want a tangy topping for tacos, chili, or potatoes.

1 cup (140 g) raw cashews, soaked in hot water for 30 minutes, then drained
⅓ cup (80 ml) water, plus more if needed
2 tablespoons (30 ml) fresh lemon juice
1 teaspoon apple cider vinegar
¼ teaspoon salt

In a high-powered blender, combine the drained cashews, water, lemon juice, vinegar, and salt. Blend until completely smooth and creamy, 2 to 3 minutes. Taste and adjust the seasonings as desired. For a thinner consistency, add a little more water, 1 tablespoon (15 ml) at a time. Transfer to an airtight container and refrigerate up to 4 or 5 days.

Cashew Cream Cheese

GLUTEN-FREE | OIL-FREE | SOY-FREE

This homemade plant-based cream cheese made with cashews can be used in any recipe calling for vegan cream cheese.

¾ cup (105 g) raw cashews, soaked in hot water for 30 minutes, then drained
1 tablespoon (15 ml) plain unsweetened plant milk
1 tablespoon (15 ml) fresh lemon juice
1 tablespoon (15 ml) apple cider vinegar
2 tablespoons (28 g) refined coconut oil, melted
½ teaspoon salt

1. In a high-powered blender, combine all the ingredients. Blend until completely smooth and creamy.

2. Transfer to an airtight container and refrigerate for at least 2 hours to chill and thicken before use. It will keep well in the refrigerator for up to 5 days.

Cheesy Sauce

MAKES ABOUT 2 CUPS (ABOUT 480 ML)

GLUTEN-FREE | OIL-FREE | SOY-FREE

This rich and creamy sauce made with cashews adds a nice cheesy flavor to recipes.

1 cup (140 g) raw cashews, soaked in water for 4 hours and drained
½ cup (30 g) nutritional yeast
1 teaspoon Dijon mustard
½ teaspoon garlic powder
½ teaspoon onion powder
½ teaspoon paprika
½ teaspoon vegetable broth powder
½ teaspoon salt
1 cup (240 ml) water or unsweetened plant milk
2 tablespoons (30 ml) fresh lemon juice

In a high-powered blender, combine all of the ingredients and process until smooth.
Transfer to an airtight container and refrigerate up to 4 or 5 days.

Mushroom Gravy

MAKES ABOUT 2½ CUPS (600 ML)

GLUTEN-FREE | OIL-FREE | SOY-FREE

In addition to being oil-free, this flavorful gravy is also gluten- and soy-free. To make a quick broth, dissolve 1 bouillon cube (vegetable or mushroom) in hot water.

¼ cup (40 g) minced yellow onion
1½ cups plus 2 tablespoons (390 ml) vegetable or mushroom broth
2 cups (140 g) sliced fresh mushrooms
½ teaspoon ground dried thyme
¼ teaspoon ground sage
2 tablespoons (30 ml) dry red or white wine (optional)
Salt and freshly ground black pepper

1. Combine the onion and 2 tablespoons (30 ml) of broth in a small saucepan over medium heat and simmer until the onion is soft. Stir in the mushrooms and cook until slightly softened, then stir in the thyme, sage, and wine (if using). Add 1 cup (240 ml) of the remaining broth and bring to a boil. Reduce the heat and simmer for 5 minutes.

2. Transfer the mixture to a high-powered blender or food processor, add the remaining ½ cup (120 ml) of broth and process until very smooth. Transfer the gravy back to the saucepan and season to taste with salt and black pepper. Simmer until the gravy is hot and the flavors are blended. If the gravy is too thick, stir in a small amount of additional broth or some unsweetened plant milk.

Almond Parmesan

MAKES ABOUT 1 CUP (134 G)

GLUTEN-FREE | OIL-FREE | SOY-FREE

This easy-to-make alternative to Parmesan cheese is a tasty topping for pasta, salads, or other dishes that would be enhanced by a few shakes of this salty, cheesy goodness.

1 cup (110 g) slivered raw almonds
⅓ cup (19 g) nutritional yeast
1 teaspoon salt

1. Combine all the ingredients in a food processor and process until finely ground. Be careful not to overprocess or you will end up with a paste.

2. Transfer to an airtight container or shaker and keep refrigerated for up to 2 weeks.

Tempeh Bacon

GLUTEN-FREE

There are many ways to make plant-based bacon using ingredients ranging from coconut and mushrooms to eggplant and rice paper. I like to use tempeh because it's protein-rich and easy to cut into thin slices. It also easily absorbs the smoky, salty marinade that gives the tempeh its bacony flavor.

1 (8-ounce, or 225 g) package tempeh, cut lengthwise into thin strips
3 tablespoons (45 ml) tamari
3 tablespoons (60 g) pure maple syrup
2 tablespoons (30 ml) apple cider vinegar
2 tablespoons (30 ml) water
1 teaspoon liquid smoke
½ teaspoon smoked paprika
¼ teaspoon freshly ground black pepper
2 tablespoons (30 ml) olive oil

1. Place the tempeh slices in a shallow baking dish, overlapping slightly if needed.

2. Combine the tamari, maple syrup, vinegar, water, liquid smoke, paprika, and pepper in a small saucepan. Heat over medium heat until it is hot.

3. Pour the hot marinade over the tempeh slices and set aside for 20 minutes so the tempeh can absorb the marinade.

4. Heat the oil in a large skillet over medium-high heat. Add the tempeh, in batches if needed, and cook, turning once, until the tempeh is browned. Pour any remaining marinade onto the tempeh as it cooks and allow it to evaporate. The tempeh bacon is now ready to serve or use in recipes. Store in the refrigerator up to 4 or 5 days.

Tofu Chorizo

GLUTEN-FREE | SOY-FREE OPTION

Ready-made soy chorizo can be found in supermarkets and natural food stores, but it's easy (and less expensive) to make your own. If you can't eat soy foods, check out the soy-free variation at the end of this recipe.

¼ cup (28.75 g) oil-packed sun-dried tomatoes, drained and finely chopped
1 tablespoon (16 g) tomato paste
2 tablespoons (30 ml) tamari, coconut aminos, or Soy-Free Sauce (page 344)
1 tablespoon (15 ml) apple cider vinegar
1 tablespoon (7.5 g) chili powder
1½ teaspoons smoked paprika
1 teaspoon garlic powder
1 teaspoon dried oregano
1 teaspoon ground cumin
1 teaspoon ground coriander
¼ teaspoon freshly ground black pepper
¼ teaspoon ground allspice or ground cinnamon
¼ teaspoon cayenne pepper (optional)
1 pound (455 g) extra-firm tofu, drained and finely crumbled
1 tablespoon (15 ml) olive oil

1. In a large bowl, combine the finely chopped sun-dried tomatoes, tomato paste, tamari, vinegar, chili powder, smoked paprika, garlic powder, oregano, cumin, coriander, black pepper, allspice, and cayenne (if using). Mix well until completely blended. Add the crumbled tofu and mix well to coat the tofu.

2. Heat the oil in a large nonstick skillet over medium heat. Add the tofu mixture and cook, stirring, until the mixture is hot and the liquid is absorbed, about 5 minutes. Taste and adjust the seasonings, if needed. The chorizo is now ready to use in recipes. If not using right away, transfer to an airtight container and refrigerate up to 4 or 5 days, or freeze until needed.

Soy-Free Sauce

MAKES 1¾ CUPS (420 ML)

GLUTEN-FREE | OIL-FREE | SOY-FREE

This excellent gluten-free, soy-free alternative to soy sauce or tamari (or even Worcestershire sauce) is from *World Vegan Feast* by Bryanna Clark Grogan (© 2011, published by Vegan Heritage Press; used with permission).

2 tablespoons (30 g) Marmite or other yeast extract
2 tablespoons (38 g) salt
1½ cups (360 ml) hot water, vegan broth, or mushroom soaking water
2 tablespoons (30 ml) soy-free vegan gravy browner (such as Kitchen Bouquet)

1. Combine the Marmite and salt in 1 cup (240 ml) of hot water, stirring until dissolved and well blended.

2. Mix in the remaining ½ cup (120 ml) of water and the gravy browner. Store the mixture in an airtight container in the refrigerator, where it will keep for several weeks.

NOTE: To replace some of the complex qualities that a good fermented soy sauce or tamari provides, try adding wine, broth, and/or mushroom broth or concentrate to your dish, in addition to using this soy-free sauce.

Balsamic Reduction

GLUTEN-FREE | OIL-FREE | SOY-FREE

When balsamic vinegar is cooked down, it becomes thick and syrupy. This balsamic reduction is a flavorful condiment that can be drizzled over anything from salads and vegetables to pasta, grains, and even fruit.

1 cup (240 ml) balsamic vinegar
1 tablespoon (12.5 g) granulated natural sugar (optional)

1. Bring the vinegar to a boil in a small saucepan over medium heat. Turn the heat to low and let it simmer until it is reduced to ½ cup (120 ml), about 10 minutes, then stir in the sugar (if using).

2. Simmer until the reduction becomes syrupy and coats the back of a wooden spoon, about 5 minutes longer. You should end up with between ⅓ cup and ½ cup (80 ml and 120 ml).

3. Store any leftover reduction in an airtight container in the refrigerator, where it will keep for several weeks.

Index